THE FORMATION OF THE
BOOK OF THE TWELVE
A Study in Text and Canon

SOCIETY
OF BIBLICAL
LITERATURE

DISSERTATION SERIES
Michael V. Fox, Old Testament Editor
Pheme Perkins, New Testament Editor

Number 149

THE FORMATION OF THE
BOOK OF THE TWELVE
A Study in Text and Canon

by
Barry Alan Jones

Barry Alan Jones

THE FORMATION OF THE BOOK OF THE TWELVE
A Study in Text and Canon

Scholars Press
Atlanta, Georgia

THE FORMATION OF THE BOOK OF THE TWELVE
A Study in Text and Canon

Barry Alan Jones

© 1995
The Society of Biblical Literature

Library of Congress Cataloging in Publication Data

Jones, Barry A.
    The formation of the Book of the twelve : a study in text and
canon / Barry Alan Jones.
        p.   cm. — (Dissertation series / Society of Biblical Literature ;
no. 149)
    Includes bibliographical references.
    ISBN 0-7885-0108-9 (cloth : alk. paper). — ISBN 0-7885-0109-7
(pbk. : alk. paper)
    1. Bible. O.T. Minor Prophets—Canon. 2. Bible. O.T. Minor
Prophets—Manuscripts. 3. Bible. O.T. Minor Prophets— Criticism,
interpretation, etc. I. Title. II. Series: Dissertation series
(Society of Biblical Literature) ; no. 149.
BS1560.J65   1995
224'.9012—dc20   95-6227
                                        CIP

Printed in the United States of America
on acid-free paper

To Beth

TABLE OF CONTENTS

PREFACE

Scholarly interest in the Book of the Twelve as a literary unit has ebbed and flowed over the course of the last century. Currently, interest in the Scroll of the Minor Prophets is again on the rise and at a level approaching flood tide. As evidence one may cite the inaugural meeting of the Book of the Twelve Consultation at the 1994 SBL Annual Meeting in Chicago, Illinois, which attracted a standing-room-only audience of scholars from widely diverging areas of specialization in the field of biblical studies.

The present volume attempts to wade into these active waters of study from the perspective of the relative abundance of ancient manuscript evidence for the Book of the Twelve. The primary conclusion of this study is that recent scholarly treatments of the Book of the Twelve assume that there was only one form of the Book of the Twelve in circulation in antiquity, and that this singular form of the book is represented by the textual witnesses preserved in the manuscripts of the Masoretic tradition. The extant manuscript witnesses, however, including the manuscripts of the Minor Prophets from the Judean Desert, suggest that at least three versions of the Hebrew text of the Book of the Twelve were in circulation in antiquity. One version of the Book of the Twelve survived only accidentally, as the result of an archaeological discovery. Another survived as a continuous manuscript tradition, but only in translation as part of the Greek Bible. The third version also survived in a continuous manuscript tradition which ultimately became the received Hebrew text of both religious and academic communities alike.

The evidence and arguments that follow will attempt to substantiate the thesis that multiple forms of the Hebrew Book of the Twelve existed in antiquity. Two further arguments are made as a result of the thesis. First, I argue that the comparative textual evidence for multiple forms of the Book of the Twelve provides a starting point for investigating the literary history of the Minor Prophets collection that is more reliable than the widely diverse results of literary and redaction-critical approaches. Second, I argue that the trajectory of the Hebrew text of the Minor Prophets from the many to the one as attested by the surviving manuscript evidence provides a tangible and reliable portrayal of the textual and interpretative dynamics of the extended, complex, yet somewhat ascertainable process of canonization.

Beyond my gratitude to Divine Providence, I am indebted to many people who have made the completion of this dissertation possible and to whom I wish to express special appreciation. I wish first of all to thank Dr. John I Durham and Dr. Elmo Scoggin, professors *emeriti* of Old Testament and Hebrew at Southeastern Baptist Theological Seminary, who taught me to read and to love the language of Moses. I am also grateful to Professors Fred Horton, Charles Talbert, and Ralph Wood of Wake Forest University for their personal interest in and invaluable contribution to my academic preparation.

Special appreciation is also owed to my dissertation advisor, Professor Eric M. Meyers, whose encouragement and guidance were catalysts for the completion of this project. I am also indebted to the members of my dissertation committee, Professors James L. Crenshaw, Carol L. Meyers, Melvin K. H. Peters, and Regina M. Schwartz. Their individual contributions to the research that lies behind the dissertation are, at least in my experience, an affirmation of the emphasis of Duke's Graduate Program in Religion upon dialogue both within and across the boundaries of academic specialization. I am also grateful to Professor James D. Nogalski of The Southern Baptist Theological Seminary, who made available to me his doctoral dissertation on the Book of the Twelve before it was accessible in its published form. Of the many classmates from whom I have learned a great deal, I wish to acknowledge the contributions of two in particular: Volker Greifenhagen, who read parts of the dissertation and whose keen bibliographical eye helped me to be alert to new research on the Book of the Twelve; and also Andrew Wakefield, who graciously created the fonts for the Hebrew and Greek transliterations used in the dissertation. They are models of friendship and collegiality and are also representative of the many classmates who have made doctoral studies a joyful enterprise.

Finally, I wish to acknowledge my deep gratitude to the members of my family who supported me during my graduate studies: my mother, Alice Jones, who taught me to value education; my father, the late Willard C. Jones, whose interest in the dissertation inspired its completion; and my daughter Claire, who kept my work on the dissertation in proper perspective. Last and most importantly, no word of gratitude is sufficient to express my appreciation for my wife Beth whose patience, encouragement, love, support, and sacrifice have helped to will this dissertation into being.

CHAPTER 1

THE FORMATION OF THE BOOK OF THE TWELVE: ANCIENT EVIDENCE AND MODERN ASSESSMENTS

The ancient manuscript remains of the Minor Prophets and the ancient references to them in extra-biblical literature are nearly unanimous in their attestation of the transmission of these twelve prophetical writings as a single compendious volume, the Book of the Twelve Prophets. The questions of the unity of the Minor Prophets collection and the history behind its compilation have been recognized and discussed by scholars of the Bible both ancient and modern, from St. Jerome and the Talmudic sages to the modern scholarly literature of the nineteenth and twentieth centuries. The present study is an attempt to approach the issue of the formation of the Book of the Twelve from the perspective of the ancient manuscript evidence for the Hebrew text of the book. The thesis of the dissertation is that the textual remains of the Book of the Twelve provide relatively objective evidence for investigating both the final stages of the book's compilation and the relationship of the book to the growth of a corpus of canonical literature in ancient Judaism.

In order to support the thesis of the dissertation, it will be necessary first to describe the ancient manuscript evidence for the Hebrew text of the Book of the Twelve. Following such a description, I will discuss the relationship between the manuscript evidence and the other surviving evidence for the existence of the Book of the Twelve in antiquity. I will also describe the role that textual evidence has played in previous research on the formation of the Book of the Twelve. The survey of ancient evidence and modern research will demonstrate both the need for and the promise of incorporating the manuscript evidence for the Book of the Twelve into the scholarly discussion of its literary and canonical history. Chapter Two of the dissertation will describe the methodological justification for using textual evidence to reconstruct the literary history of the Book of the Twelve. Chapters Three, Four, and Five will then discuss in detail the contributions of specific ancient manuscript witnesses to the issues of the history and canonical status of the Minor Prophets collection. The implications of such evidence for past and future scholarship on the Book of the Twelve will be discussed in Chapter Six. With the preceding overview of the dissertation in view, I now turn to a description of the manuscript evidence for the ancient Hebrew text of the Book of the Twelve.

The Manuscript Evidence for the Book of the Twelve

The primary manuscript evidence for the Book of the Twelve may be divided into three groups according to the three different arrangements of the Minor Prophets attested within the ancient manuscript witnesses. These groups are: (1) the medieval codices of the Masoretic textual tradition (MT) and the ancient, pre-Masoretic Hebrew and Greek manuscripts that attest this tradition; (2) the ancient manuscript evidence for the Old Greek (LXX) translation of the Minor Prophets; and (3) fragments of a single manuscript (4QXII[a]) from among the fragmentary remains of seven manuscripts of the Book of the Twelve discovered at Khirbet Qumran. The three groups of manuscripts are unanimous in their representation of the twelve Minor Prophets as a single volume and in their attestation of the antiquity of the bibliographic unity of the collection. The individual characteristics of each manuscript group may be summarized as follows.

The Masoretic Tradition

The Masoretic textual tradition is not only consistent in its treatment of the Minor Prophets as a single book but is also uniform in the sequence of the books, their order being as follows: Hosea, Joel, Amos, Obadiah, Jonah, Micah, Nahum, Habakkuk, Zephaniah, Haggai, Zechariah, and Malachi.[1] The unity of the book is attested by scribal practices such as leaving a space of three lines between the prophetic books of the Twelve as opposed to a space of four lines between other biblical books that are copied on a single scroll.[2] The unity of the book is also indicated by the Masoretic colophons, such as the one found at the end of the Book of Malachi in *BHS*, which totals the number of verses not only for that book but also for "the Twelve." By the relatively late date of the copying of the extant MT manuscripts,[3] the unity of the Book of the Twelve was an immutable scribal tradition reproduced with a consistency and uniformity that is characteristic of the religiously motivated transmission of sacred literature.

The chronological gap between the composition of the Book of the Twelve and the extant manuscripts of the MT has been partially reduced by the discoveries from Qumran and the Judean Desert. Beginning with the scroll of the Minor Prophets

---

[1]C. D. Ginsburg, *Introduction to the Massoretic-Critical Edition of the Hebrew Bible* (1st ed. 1897; reprinted New York: KTAV Publishing Co., 1966), 1–5.

[2]This practice is attested in the Talmud (*b. B. Bat.* 13b) and also in the Qumran manuscripts. See D. Schneider, "The Unity of the Book of the Twelve" (Yale University, Ph.D. dissertation, 1979), 3.

[3]For example, Codex Leningradensis, the textual basis for *BHS*, was copied in 1008 CE. Codex Cairensis, the oldest of the MT manuscripts, dates to 895 CE. See E. Würthwein, *The Text of the Old Testament*, tr. E. F. Rhodes (Grand Rapids, MI: Eerdmans, 1979), 34–35.

discovered in Wadi Murabba'at,[4] the MT text of the Book of the Twelve has been attested with far greater antiquity than previous manuscripts allowed. The Murabba'at document, a greatly deteriorated leather scroll dating from the second century CE, preserves parts of a proto-Masoretic text of the Minor Prophets that is nearly identical to the consonantal text of the MT. The remains of the scroll begin with Joel 2:20 and include partial texts from Amos, Obadiah, Jonah, Micah, Nahum, Habakkuk, Zephaniah, Haggai, and Zechariah, concluding with Zech 1:4. Each extant book is found in the same order as in the MT manuscripts.

The Septuagint Manuscript Witnesses

The surviving manuscripts of the Greek Bible further attest the antiquity and consistency of the practice of writing the Minor Prophets as a single book, albeit according to different scribal techniques and traditions. The oldest complete manuscript, the third century CE papyrus Codex Washington, gives both the name and the number of the twelve books in the superscription to each book, e.g. "*Michaias g,*" "*Malachias ib.*"[5] The same is true for the fourth and fifth century CE uncial codices Vaticanus, Alexandrinus, and Sinaiticus.[6] The LXX Minor Prophets is distinct from the MT, however, both in its text and in the sequence of the prophetic books. The arrangement of the books in the LXX manuscripts differs from the MT with respect

---

[4]Published in P. Benoit, J. T. Milik, and R. de Vaux, *Les Grottes de Murabba'at*, DJD II (Oxford: Clarendon Press, 1961), *Texte*, 181–208; and *Planches*, 55–73.

[5]*Facsimile of the Washington Manuscript of the Minor Prophets in the Freer Collection and Berlin Fragment of Genesis* (Ann Arbor, MI: University of Michigan Press, 1927), 14–63. See also H. A. Sanders, *The Minor Prophets in the Freer Collection* (Ann Arbor, MI: University of Michigan Press, 1927) 10–15.

[6]See the apparatus of J. Ziegler's critical edition in *Septuaginta. Vetus Testamentum Graecum*, Vol. *XIII Duodecim Prophetae*, 3rd ed. (Göttingen: Vandenhoeck & Ruprecht, 1984).

to the first six books, which follow the order Hosea, Amos, Micah, Joel, Obadiah, and Jonah.[7] The order of the remaining six books is identical to that of the MT.

The fragmentary remains of a Greek scroll from the Judean desert designated as 8 Ḥev XIIgr further attest the antiquity of both the Hebrew and Greek textual witnesses to the Book of the Twelve and also underscore the textual differences between the MT and the LXX manuscripts of the Minor Prophets. The remains of this scroll, found in Naḥal Ḥever in 1952 and dated to the middle of the first century BCE, contain parts of the books of Jonah, Micah, Nahum, Habakkuk, Zephaniah, and Zechariah.[8] D. Barthélemy argued convincingly that 8 Ḥev XIIgr represents a rescension of the LXX Minor Prophets toward a proto-MT text. The rescension was apparently made by bilingual Palestinian Jews who wanted a Greek translation that was closer to the proto-MT Hebrew text than was the Old Greek translation. E. Tov reports in the recent *editio princeps* of the scroll that the fragments containing the end of the Book of Jonah and the beginning of the Book of Micah fit credibly together, thus supporting the assumption that the sequence of the first six books

---

[7]The eighth century CE Codex Venetus has the order Hosea, Amos, *Joel, Jonah, Obadiah*, Micah, etc. H. B. Sweet, *Introduction to the Old Testament in Greek* (Cambridge: Cambridge University Press, 1914), 227.

[8]D. Barthélemy, "Redécouverte d'un chaînon manquant de l'histoire de la Septante," *RB* 60 (1953): 18–29. Prior to his anticipated *editio princeps* of the text, Barthélemy published a thorough preliminary report in *Les Devanciers d'Aquila: Premiere Publication Integrale du Texte des Fragments du Dodecapropheton. VTSup* 10 (Leiden: E. J. Brill, 1963). The critical edition of the text has been published by E. Tov in *The Greek Minor Prophets Scroll from Naḥal Ḥever (8ḤevXIIgr)*, DJD VIII (Oxford: Clarendon Press, 1990). For the archaeological context of the discovery of the scroll, see Y. Aharoni, "Expedition B—The Cave of Horror," *IEJ* 12 (1962): 186–99; and idem, "The Caves of Naḥal Ḥever," *Atiqot* 3 (1961): 158. The fragments recovered in the Naḥal Ḥever excavations were published in B. Lifshitz, "The Greek Documents from the Cave of Horror," *IEJ* 12 (1962): 201–7.

was identical to the MT sequence.[9] Since the order of the books of the LXX Book of the Twelve differs from the MT, it is probable that the sequence of the books in 8 Ḥev XIIgr is also the result of rescensional activity.

4QXII[a]

Among the manuscript discoveries from Khirbet Qumran are fragments of seven different scrolls of the Minor Prophets from Cave IV.[10] The oldest of the seven scrolls, 4QXII[a], contains parts of the books of Zechariah, Malachi, and Jonah and has been dated on paleographic grounds to the middle of the second century BCE.[11] This manuscript apparently exhibits a previously unattested sequence of books. The end of the Book of Malachi is preserved at the bottom of column four in Fuller's reconstruction. The scroll, however, contained writing beyond the end of the Book of Malachi. The Book of Jonah begins on a separate fragment at the top of a column following a blank space of two or three lines.[12] Fuller has labeled this Jonah fragment Column V, concluding that Jonah most likely followed Malachi as the final book of the scroll.

The history of textual transmission attested by the ancient manuscript evidence for the Book of the Twelve demonstrates the antiquity of both the textual unity and sacred status of the Minor Prophets. Concurrently, however, the manuscripts of the LXX Minor Prophets and 4QXII[a] show that a degree of fluidity

---

[9]Tov, *The Greek Minor Prophets Scroll*, 8.

[10]These fragments have been edited by R. Fuller ("The Minor Prophets Manuscripts from Qumran, Cave IV" [Ph.D. thesis, Harvard University, 1988] and are scheduled for publication in the series *Discoveries in the Judean Desert*. Information concerning the fragments has been communicated to me by Fuller and by Prof. E. M. Meyers.

[11]F. M. Cross, Jr., "The Development of the Jewish Scripts," *The Bible and the Ancient Near East: Essays in Honor of William Foxwell Albright* (Garden City, NY: Doubleday, 1965), 170–254; and idem, *The Ancient Library of Qumran and Modern Biblical Studies* (Westport, CT: Greenwood Press, 1976), 121.

[12]Fuller, "The Minor Prophets Manuscripts," 5.

existed both in the text and in the arrangement of the prophetic books within the scroll. These manuscripts suggest that variant arrangements of the Book of the Twelve were in circulation in Hebrew as late as 150-100 BCE, the approximate date of both 4QXII^a and the Old Greek translation of the Minor Prophets. The thesis of the present dissertation is that both 4QXII^a and the Hebrew source text of the LXX represent examples of variant literary editions of the Book of the Twelve and that these textual traditions may be used to reconstruct part of the literary history of the book. Subsequent chapters of the dissertation will attempt to support this thesis by means of recent methodological developments in textual criticism and by a thorough textual and literary examination of the ancient manuscripts of the Book of the Twelve. The background for such an investigation, however, may be provided by a discussion of the ancient literary evidence for the Book of the Twelve and by a summary of the scholarly research on the formation of the book. The remainder of Chapter One will be devoted to a survey of ancient evidence and modern scholarship on the Book of the Twelve that will indicate how the manuscript evidence described above might contribute to the current picture of the formation and history of the collection.

Ancient Evidence for the History of the Book of the Twelve

The remarks of the nineteenth century biblical scholar K. F. Keil well characterize the earliest literary evidence for the Book of the Twelve:

> As early as the collection of the canon the twelve Minor Prophets were combined onto a single scroll and *in the canon* they have ever been regarded and enumerated as one book.[13]

---

[13] *Manual of Historico-Critical Introduction to the Canonical Scriptures of the Old Testament*, Vol. I, tr. G. Douglas (1st ed. 1892, reprinted Grand Rapids, MI: Eerdmans, 1952), 364 (emphasis added).

All of the ancient literary attestations of the Minor Prophets confirm the evidence of the ancient manuscripts concerning the antiquity of the literary unity and sacred status of the Book of the Twelve. This evidence includes references found in extra-biblical literature and in lists of the books of the Hebrew canon.

Ancient Literary References

Sirach. Jesus Ben Sira's brief benediction in Sir 49:10 provides the earliest external reference to the Book of the Twelve.

> May the bones of the Twelve Prophets send forth new life from where they lie, for they comforted the people of Jacob and delivered them with confident hope (NRSV).

The renowned Jerusalem scribe, writing near the beginning of the second century BCE, knew the Minor Prophets as a collection unified both in name and in message. In 48:10, Ben Sira concluded his remarks about the prophet Elijah by citing ("it is written") from the text of Mal 3:23-24. This citation from the last two verses of the (Hebrew)[14] Book of the Twelve supports the reasonable assumption that Ben Sira knew the collection of the Twelve in essentially its completed form. Allowing some time for such a collection to gain circulation, his remarks provide a *terminus ad quem* for the Book of the Twelve of approximately 250 BCE.

The context of Ben Sira's remarks within the *laus patrum* of chapters 44–50 is suggestive for the relationship between the Book of the Twelve and the history of the biblical canon. Ben Sira's "praise of the ancestors" was not an enumeration of the books of the Hebrew Scriptures; rather it was an account of the heroes of Israel's history that demonstrated a continuous succession of religious leaders.[15] The array of biblical heroes listed in Sir 44–50, however, bears out the remarks of his

---

[14]MT Mal 3:22 follows rather than precedes MT Mal 3:23–24 in the LXX.

[15]J. C. H. Lebram, "Aspekte der alttestamentlichen Kanonbildung," *VT* 18 (1968): 173–89.

grandson that Ben Sira "had devoted himself to the study of the Law and the Prophets and the other books of the ancestors" (Prologue, lines 8–10). Ben Sira's blessing of the Twelve follows similar words of praise for the prophets Isaiah, Jeremiah, and Ezekiel. The Twelve were arranged within this historical schema according to the events that are chronicled in the works at the end of the book, namely the rebuilding of the Temple by Zerubbabel and Joshua ben Jehozadak under the guidance of Haggai and Zechariah, and the reforms of Nehemiah, possibly associated with material in the book of Malachi. Ben Sira's references to ancient Israel's sacred literature and traditions and the remarks of his grandson indicate that he was familiar at the least with a collection of sacred texts that included the Torah, the prophetic books, and other writings whose identity and number are not explicitly stated.

Qumran. A number of texts from the Minor Prophets are cited in the literature of the Qumran community.[16] No specific reference, however, is made to their existence as a unified collection. The discovery of seven fragmentary manuscripts of the Book of the Twelve, however, shows that this silence is not an indication that the Qumran covenanters did not know of the book. As the scriptural citations in the Qumran literature show, the Qumran community assumed the unity, not only of the Minor Prophets, but of all of Scripture as divinely inspired oracles. Texts were cited and interpreted in the Qumran documents as "Scripture" rather than as individual units, with little attention given to the immediate context of a given passage.[17] The unity of Book of the Twelve is taken for granted

---

[16]For a complete list see T. N. Swanson, "The Closing of the Collection of the Holy Scriptures: A Study in the History of the Canonization of the Old Testament" (Ph.D. diss., Vanderbilt University, 1970), 166.

[17]M. Fishbane, "The Use, Authority, and Interpretation of Mikra at Qumran," *Mikra: Text, Translation, Reading and Interpretation of the Hebrew Bible in Ancient Judaism and Early Christianity*, ed. M. J. Mulder (Philadelphia: Van

in the Qumran literature, and yet its particularity is lost within the larger context of "Scripture."

The New Testament. A similar situation presents itself in the use of the Minor Prophets among the NT writers. The NT cites or alludes to numerous passages from the Minor Prophets and employs a variety of citation formulas for introducing these scriptural quotations. The words of the prophets are sometimes cited as the words of the deity, "what was spoken by the Lord,"[18] or simply as the words of Scripture, "as it is written,"[19] or "as Scripture says."[20] On three occasions the NT author cites a text from the Book of the Twelve by the name of the individual prophet, twice in Romans ("as in Hosea," 9:25, 26) and once in Acts ("what was spoken through the prophet Joel," 2:17). The only explicit references to the Minor Prophets as a collection are found in the book of Acts. In Acts 7:42–43 the author introduces a quotation from Amos 5:25–27 with the citation *kathōs gegraptai en bibliō tōn prophetōn*, "as it is written in the book of the prophets," a clear reference to the Book of the Twelve. Acts 15:15 cites Amos 9:11–12 as "the words of the *prophets.*" Again in Acts 13:40–41, Hab 1:5 is cited as "what the *prophets* said." Since the citation in Acts 7:42 makes reference to the "book of the prophets," the use of the plural term "prophets" in Acts 13:41 and 15:15 most likely also refers to the Book of the Twelve rather than to the entire prophetic corpus. The NT writers knew the Minor Prophets as a single literary unit but, as with the Qumran literature, the larger context of Scripture received primary attention over the secondary context of the Book of the Twelve.

Apocrypha and Pseudepigrapha. Outside of Sir 48:10 and 49:10, citations and references to texts from the Minor Prophets are quite rare in apocryphal literature. Tob 2:6 explicitly cites the

---

Gorcum/Fortress Press, 1990), 347–55; see also G. J. Brooke, *Exegesis at Qumran* (Sheffield: JSOT Press, 1985).

[18]Matt 2:11; 21:4; Acts 2:17; Heb 12:26.

[19]Matt 26:31; Luke 7:27; 21:22; John 12:15; Rom 1:17; 9:13; 10:15.

[20]John 7:38, 42; 19:37; 1 Cor 15:4, 55.

text of Amos 8:10 and Tob 14:4 refers directly to Nahum's prophecy of doom for Nineveh.[21] Both texts are cited as direct speech rather than as words of Scripture, as if the hero Tobit had actually heard the prophets speak these words. This device is in harmony with the historical fiction and compressed chronology of the book.

The books of the Minor Prophets are also rarely cited in the Pseudepigrapha, although there are three texts in which the twelve prophetic individuals are listed by name. In 4 Ezra 1:39–40, the twelve are listed, following the sequence of the LXX, along with the three patriarchs as leaders of the peoples of the East. The context of this listing is concerned more with the prophets as individuals than with their literary remains. The second listing of the twelve prophets occurs in the work *The Lives of the Prophets.* As is expected, this work lists the events surrounding the death and burial of each of the twelve. The prophets are listed in the same sequence as in the LXX, except that the prophet Micah precedes rather than follows Amos. In *The Martyrdom and Ascension of Isaiah* 4:22, which is part of a late Christian interpolation, the twelve prophets are listed in the order Amos, Hosea, Micah, Joel, Nahum, Jonah, Obadiah, Habakkuk, Haggai, Zephaniah, Zechariah, and Malachi. This order, although unlike that of either the MT or the LXX, is closer to the LXX.[22] Although it is possible that the variant sequences in *Lives of the Prophets* and *Martyrdom of Isaiah* are based upon textual witnesses, they appear to be random listings of individual names rather than a reflection of alternative textual

---

[21]The reference to Nahum's oracle against Nineveh is found in Codex Sinaiticus. Codices Alexandrinus and Vaticanus, however, refer to Jonah's oracle against Nineveh. See the text and apparatus in R. Hanhart, ed. *Septuaginta. Vetus Testamentum Graecum, Vol. VIII/5 Tobit* (Göttingen: Vandenhoeck and Ruprecht, 1982).

[22]Instead of Hosea-Amos as in the LXX, *Mart. Isa.* reverses the order. Again, the LXX's Obadiah-Jonah-Nahum is reversed as Nahum-Jonah-Obadiah. Finally, the LXX's Zephaniah-Haggai is reversed as Haggai-Zephaniah.

arrangements of the prophetic books. That these listings reflect the sequence found in the LXX more so than that of the MT is a reminder of the authoritative status that the text of the LXX possessed in antiquity.

Lists of Canonical Books

Like the references to the Book of the Twelve in ancient texts, the earliest extant lists of canonical books also treated the Minor Prophets as a single volume. The earliest reference to the Book of the Twelve in an enumeration of biblical books is an indirect one and occurs in Josephus's remarks about the books of the Jewish Scriptures in *Against Apion* I.8. Dating to roughly the end of the first century CE, Josephus's reckoning of the number of books as twenty-two presupposes counting the Minor Prophets as one book. The number of the holy books reported to be transcribed by Ezra in 4 Ezra 14:41, twenty-four, also reflects this reckoning. This text also probably originated toward the end of the first century CE.

The earliest surviving list of books of the Hebrew Scriptures in Christian literature is that of Melito, bishop of Sardis, as preserved by Eusebius (*Eccl. Hist.* IV, xxvi.). There Melito lists the Minor Prophets as *tōn dodeka en monobiblō*, "the Twelve in one book." The next oldest extant list, that of Origen, also preserved by Eusebius (*Eccl. Hist.* VI, xxv) attests the unity of the Book of the Twelve in an unusual way. Origen's list intends to name the twenty-two books of the Jewish Scriptures. The list, however, contains only twenty-one items. The *dodekaprophelon*, missing from Origen's list presumably by accidental omission, would provide the twenty-second canonical book.[23]

The references to the Book of the Twelve in ancient texts and in lists and enumerations of the books of the Hebrew Scriptures demonstrate the continuity over several centuries of the treatment of the Book of the Twelve as a single book. They also confirm the frequent observation that the phenomenon of

---

[23]For other ecclestiastical lists of biblical books see Sweet, *Introduction to the Old Testament in Greek*, 201–205.

the Book of the Twelve was closely related in antiquity with the preservation of the sacred books of the Hebrew Scriptures. Both of these characteristics, the unity of the Twelve and its ancient scriptural status, are attested in the ancient manuscript remains. A survey of the scholarly literature on the Book of the Twelve will show that these two issues are also recurrent themes within the history of scholarship.

The Formation of the Book of the Twelve: History of Scholarship

Two general observations may be made about the treatment of the Book of the Twelve in previous research. First, scholars who have addressed the issue of the unity of the Book of the Twelve have dealt almost exclusively with the form and arrangement of the book in the MT. The variant arrangement of the LXX is either generally ignored or dismissed as a secondary alteration. The variant arrangement of 4QXII^a has not been addressed for the obvious reason that it has yet to be published. The existence of 4QXII^a, however, along with a fresh appraisal of the textual and literary distinctives of the LXX Book of the Twelve, provides an opportunity to review the results of previous scholarship in light of the full range of the manuscript evidence. The possible contributions of this manuscript evidence and the need to incorporate it into a study of the literary and canonical history of the Book of the Twelve will be demonstrated in the survey of research below.

The second general observation to be made about previous treatments of the unity of the Book of the Twelve is that scholars tend to characterize it in one of two ways: (1) as the result of extensive redactional composition, or (2) as the result of editorial compilation. Those who describe the unity of the Book of the Twelve as a redactional composition see it primarily as the work of ancient editors who unified the books of the Minor Prophets by composing numerous textual insertions into the seams of the text and thereby created either structural, thematic, or verbal relationships among the respective books. Those who view the Book of the Twelve as a compilation describe it primarily as the work of editors who collected the books of the Minor Prophets into a single volume because of pre-existing structural, thematic, or verbal ties that were perceived as unifying the respective books. Both characterizations are correct to some extent and most scholars recognize that the Book of the Twelve is the result of some degree of both compilation and redactional composition. As the following discussion will show, however, differences of opinion exist concerning the precise relationship between these two alternative views of the formation of the Book of the Twelve.

The Book of the Twelve as a Redactional Composition

K. Budde was the first scholar of the modern period to describe the Book of the Twelve as primarily a redactional creation.[24] Budde sought an explanation for the fragmented and disconnected nature of the contents of the Minor Prophets. He found most frustrating the scant amount of historical or narrative material that would provide the background for the prophets' utterances. Important events in the prophets' careers such as Hosea's marriage (Hos 1–3), Amos's confrontation with Amaziah (Amos 7:10–17), and Micah's disputation against unnamed prophets (Mic 3:1) received only the barest traces of narration required to report the divine words spoken on those occasions. Budde concluded that the enigmatic form of the Minor Prophets was the result of a systematic redaction of the prophetic traditions that sought to eliminate any "merely human" words in order to create a book consisting entirely of divine speech.

Budde identified the formation of the prophetic canon as the occasion for this redaction.[25] The purpose of the redaction was to produce a collection of prophetic materials of suitable holiness to be accepted into the corpus of sacred writings. Such a

---

[24]"Eine folgenschwere Redaktion des Zwölfprophetenbuchs," *ZAW* 39 (1922): 218–29.

[25]Ibid., 225–26. Budde employed the term "Kanon" but admitted that his use of the term was an anachronistic one, referring to what later became the canon of Hebrew Scripture.

redaction sought to placate the forerunners of groups such as the Samaritans and the Sadducees who viewed only the Torah as authoritative. The initial stage of the Priestly source, Pg, with its mere skeleton of narrative background, provided for Budde a parallel example of an abbreviated redaction of traditional materials. He argued that the proposed redaction must have taken place not only before the Minor Prophets were translated into Greek but also before the addition of the Book of Jonah, whose narrative form contradicts the aim of the entire redaction. He proposed a date in the fourth or third century BCE.

Budde's arguments have found little support in subsequent scholarly literature.[26] The lack of direct evidence for the supposedly excised material, the presence of some remaining biographical material (e.g. Hos 1–3, Amos 7:7–14), and the lack of historical evidence for the group(s) who would have questioned the sanctity of the prophetic literature make his theory difficult to accept. Nevertheless, Budde's observations have been too hastily dismissed. First, Budde was accurate in his description of the fragmented, aphoristic literary form of the Minor Prophets. His exasperation with the juxtapositions, elliptical references, and enigmatic symbolism of the Book of the Twelve provides a more straightforward assessment of the contents of the book than do other recent works that emphasize its literary unity to the point of ignoring the incongruities within the texts of the Minor Prophets.[27] Second, Budde's description of the "canonical" form of the Book of the Twelve as exclusively divine speech anticipated the discovery of the Qumran *pesharim* in which the words of the prophetic texts were interpreted exactly as Budde

---

[26]D. Schneider ("The Unity of the Twelve," 11) called Budde's article "irrelevant." W. Rudolph (*Haggai-Sacharja 1–8–Sacharja 9–14–Maleachi,* KAT XIII/4 [Gütersloh: Gerd Mohn, 1976], 298) also dismissed Budde's article as "in die Luft gebauen." For a more sympathetic treatment of Budde's arguments, see the comments of J. W. Rogerson, "Dodekapropheton," *TRE* Bd. IX (Berlin, New York: Walter de Gruyter, 1982), 18–20.

[27]For example, see the discussion below of P. House, *The Unity of the Book of the Twelve* (Sheffield: JSOT Press, 1990).

described them, i.e., as divine words having little relation to their human transmitters.[28] Finally, and most significantly, Budde's remarks about the late addition of the Book of Jonah take on new significance in light of the discovery of 4QXII[a], in which Jonah follows Malachi presumably at the end of the scroll.[29] The present study will seek to discover whether 4QXII[a] confirms Budde's argument about the relationship of Jonah to the Book of the Twelve.[30]

Budde's ingenious, but ultimately flawed, proposal of a comprehensive redaction of the Book of the Twelve inspired R. E. Wolfe's description of the Book of the Twelve as a redactional construct.[31] Rather than describing the Book of the Twelve as the result of the deletion of prophetic traditions, as Budde suggested, Wolfe saw the book as a result of an extended series of editorial additions. Based on his own reading of the individual books of the Minor Prophets and his (subjective) identification of the distinct characteristics of each prophet, Wolfe separated what appeared to him as "authentic" and "secondary" materials. Wolfe compared the "secondary" materials for similarity in content, language, and historical context. The result was a series of successive editions of what eventually became the Book of the Twelve, beginning with a Judaistic editor of the Book of Hosea

---

[28]See, for example, the view stated in 1QpHab vii.1ff. that Habakkuk's prophecies had no relation to the events of the prophet's day but were instead oracles written to be interpreted by the Teacher of Righteousness expressly for the needs of the Qumran community. For a thorough treatment of various views of prophecy in post-biblical literature, see J. Barton, *Oracles of God* (New York and Oxford: Oxford University Press, 1986).

[29]Budde had previously argued that Jonah was the final book to be added to the Book of the Twelve and was added to make the number of books total the sacred number twelve. See "Vermutungen zum 'Midrasch des Büches der Könige,'" *ZAW* 11 (1892): 37–51.

[30]See below, Chapter Four.

[31]"The Editing of the Book of the Twelve" (Ph.D. dissertation, Harvard University, 1933); idem, "The Editing of the Book of the Twelve," *ZAW* 53 (1935): 90–129.

and ending with the thirteenth and final editorial layer produced by the scribes who made the minor changes reflected in the differences between the MT and the LXX texts. The editorial activity described by Wolfe began in the mid-seventh century and was completed by 225 BCE. The acceptance of the Book of the Twelve as canonical, which Wolfe dated to approximately 200 BCE, precluded any further emendations to what was thereafter a sacrosanct text.

Before assessing the contributions of Wolfe's study to the issue of the Book of the Twelve and canon formation, a discussion of the flaws in his source-critical methodology is in order. First, Wolfe's criteria for identifying the "authentic" prophetic writings, which he identified as his "feeling and appreciation for the distinct views of each prophet,"[32] were entirely subjective; therefore, his resulting analysis, even if it were correct, could not possibly be validated. Texts which he identified as secondary have been labeled original by others possessing different literary sensibilities. No reliable method of adjudicating such differences exists. Secondly, Wolfe assumed that similar materials among the Minor Prophets were the result of common authorship rather than the result of quotation or prophetic tradition.[33] To assume that some similar materials are the result of common authorship is a legitimate assumption and in some cases this assumption may have a high degree of probability. To conclude, however, that all similar materials bear this single explanation is a mechanical and simplistic approach to an extremely complex literary corpus.

The obvious flaws in Wolfe's methodology and the excesses of his literary analysis, however, should not obviate his contributions to the issue of the unity of the Book of the Twelve. First, Wolfe argued that much of the material in the Book of the Twelve, in fact a majority of it, is the result of redactional activity. Although the means of identifying the precise extent

---

[32]Ibid., 90.

[33]Ibid., 125. Wolfe based this assumption on a view of prophets as religious innovators who eschewed religious tradition.

and origin of such material have yet to be found, the view is widely accepted in biblical scholarship that the process of transmission has not only preserved the texts of the Minor Prophets but has contributed to them as well.[34] A second important issue raised by Wolfe's study is the relationship that he posited between the redactional growth of the Book of the Twelve and its eventual canonical status. Wolfe argued that one of the editors' motives for collecting the prophetic literature was to preserve the literature of Israel's past, first during the exile, and secondly as the prophetic movement began to wane. Only later as the literature developed a history of preservation did it come to be recognized as sacred and authoritative. The issue of canonicity, which for Budde was the impetus for the redaction of the Book of the Twelve, was instead for Wolfe the terminal point of the redactional process. Although Wolfe's description of the relationship between redaction and the canonical process is speculative, his identification of this issue is an important contribution.

A final contribution of Wolfe's study is significant for the methodology of the present work. At least one of Wolfe's thirteen layers of redaction does possess some means of external validation, namely, those changes which he identified by comparison of the LXX and the MT texts of the Minor Prophets. Wolfe's "final" redactional stage suggests that the textual evidence of the LXX provides a concrete starting place for a redaction-historical study that would work backward from textual evidence to earlier, more conjectural levels of composition. Such a methodology, and its implications for the canonical process, is explored in Chapters Two and Three of this dissertation.

Research on the unity of the Book of the Twelve from a redaction-critical perspective waned in the decades following

---

[34]The recent trend, however, to reject redactional schemes of the growth of the Minor Prophets may be seen in S. Paul's recent commentary (*Amos*, [Minneapolis: Fortress Press, 1992]) in which he attributes the entire book to the eighth century prophet.

Wolfe's dissertation. Recent scholarship, however, has again taken up Wolfe's quest for the literary history behind the received Hebrew text of the Book of the Twelve. The renewed quest for the redactional history of the Book of the Twelve has employed more refined literary-critical tools, a more sophisticated methodology, and has achieved a more complex description of the editorial history of the text than previous studies. Whether the conclusions reached by means of these new approaches will be agreeable to a wide audience of scholars remains to be seen.

The methodology employed in the new redaction-critical investigations of the Book of the Twelve is primarily the one described in H. Barth and O. Steck's *Exegese des Alten Testaments*.[35] By the term redaction history, this methodology refers to the entire history of the text as a written document, from the first compositional layer to its last textual gloss. The redaction history of a given text may be constructed only after making a thorough literary-critical analysis of the various levels of the text's composition.

P. Weimar's description of the redaction history of the Book of Obadiah represents such a renewed attempt at a redactional explanation for the Book of the Twelve.[36] Weimar identified six layers of composition within the brief Book of Obadiah. By comparing the latest layers of redaction with supposedly secondary language found elsewhere in the Book of the Twelve, he suggested that the composition of the final form of the Book of Obadiah was connected to the larger context of the Book of the Twelve by means of verbal cross-references with other redactional texts within the Minor Prophets corpus.

Based upon an approach similar to that of Weimar, E. Bosshard has compared the structure of the Book of the Twelve with the Book of Isaiah and has argued that the final forms of the two books were the products of the same redactional tradents.[37]

---

[35]4th edition (Neukirchen-Vluyn: Neukirchener Verlag, 1973).

[36]"Obadja: Eine redaktionskritische Analyse," *BN* 27 (1985): 94–99.

[37]"Beobachtungen zum Zwölfprophetenbuch," *BN* 40 (1987): 30–62.

Bosshard identifies numerous examples of what appear to be
sequential parallels between the (MT) Book of the Twelve and
Isaiah. Concluding that these parallels must have arisen from a
common editorial history, Bosshard identifies three significant
texts within the Book of the Twelve that form key linkages with
Isaiah. On the basis of *Stichwörter* between the three texts, the
other Minor Prophets, and Isaiah, Bosshard identifies Joel 1:15,
2:1–11, Ob 5f., 15ff., and Zeph 2:13–15 and 3:14–18 as a single
redactional layer, whose purpose was to unify the Minor
Prophets in a way that reflects the parallel structure of the Book
of Isaiah.[38] The books of Jonah and Malachi, which bear no
parallels to Isaiah in Bosshard's analysis, are argued to belong to
yet another, later, redactional layer.

In a subsequent essay, Bosshard collaborates with R. G. Kratz
to describe the redactional incorporation of Malachi into the
Book of the Twelve, which they conclude to be the final level of
literary activity in the development of the book.[39] Again verbal
cross references are used to identify what Bosshard and Kratz
designate as redactional stages. Three such layers are isolated in
Malachi. The first redactional layer, Mal 1:2–5, 1:6–2:9 and 3:6–
12, has literary ties to Hosea 11–13 and Haggai-Zechariah 1–8,
encompassing a supposed pre-existing form of the Minor
Prophets.[40] The second layer proposed by Bosshard and Kratz is
Mal 2:17–3:5, 13–21. The third layer in Malachi is composed of
Mal 1:1,14a; 2:10–12; and 3:22–24. This redactional layer created
a twelfth prophetic book by means of the superscription in 1:1
and also encompassed the entire prophetic corpus by creating
verbal parallels between 3:22–24 and Jos 1:2, 7.[41]

The work of Bosshard and Kratz served as a point of
departure for O. Steck in his attempt to describe the final

---

[38]Ibid., 38.

[39]"Maleachi im Zwölfprophetenbuch," *BN* 52 (1990): 27–46.

[40]Ibid., 37–8.

[41]Ibid., 46.

redactional stages in the formation of the prophetic canon.[42] Based on his own redaction-critical work on the book of Isaiah and the conclusions of Bosshard and Kratz, Steck outlined the redactional development of the final chapters of Isaiah and the conclusion to the Book of the Twelve (Haggai, Zechariah, and Malachi) from an initial stage in the Persian period through seven consecutive rescensions dating from 332 to 200–190 BCE. The final rescension, Mal III in Bosshard and Kratz's scheme, created at one stroke the separate Book of Malachi, the Book of the Twelve, and the canonical collection of prophetic literature, which included Isaiah, Jeremiah, Ezekiel, and the completed Book of the Twelve.[43]

Although Weimar, Bosshard, Kratz, and Steck employ a more refined methodology than did R. Wolfe, their work shares many of the weaknesses of his literary-critical analysis. For example, although these scholars employ a consistent methodology and detailed literary analyses of the biblical text in identifying redactional materials, the sheer volume of secondary materials that they isolate makes a reconstruction of the redactional history extremely complex. As the amount of redactional material that is isolated from its present context increases, the number of possibilities for how the final form of the text came into being also increases. Concurrently, the increased amount of redactional material in the book also decreases dramatically the possibility that the redactional reconstructions of these scholars are correct. The redactional reconstructions of Weimar, Bosshard, Kratz, and Steck therefore suffer from their own success at identifying proposed redactional materials within the text of the Book of the Twelve.

Another weakness of the methodology of Weimar, Bosshard, Kratz and Steck is the hypothetical nature of their redactional reconstructions. Although their redactional stratification of the text does follow a detailed analysis of the literary structure of

---

[42]*Der Abschluss der Prophetie im Alten Testament* (Neukirchen: Neukirchener Verlag, 1991).

[43]Ibid., 132–36.

the final form of the book, their description of the redactional layers begins with the earliest reconstructed compositional layer and moves to the latest layer; they therefore build their case on a hypothetical initial stage that exists only in their own respective reconstructions.[44] The speculative nature of such reconstructions accounts for the widespread disagreement among scholars on the details of the texts' redactional history.

A third weakness in the redactional approach to the Book of the Twelve described above is one of logic. After demonstrating through literary analysis that a passage or a phrase does not fit literarily within its present context, the literary critics discussed above argue that the isolated text nevertheless coheres with other similar texts in disparate contexts and that these scattered texts belong to a single redactional hand. For example, in Bosshard's comparison between the Book of the Twelve and Isaiah, Joel 1:15, 2:1–11, Obad 5f., 15ff., and Zeph 2:13–15, 3:14–18 do not cohere to their present contexts, but bear sufficient similarity with each other and with texts in Isaiah to belong to the same redactional layer. It would seem that the same analysis that separated these texts from their present contexts would also advise caution in assigning a redactional unity to such disjointed texts. Contemporary redaction critics, however, appear to be far less analytical regarding the literary unity of their reconstructed redactional layers than toward the literary unity of the text in its final form.

These criticisms do not mean that some of the redaction-historical observations do not convince. One benefit of the studies cited above is that they demonstrate the numerous and complex verbal and literary relationships among the texts within the Book of the Twelve. Nevertheless, the conclusion that such complex relationships are uniformly the results of common redactional shaping is only one possible explanation of these

---

[44]The opposite approach of beginning with the more concrete redactional layer of the final form and moving backward toward earlier, more hypothetical layers is described and employed in G. Yee, *Composition and Tradition in the Book of Hosea* (Atlanta: Scholars Press, 1987), 1–50.

phenomena. Literary dependency, shared traditions, the often limited vocabulary of classical Hebrew, and even coincidence are some of the alternative explanations. Often a precise judgment between these options is impossible to achieve. Stricter controls than those employed by the authors cited above are needed to adjudicate reliably the questionable cases. For example, Steck, Bosshard, Weimar and others do not offer a range of probability, from very likely to less likely, for their suggested redactional stages. They also do not say what constitutes a critical mass of cross references with other texts or inconsistencies with the immediate context that would tip the scales of judgment in favor of identifying a text as evidence of an independent redactional stage. Often, a subjective judgment about a text's redactional origins becomes an accepted fact upon which further judgments are made. Finally, the basis for these scholars' precise dating of reconstructed redactional stages, especially within the fourth and third centuries BCE when little historical evidence is available, is difficult to ascertain.

The Book of the Twelve as a Literary Compilation

Scholars who judge the Book of the Twelve to be a literary unity are generally more skeptical about either the existence of comprehensive redactional layers within the text, or the possibility of reliably identifying such layers. Instead, these scholars view the Book of the Twelve as a compilation of pre-existing materials that were recognized as already possessing literary, thematic, or structural affinities. This description includes those who employ methodologies from the discipline of literary studies and also those who argue for the "canonical" unity of the Book of the Twelve.

Possibly the earliest example in modern critical scholarship of the view of the Book of the Twelve as a literary compilation is found in the work of H. Ewald.[45] Ewald used the evidence of the prophetic superscriptions to reconstruct pre-exilic and post-

---

[45] *Die Propheten des Alten Bundes*, Vol I (Göttingen: Vandenhoeck and Ruprecht, 1867), 73–81.

exilic collections of the prophetic books. According to Ewald, the editors who created this collection did insert some material into the text; the name "Malachi" in Mal 1:1 was one such insertion which was intended to create a twelfth named prophet. Although Ewald allowed for some editorial additions, however, these were of a far more limited nature than the comprehensive redactions discussed above. The editors of the Book of the Twelve were in Ewald's view primarily compilers.[46]

By far the most comprehensive argument for the literary compilation of the Book of the Twelve is the 1979 Yale dissertation of D. Schneider. Intrigued by the lack of scholarly attention to the received, "canonical" form of the Minor Prophets and dissatisfied with the excesses of previous literary analysis, Schneider sought to discover the significance of the Book of the Twelve as a textual unity by investigating its origins. The result was a description of a four-stage process of development beginning in the eighth century BCE and concluding during the career of Nehemiah in the last half of the fifth century.

Schneider proposed that a collection of the books of Hosea, Amos, and Micah in the time of King Hezekiah formed the nucleus of the Book of the Twelve.[47] He argued that this early collection, reflected in the order of these three books in the LXX, was united by (1) evidence of literary dependence of Hosea upon Amos and of Micah upon both Hosea and Amos; (2) the use of catchword associations; and (3) thematic and theological unity among the three respective books.[48] A second collection consisting of Nahum, Habakkuk and Zephaniah was compiled by

---

[46]For a similar explanation of the history of the Book of the Twelve, see C. Steuernagel, *Lehrbuch der Einleitung das Alte Testament* (Tübingen: J. C. B. Mohr, 1912), 669–72.

[47]"The Unity of the Book of the Twelve," 38–42.

[48]D. N. Freedman has argued for a similar collection during Hezekiah's reign based on the evidence of the superscriptions to these books. See "Headings in the Books of the Eighth Century Prophets," *AUSS* 25 (1987): 9–26.

a Josianic reform party and added to the prior collection probably during the exile.[49] Thematic development, literary dependence, and verbal associations give unity and order to these three works. In Schneider's third stage of development, the books of Joel, Obadiah, and Jonah were added to the six previously named books at a late stage of the exilic period.[50] In arriving at this date, Schneider located the origin of Joel in the late seventh century and Jonah in the sixth century. Schneider not only based these dates on the usual internal and linguistic evidence, but also employed the sequence of the Twelve as a clue to their date of composition. Schneider's fourth and final stage consisted of the addition of Haggai, Zechariah, including chapters 9–14 (early fifth century), and Malachi, an addition accomplished no later that the end of the fifth century BCE.[51]

Schneider has carefully argued for a plausible reconstruction of the origins of this collection. His arguments for an early collection consisting of Hosea, Amos, and Micah are for the most part convincing ones that explain both the LXX sequence of these books as well as the original impetus for combining prophetic texts together. His early date for Zechariah 9–14 was based on sound arguments and has been echoed in recent scholarship.[52] He gave a thorough discussion of the role that inner-biblical allusions and citations played in the creation of the sequence of the books among the Twelve. He also argued for a literary component of the prophetic task, claiming that the books of Joel and Habakkuk in particular were primarily literary compositions designed to occupy their respective positions in the prophetic corpus.[53] Schneider's account is a balanced

---

[49]Schneider, "The Unity of the Book of the Twelve," 55–56.

[50]Ibid., 112–14.

[51]Ibid., 143–45.

[52]A. E. Hill, "Dating Second Zechariah: A Linguistic Reexamination," *HAR* 6 (1982): 105–34; C. L. Meyers and E. M. Meyers, *Zechariah 9–14*, The Anchor Bible Vol. 25B (Garden City, NY: Doubleday, 1993), 18–28.

[53]Examples of recent studies emphasizing the literary activity of some prophets include E. Davis, *Swallowing the Scroll: Textuality and the Dynamics of*

treatment of both the unity and the complexity of the Book of the Twelve.

An appreciation of the far-reaching scope of Schneider's investigation and reconstruction is nevertheless diminished by the scarcity of external historical evidence for the origin and prehistory of the Book of the Twelve and thus the necessity of reliance on internal clues alone, conditions which literary-critical approaches to the Book of the Twelve also faced. Therefore even Schneider's cautious treatment of the issue is vulnerable to the following assessment:

> Schneider's [work] is an excellent background to the topic as well as a thorough discussion of various theories on the order of prophets in the Twelve. His own theory is ingenious; *but so are most other proposals.*[54]

One difficulty that Schneider and others face is the problem of explaining literary parallels between the various prophetic books. Schneider attributed nearly all similarities in the text to the explanation of literary dependence of one prophet/text upon another. He describes an almost unbroken chain of prophetic tradition from the earlier "writing" prophets through the so-called end of prophecy concluding with Malachi. If one concedes that far more prophetic speech and writings existed in ancient Israel than what is preserved in the relatively few texts that are now extant, then it is equally likely that the shared language and themes among the prophets are a result of their

---

Discourse in Ezekiel's Prophecy (Sheffield: Almond Press, 1990); S. Bergler, *Joel als Schriftinterpret* (Frankfurt an Main, New York, Paris: Peter Lang, 1990); H. Utzschneider, *Künder oder Schreiber? Eine These zum Problem der "Schriftprophetie" auf Grund von Maleachi 1,6–2,9* (Frankfurt an Main, New York, Paris: Peter Lang, 1989); and D. Christensen, "The Book of Nahum: The Question of Authorship within the Canonical Process," *JETS* 31 (1988): 51–8.

[54]J. Sasson, *Jonah*, The Anchor Bible Vol. 24B (New York: Doubleday, 1990) 15, n. 9 (emphasis added).

mutual appropriation of independent traditions or speech forms rather than direct borrowing from one writing prophet by another writing prophet. For example, does Hosea's use of lion imagery for God (Hos 5:24) necessarily imply a dependence upon Amos's use of the same (Amos 1:2, 3:8), as if Amos held a monopoly on this metaphor?[55] Schneider's assumption of literary dependence in every instance of parallel language is too woodenly applied to an extremely complex literary corpus.[56]

Schneider's work points out another difficulty in dealing with the internal evidence of the Book of the Twelve, namely, the question of how to judge the literary history of the various textual units. Although I have criticized Wolfe, Steck, and others for too subjectively judging many texts to be secondary additions, others would likewise be critical of Schneider's conservatism in attributing nearly all of the Book of the Twelve to its named prophetic authors.[57] Such mutually exclusive criticisms of Wolfe, Steck, and Schneider highlight the difficulty of identifying stages of literary composition that preceded that of the received text. Only if one has at hand a previous or at least differing version of the text under consideration would it be possible to discuss concretely the reality of redactional changes to the text.

For this reason, the most severe limitation of Schneider's work is the lack of attention he devotes to the differences between the LXX and the MT texts of the Book of the Twelve.

---

[55]Schneider, "Unity of the Twelve," 21. For examples of the use of this imagery in Ancient Near Eastern literature and iconography, see S. Paul, *Amos*, 21.

[56]Cf., however, Schneider's rejection of literary dependence between Joel 2:13–14 and Jonah 3:9, 4:2 ("Unity of the Twelve," 104) when such a relationship does not fit his reconstruction.

[57]To Schneider's credit he did identify some material, namely, the references to Judah in Hosea and the doxologies in Amos, as redactional ("Unity of the Twelve," 38–40). Few scholars would agree, however, with either his eighth century date for this material or with his reasoned but unconvincing argument for the integrity of Micah.

Schneider plays down the varying sequence of books in the LXX, arguing that the LXX order is a variant sequence dependent upon the MT. Unfortunately, after much effort to discern the literary unity of the MT Book of the Twelve, he does not investigate the possible literary unity of the LXX arrangement. If Schneider had attempted to find the literary unity of the LXX Book of the Twelve, he would have found, following his own methodology, much evidence that the LXX order of the first six books of the Twelve is also a unified literary corpus. Chapter Five of this dissertation will demonstrate that the literary, thematic, and structural relationships among the first six books in the LXX arrangement are equally coherent and cohesive as those that Schneider has identified for the MT Book of the Twelve. The same argument will be made in Chapter Four for the order attested in 4QXII[a], to which Schneider understandably did not have access.

Another approach to the question of an underlying unity within the Book of the Twelve takes as its starting point the recent scholarly emphasis on the Bible as canon. An article on the canonical unity of the Book of the Twelve by R. Clements has been particularly influential in this regard.[58] Taking a clue from ancient texts such as Sir 49:10 and Acts 3:24 that describe the prophets as speaking with a unified voice, Clements identified a hermeneutical tendency to harmonize varied prophetic texts into a single prophetic *message*. Clements argued that for early Judaism and Christianity, the essential message of the canonical prophets was one of judgment followed by restoration, with an emphasis on the latter.[59] This unified message of hope for restoration, which was predominant mostly after 587 BCE, was nonetheless recognized by later tradents and collectors of prophetic literature as a natural outgrowth of hopeful elements evidenced within the earlier prophetic

---

[58]R. Clements, "Patterns in the Prophetic Canon,"in *Canon and Authority*, ed. George W. Coats and Burke O. Long (Philadelphia: Fortress Press, 1977), 43–56.

[59]Ibid., 45.

traditions themselves. Clements argued that the prophetic writings were collected and edited in such a way as to highlight the full prophetic message within each text, including the crucial element of hope for restoration.[60] Although Clements's remarks are highly suggestive for understanding the origins of the Book of the Twelve, he does not spell out the implications of his observations for understanding specifically how the collection came together, nor does he discuss more specific examples of unifying features within the corpus beyond the general pattern of judgment and restoration.

A. Y. Lee's dissertation on the Book of the Twelve sought to expand upon Clements's comments about hopeful endings within the prophetic corpus.[61] Following Clements, Lee argues that the Book of the Twelve was unified by the theme of hope that characterizes the concluding sections of many of the books of the Minor Prophets.[62] Contrary to the arguments of numerous commentators, Lee concludes that the hopeful elements in the pre-exilic prophetic books of Hosea, Amos, and Micah were for the most part not redactional additions but rather integral parts of the proclamation of the individual prophets. The collectors of the remaining books of the Minor Prophets found comfort in these hopeful texts and shaped the entire collection in light of the pattern of judgment and hope.

Although a treatment of the canonical context of the Book of the Twelve seems an obvious result of the scholarly emphasis on canonicity, Lee's work in that direction has some serious difficulties. First, Lee makes no use of Schneider's dissertation because he claims that it does not employ a "canonical

---

[60]A similar point is made by B. Childs in his article, "The Canonical Shape of the Prophetic Literature," *Interpretation* 32 (1978): 46–55. Childs, however, prefers to discuss individual books and does not extend his argument to the Book of the Twelve.

[61]"The Canonical Unity of the Scroll of the Minor Prophets" (Ph.D. dissertation, Baylor University, 1985).

[62]These "hopeful endings" include Hos 14:1–8; Amos 9:11–15; Mic 7:8–20; Joel 4:16–21; Obad 17–21; and Zeph 3:8–20.

approach," even though Schneider's work is based upon a conscious attempt to understand the received form of the Minor Prophets as a single volume. Secondly, although Lee's work primarily reflects the influence of Clements's article, he identifies his method as the canonical approach of B. Childs. Childs, however, deliberately avoids the issue of the unity of the Book of the Twelve except to say that it remains an unresolved problem.[63] Ultimately, Lee's dissertation adds little to the previous observations of Clements.

Clements's article also served as a partial model for a recent monograph on the Book of the Twelve by P. House.[64] Although expressing a common cause with canonical criticism, House employs "literary criticism" to identify the genre, structure, themes, and plot of the Book of the Twelve in an attempt to demonstrate its unity. House identified the Book of the Twelve as comprised of three elements or movements: sin (Hosea to Micah); punishment (Nahum to Zephaniah); and restoration (Haggai to Malachi).

House's description of the unity of the Book of the Twelve takes Clements's balanced thesis to unacceptable extremes by reducing the rich diversity of the contents of Minor Prophets to an overly simplistic scheme. Although the pattern of judgment and hope is readily identifiable within the Minor Prophets and may have been one unifying factor, as Clements argues, the texts are far more complex and diverse than the description of House allows. For example, although the final movement of the Book of the Twelve is said to be that of hope for restoration, the final line of the (MT) Book of Malachi, "lest I come and strike the land with a curse," is somewhat less than a hopeful peroration. House's reductionistic tendency is demonstrated by his redundant use of the pattern "sin-judgement-restoration" as the basis for three different chapters of his book, describing respectively the structure, the theme, and the plot of the Book of

---

[63] *Introduction to the Old Testament as Scripture* (Philadelphia: Fortress Press, 1979), 308–9.

[64] *The Unity of the Twelve* (Sheffield: JSOT Press, 1990).

the Twelve. The "dark riddle" of the Minor Prophets described by Budde appears to be a more accurate description of the Book of the Twelve than House's *a priori*, theologically-determined scheme of "literary" unity.

House's work is also flawed by an overt polemic against "historical criticism," claiming that "historical research has not successfully uncovered the structure of the Twelve because that structure is governed by literary principles."[65] This statement not only shows that House has ignored Schneider's balanced treatment of literary issues in his dissertation (not cited in House's bibliography), but also reveals House's assumption that all "historical" critics are literary boors.[66] House's innovative attempt to describe the Book of the Twelve in formalist categories is ultimately inferior to Schneider's treatment and succeeds primarily in demonstrating the limitations of such an approach to the Minor Prophets.

Two other treatments of the Book of the Twelve as a unit do, however, demonstrate the merits of a strictly "literary" approach to the text. N. Gottwald's article on "Tragedy and Comedy in the Latter Prophets"[67] addresses concerns similar to those of House such as issues of genre and plot. Gottwald, however, recognizes that prophetic books "as a whole are not coherent narratives, but mixtures of genres written compositely over centuries of time."[68] Gottwald chooses to speak, therefore, of the plot of the "implied narrative" lying behind the formally diverse prophetic materials. The implied narrative, namely that "both Israelite kingdoms were destroyed but that the national identity continued both in a restoration to Palestine and in a

---

[65]Ibid., 67.

[66]Ibid., 109. House cites none other than G. von Rad's (!) comments concerning the enigmatic arrangement of the prophetic corpus as an example of such exclusively historically-minded scholarship. It remains to be seen whether House's literary sensitivities are to be preferred over those of von Rad.

[67]*Semeia* 32 (1984): 83–96.

[68]Ibid., 83.

thriving Jewish life in dispersion," allows Gottwald to address both the overarching comic shape of the Minor Prophets and its dark, tragic character as well.

H. Marks's treatment of the Book of the Twelve[69] also employs literary perspectives without diminishing the diversity or complexity of the texts. Marks describes the Book of the Twelve in relation to the interplay of "text" and "voices." The "text" refers to the overarching structure of the single "book" of the Twelve, thus encompassing the unifying features that scholars such as Schneider, Clements, and House have identified. Marks also, however, gives attention to the "voices" within the text, the individual and diverse elements of the Minor Prophets that do not fit into any unifying scheme. Marks argues that although the canonical form of the book is designed to consolidate its complex contents into a literary unity, the discordant features of the book cannot altogether be silenced.

The works of Marks and Gottwald provide models of literary assessments of the Book of the Twelve that do not reduce the possible play of interpretations preserved within the canonical form of the book. They also demonstrate that a literary assessment of the Book of the Twelve can be valid without denying the composite nature of the book or the presence of redactional materials within the individual texts of the collection. Their works recognize the paradox that although it is most likely that some if not much of the text of the Minor Prophets is redactional in origin, attempts to identify these texts and their relationships to one another is difficult if not impossible to accomplish. In spite of such a situation, Gottwald and Marks conclude that a reading of the texts as a unified corpus is both possible and fruitful.

A Recent Synthesis of Previous Approaches

The most recent treatment of the formation of the Book of the Twelve, J. Nogalski's doctoral dissertation, attempts to bring

---

[69]"The Twelve Prophets," in *The Literary Guide to the Bible*, ed. R. Alter and F. Kermode (Cambridge: Harvard University Press, 1987), 207–32.

together the best elements of previous redactional and literary approaches into a new synthesis that explains the unifying elements of the book and their origins as well.[70] A student of Steck's, Nogalski approaches the text from the perspective of a literary and redaction-critical methodology. His recognition of the inconclusive and unsatisfactory nature of previous literary-critical approaches, however, including those of Weimar and Bosshard, is demonstrated in his stated goal of establishing "a *more objective starting point* for a discussion of the unity of the Book of the Twelve."[71] The objective starting point of which he speaks is the phenomenon of catchword associations that are shared in common by contiguous books in the MT order of the Minor Prophets.[72]

The catchwords that are the basis of Nogalski's work occur in the concluding and beginning sections of contiguous books within the Minor Prophets collection. The texts of Hosea 14 and Joel 1 may be cited as an example of his methodology and argument. The words *yŏšĕbîm* "inhabitants," *dāgān* "grain," *gepen* "vine," and *yayin* "wine" occur in Hos 14:8 and also in the first chapter of Joel at 1:10, 1:7, and 1:5 respectively. Nogalski begins his study of these word tallies with a thorough treatment of the relationship of Hosea 14 to the larger context of the Book of Hosea and also the relationship of Hos 14:8 to the structure and syntax of its

---

[70]"Redactional Layers and Intentions: Uniting the Writings of the Book of the Twelve" (Ph.D. dissertation, University of Zürich, 1991). Nogalski's dissertation has recently been reedited for publication in two volumes: *Literary Precursors to the Book of the Twelve*, BZAW 217 (Berlin: Walter de Gruyter, 1993); and *Redactional Processes in the Book of the Twelve*, BZAW 218 (Berlin: Walter de Gruyter, 1993).

[71]"Redactional Layers and Intentions," 17 (emphasis added). This stated aim of Nogalski has been removed from the published edition of the dissertation and is therefore cited from the text of the dissertation itself.

[72]Nogalski dismisses the LXX order of the Twelve as secondary and discounts the sequence of 4QXII[a] until publication of the text (*Literary Precursors to the Book of the Twelve*, 2, nn. 5 and 8). See the criticism below regarding his exclusive dependence upon the MT sequence.

immediate context in Hos 14:2–10.[73] Based upon such an analysis, Nogalski argues that Hos 14:8 does not suit the structure and message of its immediate context and therefore concludes that it is a redactional insertion, the purpose of which is to connect the Book of Hosea with the Book of Joel by means of redactional catchwords. A similar analysis of Joel 1:1–14 results in the conclusion that the catchwords from Hos 14:8 are integral to the structure and context of Joel 1. Nogalski thus concludes that the author of Joel not only constructed his text to connect with the end of Hosea, but he also inserted Hos 14:8 in order to solidify that connection by means of *Stichwörter.*[74]

Nogalski seeks answers to the origin of the Book of the Twelve by a thorough examination of the catchword phenomenon in all twelve books of the Minor Prophets. Although he recognizes Schneider's extensive use of catchwords to explain the sequence of the Twelve, Nogalski criticizes Schneider's unilateral rejection of the possible redactional origins of the numerous catchwords. In light of the shortcomings of previous redactional approaches to the Minor Prophets, however, Nogalski also refuses to explain all of the catchwords between contiguous books by a single explanation of redactional activity. As seen in the example from Hosea and Joel, Nogalski evaluates each occurrence of catchwords in the Book of the Twelve on the basis of: (1) their immediate literary context; (2) the transmission history of the individual writing to which they belong; (3) their function within the context of the Book of the Twelve; and (4) relationships between the contexts of the catchwords and other texts within the Hebrew Bible.[75] The result of such analysis, therefore, is a balanced, methodologically consistent treatment of the redactional history of the Book of the Twelve.

Based upon his analysis of the catchwords in the text of the Book of the Twelve, Nogalski reconstructs the redactional history of the book as follows. First, initial forms of the books of

---

[73]*Literary Precursors,* 58–69.

[74]*Redactional Processes,* 13–22.

[75]*Literary Precursors,* 15.

Hosea, Amos, Micah, and Zephaniah were united by a Deuteronomistic layer of editing at some point during the sixth century.[76] This corpus was united primarily by the chronological schema employed in the superscriptions, which, like the Deuteronomistic History, connects the works of the prophets with the reigns of Israelite and Judean kings.[77] Second, early forms of the books of Haggai and Zechariah 1–8 formed a pre-existing corpus in addition to the Deuteronomistic corpus.[78]

The two pre-existing corpora described above were united, according to Nogalski, by a sweeping redactional stage that inserted the books of Joel, Obadiah, Nahum, Habbakuk, and Malachi into the chronological framework of the two previous collections, and thereby created a single unified book of eleven prophetical writings.[79] Nogalski dates this layer of redactional expansion to the fourth century BCE. Zechariah 9–14 is thought to have been added to the eleven-book corpus after the expansive insertion of the Joel layer of texts, although a more precise dating of this addition is difficult to determine.[80] The twelfth and last independent writing to be added to the Book of the Twelve was the Book of Jonah.[81]

---

[76]Ibid., 85–88.

[77]Ibid. Nogalski's observations about the overlap between the superscriptions of Hosea, Amos, and Micah were reached independently of similar conclusions in Freedman, "Headings in the Eighth Century Prophets." Nogalski observes that Zephaniah extends the chronological span of the Hosea-Amos-Micah corpus from the reign of Hezekiah (Mic 1:1; Zeph 1:1) to the reign of Josiah (Zeph 1:1).

[78]*Literary Precursors*, 240–72. Again, Nogalski apparently arrived at this conclusion about a Haggai-Zechariah 1–8 corpus independently of the extensive arguments for the same conclusion by Meyers and Meyers, *Haggai, Zechariah 1–8*, Anchor Bible Vol. 25A (Garden City, NY: Doubleday, 1987), xliv–xlvii and passim.

[79]Nogalski, *Redactional Processes*, 275–77.

[80]Ibid., 241–47.

[81]Ibid., 270–73.

Of the expansions of the Minor Prophets collection that resulted in the Book of the Twelve, the most important by far for Nogalski was the layer that incorporated the Book of Joel into the collection. Not only were the books of Joel, Obadiah, Nahum, Habbakkuk, and Malachi supposedly added to the previous collections, but Nogalski claims that the addition of these books was also the primary occasion for extensive redactional work that sought to unify the entire corpus of the Minor Prophets by means of redactional catchwords. Most important in this unifying redactional work, according to Nogalski, was the Book of Joel. The series of locust-like invaders in Joel 1 served as a quasi-apocalyptic schema for the numerous invasions of Israel and Judah depicted in the chronological schema of the Book of the Twelve.[82] Redactional insertions within Hos 14:8, Amos 9:12–13, and Micah 1 incorporated the books of Joel and Obadiah into their present contexts in the Book of the Twelve.[83] Allusions to locusts in Nah 3:15, 17 and Hab 1:9 served to incorporate these two books into the chronological schema of the Twelve by identifying the enemies depicted within these books as Assyria and Babylon, respectively.[84] Finally, the recurrence in Haggai, Zechariah, and Malachi of agricultural motifs present in the Book of Joel is explained as the result of further unifying redactional activity on the part of the editor(s) of the Minor Prophets collection.

The scope of Nogalski's work and his detailed and thorough treatment of the redactional seams between the books of the Twelve Prophets do not allow a thorough summary of his work within the framework of the present chapter. His analyses will be treated in subsequent chapters as they impinge upon the discussion of individual texts. Nevertheless, a few general observations are necessary. Nogalski's exhaustive analysis and sensitivity to literary and theological issues are exemplary. His aim of calling scholarly attention to the role of catchwords in the

---

[82]Ibid., 276.

[83]Ibid., 43–46, 72–73, 82–84.

[84]Ibid., 116, 142–43.

formation of a unified Book of the Twelve should certainly meet with success. More than any scholar since Schneider, Nogalski's work will challenge future scholars to take seriously the unifying elements within the Minor Prophets collection. Perhaps the most laudable aspect of Nolgalski's work is the clarity and consistency of his methodology. He elucidates a self-conscious and balanced methodological approach to the problem of the formation of the Book of the Twelve and follows this methodology throughout the course of his treatment.

In light of Nogalski's thorough analysis and careful research, criticism of his work arises primarily from the limitations of his methodology rather than the quality of his investigation. First, although Nogalski seeks to give a balanced treatment of the question of whether verbal parallels between texts were the result of redactional insertion, or whether the catchwords were already present in the texts when the various books were joined together, which was the general conclusion of Schneider, Nogalski's conclusions are almost without exception that the catchwords are the result of redactional activity. Although he does distinguish between texts that have relatively objective evidence for their redactional status and texts whose redactional status is less well attested, even in the more questionable cases Nogalski opts for the explanation of redactional insertion. For example, Nogalski argues that the use of agricultural motifs in the texts of Haggai, Zechariah 1–8 and Malachi are the result of redactional unification with similar motifs in the Book of Joel.[85] The possibility that the frequent use of agricultural imagery is a result of concerns during the Persian period with food production in the war-ravaged province of Yehud is not considered by Nogalski.[86] The tendency toward redaction as the explanation for all parallel language in the Book of the Twelve

---

[85]Ibid., 204–207. Examples of such texts include Hag 2:19; Zech 8:12; and Mal 3:10–11.

[86]For a discussion of the economic context of late sixth and early fifth century Yehud, see Meyers and Meyers, *Haggai, Zechariah 1–8*, 41–42; idem, *Zechariah 9–14*, 22–25.

appears to derive from the orientation of Nogalski's redaction-critical methodology.

Another criticism of Nogalski's work has to do with some of the words that he accepts as unifying catchwords. Although many of his examples are convincing, many other words occur far too frequently within the Hebrew Bible to conclude that their presence within the seams of the Book of the Twelve is the result of intentional redaction. In the example cited above, Nogalski cites the word "inhabitants" in Hos 14:8 and Joel 1:2 as a redactional catchword, even though the word occurs more than two hundred times in the Hebrew Bible. Elsewhere, Nogalski lists thirteen words shared by both Nahum 1 and Mic 7:8–20, texts that are contiguous in the MT Book of the Twelve.[87] He argues that these shared words are evidence of redactional unification of these two texts. He includes among his word tallies, however, words such as "anger," "sea," "rivers," "mountains," "land," and "day," each of which occurs at least one hundred times in the Hebrew Bible. It is difficult to see how words such as *yôm* and *'ereṣ*, each of which occurs over 2200 times in the Hebrew Bible, can reasonably be identified as redactional insertions. The presence of such words adds little to Nogalski's argument.

Finally, and most importantly for the present study, like all other treatments of the Book of the Twelve described above, Nogalski's work depends exclusively upon the MT sequence of the Book of the Twelve for the reconstruction of its redactional history. This dependence limits Nolgalski's work in two ways. First, Nogalski concludes that for the books of Hosea, Joel, Amos, and Obadiah, the presence of catchwords demands that the books must be contiguous within the scroll of the Twelve, and that deviations that create a displacement of the catchwords, such as the sequence of the LXX, must represent a secondary arrangement. For example, the presence of catchwords with Joel

---

[87]This portion of Nogalski's dissertation is summarized in the article "The Redactional Shaping of Nahum 1 for the Book of the Twelve," in *Among the Prophets*, ed. P. R. Davies and D. J. A. Clines, JSOTSup 144 (Sheffield: JSOT Press, 1993), 197.

1 in the text of Hos 14:8 demands, according to Nogalski, that Joel 1 follow the Book of Hosea in the original sequence of the Book of the Twelve. The arrangement of Hosea and Joel in the LXX must therefore be a secondary displacement. This conclusion, however, is undermined by claims made elsewhere by Nogalski himself. Nogalski identifies a number of texts within the Minor Prophets such as Nah 3:15, 17, Hab 3:17, and Hag 2:19 as redactional glosses that are intended to link those books with similar language in the distantly removed Book of Joel. Based on this argument, the text of Hos 14:8 could just as easily be explained as such a redactional gloss, without prejudging the sequence of the MT as the original or exclusively meaningful sequence of books.

A second limitation of Nogalski's work that is the result of his exclusive focus on the MT is that a number of his conclusions about the redactional history of the Book of the Twelve could be strengthened by a consideration of the variant sequences contained in the LXX and 4QXII[a]. For example, Nogalski concludes, much as did Budde earlier, that the Book of Jonah is the final independent writing to enter the corpus of the Book of the Twelve. This conclusion appears to be strengthened by the fact that Jonah occurs in three different positions in manuscripts of the Book of the Twelve, and also by the sequence of 4QXII[a], in which Jonah is presumably the final book of the scroll. In another example, Nogalski concludes that the books of Joel, Obadiah, Nahum, and Habakkuk share so many common verbal and thematic similarities that they most likely entered the corpus of the Minor Prophets at the same time and from the same redactional hand. Interestingly, if on the basis of the sequence of 4QXII[a] one removes the Book of Jonah from the LXX arrangement of the Twelve, the result is a sequence of Joel, Obadiah, Nahum, and Habakkuk. In this case the evidence of the LXX and 4QXII[a] highlights the many literary affinities between Joel, Obadiah, Nahum, and Habakkuk that are identified by Nogalski. These two examples alone suggest that further scrutiny of the variant arrangements preserved within the manuscripts of the Book of the Twelve might yield new information about the formation and history of the book.

Conclusion

The history of scholarship on the issue of the unity of the Book of the Twelve demonstrates a degree of disagreement on the origin of the book and the kind of literary activity that produced it. The two primary views of the book's origin are that it is either the result of redactional composition or editorial compilation. Even among scholars who agree on the nature of the book's unity, a wide variety of opinions exists concerning the details of its literary history and its internal relationships.

Such disagreements notwithstanding, a fair amount of agreement exists on certain issues related to the unity of the Book of the Twelve. For example, most scholars agree that there are numerous literary relationships between the various texts within the Book of the Twelve and that these relationships contribute to the book's cohesiveness. Also, most scholars agree that the arrangement of the Book of the Twelve, at least in its MT sequence, represents a coherent, intentional ordering of the material. Most scholars surveyed above, with few exceptions, also admit that the Book of the Twelve is an extremely complex corpus and that an understanding of the precise nature of all of its relationships has thus far eluded scholarly investigation. Finally, all of the scholars reviewed above posit some connection between the formation of the Book of the Twelve and the history of the canon of Hebrew Scriptures, a connection to be explored in detail in the following chapter.

The ancient evidence for the Book of the Twelve, including the ancient manuscript witnesses and the scholarly literature on its formation and unity reveal three questions that require further investigation. These questions are: (1) What is the significance of the variant arrangements found in the LXX manuscripts and in 4QXII[a]? (2) By what method can the various redactional schemes proposed for the Book of the Twelve be reliably evaluated? (3) What impact does a consideration of the manuscript evidence have upon previous claims about the relationship between the Book of the Twelve and the formation of the prophetic canon?

(1) The issue of the variant arrangement of the LXX Book of the Twelve is noticeably absent from the scholarly discussion. The previously unknown sequence of books discovered in 4QXII[a] invites renewed attention to the evidence of the LXX text and also requires investigation of its own internal arrangement in relation to the formation of the Book of the Twelve. If scholars agree that the sequence of the MT Book of the Twelve possesses an internal coherence and a degree of literary unity, then the same possibilities should be explored for the LXX and Qumran arrangements.

(2) A methodology is needed for evaluating the variety of proposed comprehensive redactional stages within the Book of the Twelve. At present, no external controls are available by which to judge the extent to which redactional activity was responsible for the received text of the Book of the Twelve. This lack of external evidence explains the great diversity of opinion on the redactional history of the Minor Prophets.

(3) The numerous claims made by scholars studying the Book of the Twelve that the final redactional shaping or compilation of the book was also the final step in the completion of the prophetic canon needs to be reconsidered in light of recent studies in the canonization of Hebrew Scriptures. As I will discuss in Chapter Two, the entire question of the existence before the Common Era of the prophetic canon as it is known in the Masoretic tradition has been called into question in the scholarly literature on the history of the canon. Previous claims about the relationship between the Book of the Twelve and the history of the canon need to be weighed against a full consideration of the evidence of the LXX and the new evidence of 4QXII[a].

Although these three questions seem to lead in disparate directions of investigation, they actually share a great deal of common ground. Recent research in the field of textual criticism has suggested a methodology for using manuscript evidence such as that for the Book of the Twelve to illuminate the literary history of biblical books. The textual variants attested among the manuscript witnesses to the Book of the Twelve may present concrete examples of ancient editorial alterations and thereby provide external evidence for evaluating proposed redactional stages in the history of the Book of the Twelve. The three arrangements of the Book of the Twelve preserved in ancient manuscripts may also provide evidence for the latter stages of the literary history of the Book of the Twelve and therefore attest to an identifiable stage in its canonical development. Chapter Two now turns to a discussion of how the discipline of textual criticism offers a methodological framework for addressing the questions of the manuscript evidence for the Book of the Twelve, the evaluation of its literary history, and the relationship of the Book of the Twelve to the history of the canon.

CHAPTER 2

TEXTUAL CRITICISM, THE BOOK OF THE TWELVE, AND THE CANONICAL PROCESS

The survey in Chapter One of previous scholarly attempts to trace the development of the Book of the Twelve sought to demonstrate the need and the promise of incorporating the evidence of the LXX and Qumran manuscripts of the Minor Prophets into a reconstruction of the book's literary formation. The present chapter will discuss the methodological grounds for using textual witnesses as evidence for the literary history of the Book of the Twelve. I will argue that the ancient manuscript evidence for the Book of the Twelve provides the most objective starting point for such a reconstruction.

Textual evidence has also been employed in recent discussions on the question of the development of canonical literature in ancient Judaism. As was seen in the studies surveyed in Chapter One above, a relationship has often been suggested between the completion of the Book of the Twelve and the completion of the prophetic section of the Hebrew canon. The present chapter will discuss the validity of this suggested relationship and will also attempt to demonstrate how textual evidence may contribute concretely to a description of the place of the Book of the Twelve within the process of the canonization of Hebrew Scripture during the Second Temple period.

Text-Critical Evidence and the Literary Criticism of Biblical Books

The historical and theoretical bases for the use of text-critical evidence in the reconstruction of the literary history of biblical books are described in S. Talmon's groundbreaking article, "The Textual Study of the Bible—A New Outlook."[1] For Talmon, a significant aspect of the Qumran discoveries is that the antiquity of some manuscripts has allowed scholars to trace the transmission history of the biblical text to a time in which the composition of many biblical texts was still in process. The overlapping of the literary and transmission histories of the Hebrew Bible caused him to reexamine the previous distinctions between the activities of authors and editors on the one hand, and the techniques of scribes and copyists on the other. Talmon concluded that the textual variety in evidence in the Qumran manuscripts was the result of a limited freedom enjoyed by most ancient copyists to introduce variation into the texts that they were copying.[2] Through a nearly exhaustive array of examples, Talmon thoroughly demonstrated that the stylistic techniques of ancient authors and the techniques used by copyists to introduce variations into the text were essentially identical. In showing the continuity between stylistic techniques operative on both the literary and textual levels, Talmon effectively blurred the strict distinction between higher and lower criticism and argued for a role for textual criticism in tracing the literary history of biblical texts.

A result of the conclusions of Talmon is that textual criticism may be seen to offer direct, concrete evidence of the kind of literary and editorial activity proposed by literary-critical investigations. By "concrete evidence," one should not imply that textual evidence is incontrovertible or unambiguous. The

---

[1] In *Qumran and the History of the Biblical Text*, ed. Talmon and F. M. Cross, Jr. (Cambridge: Harvard University Press, 1975), 321–99.

[2] Talmon described the controlled fluidness in the ancient textual witnesses as "a legitimate and accepted phenomenon of ancient scribal tradition." Ibid., 326.

textual evidence of ancient manuscripts and versions, however, where available, may provide a more tangible starting point for the literary history of biblical texts than does literary analysis alone.

An approach to the literary history of the Hebrew Bible that takes text-critical evidence as its starting point has antecedents in previous biblical scholarship. M. Smith, for example, prefaced his treatment of the literary growth of the Hebrew Bible by arguing that the best method for developing such a history would be to base all claims of textual redaction or alteration on analogies from parallel texts such as the Deuteronomistic History and the work of the Chronicler.[3] An older example of such a methodology is W. R. Smith's use of the LXX text of Jeremiah to support the validity of the nascent science of biblical literary criticism.[4] As M. Goshen-Gottstein has observed, J. Wellhausen's literary-critical insights were honed by his extensive work in textual criticism, particularly in the text of the Book of Samuel.[5]

Some of the results of the use of text-critical evidence for tracing the literary history of biblical texts have been summarized in E. Ulrich's recent essay on textual criticism and the composition of the Hebrew Bible.[6] Ulrich discusses several examples of biblical texts for which identifiable stages in their literary history are attested by text-critical evidence. These examples are: (1) the well-known example of the Book of Jeremiah, in which the editors of the MT edition varied the arrangement of the book and added sub-headings and other

---

[3]M. Smith, *Palestinian Parties and Politics That Shaped the Old Testament* (New York and London: Columbia University Press, 1970), 3.

[4]Cited in J. Tigay, *Empirical Models for Biblical Criticism* (Philadelphia: University of Pennsylvania Press, 1985), 4.

[5]Goshen-Gottstein, "The Textual Criticism of the Old Testament: Rise, Decline, Rebirth," *JBL* 102 (1983): 380–81.

[6]"The Canonical Process, Textual Criticism, and Latter Stages in the Composition of the Bible," in *"Sha'arei Talmon." Studies in the Bible, Qumran, and the Ancient Near East Presented to Shemaryahu Talmon,* ed. M. Fishbane and E. Tov (Winona Lake, IN: Eisenbrauns, 1992), 267–91.

minor expansions of an explanatory nature;[7] (2) the Book of
Exodus, for which a second edition outside of the MT is
represented in the Samaritan Pentateuch and 4QpaleoExod[m];[8]
(3) the two editions of the David and Goliath story preserved in
the MT and the LXX, which give evidence of the expansion of
the narrative by introducing alternative traditional materials into
the text;[9] (4) the variant versions of Samuel's birth preserved in
the MT and the LXX of I Samuel;[10] and (5), the book of Daniel, in
which the LXX and MT texts of chapters four and five appear to
contain independent expansions of a shorter form of the text
that is no longer attested in extant manuscripts.[11] These examples
demonstrate that text-critical evidence may not only reveal
previous stages of the literary growth of biblical texts, but may
also provide concrete illustrations of editorial and interpretative
strategies employed by the ancient tradents of the Hebrew Bible.

E. Tov's 1992 textbook on textual criticism shows the full
emergence of a self-conscious text-critical methodology for
reconstructing part of the literary history of the biblical text.[12]
Tov devotes an entire chapter to the role of textual criticism in

---

[7]See, for example, the discussion in E. Tov, "The Literary History of the
Book of Jeremiah in the Light of its Textual History," in *Empirical Models for
Biblical Criticism*, 213–37. Cited in Ulrich, "The Canonical Process," 283.

[8]P. W. Skehan, "Qumran and the Present State of Old Testament Text
Studies: The Masoretic Text," *JBL* 78 (1959): 22; and J. Sanderson, *An Exodus
Scroll from Qumran: 4QpaleoExod[m] and the Samaritan Tradition*, HSM 30 (Atlanta:
Scholars Press, 1986). Cited in Ulrich, "The Canonical Process," 279.

[9]D. Barthélemy, D. W. Gooding, J. Lust and E. Tov, *The Story of David and
Goliath: Textual and Literary Criticism. Papers of a Joint Research Venture*, OBO 73
(Freiburg and Göttingen: Van Goren, 1986). Cited in Ulrich, "The
Canonical Process," 280.

[10]See S. Walters, "Hannah and Anna: The Greek and Hebrew Texts of 1
Samuel 1," *JBL* 107 (1988): 385–412. Cited in Ulrich, "The Canonical
Process," 281.

[11]Ulrich, "The Canonical Process," 284–85.

[12]Tov, *Textual Criticism of the Hebrew Bible* (Minneapolis/Assen/Maastricht:
Fortress/Van Gorcum, 1992).

literary analysis of biblical texts.[13] Another significant feature of Tov's textbook is his thorough description of the kinds of variant readings that were intentionally created by ancient scribes/copyists.[14] These intentional changes reflect many of the literary and interpretative techniques described by Talmon and Ulrich.

The text-critical evidence for the existence of multiple literary editions of biblical books and for the intentional alterations made by ancient scribes has great significance for evaluating the literary history of the Book of the Twelve and for understanding its relationship to the canonical process. First, textual evidence may provide concrete examples of the ways in which ancient editors and redactors expanded or altered their source texts. *Text-critical materials therefore may provide an objective database for evaluating the kind of redactional changes that scholars have suggested for the Book of the Twelve.* Examples of textual alterations that are preserved in manuscript remains may be used to establish a range of probability for redactional schemes proposed for the Book of the Twelve. Redactional arguments that have directly supporting textual evidence would of course be the most probable if not almost certain. Redaction-critical reconstructions that are not attested directly by textual evidence but that are analogous to scribal or editorial activities attested elsewhere would have a lesser, yet still somewhat high, degree of probability. Claims for redactional alterations that are based on literary-critical analysis but have no direct or analogous supporting textual evidence would belong to a tertiary level of probability.

The second advantage of approaching the literary history of the Book of the Twelve from the perspective of its textual witnesses is that such a procedure makes full use of the available manuscript evidence of the LXX and 4QXII[a]. Beyond the

---

[13]Tov lists twelve examples of biblical texts, including four of those cited by Urlich, in which some stage(s) of literary growth is (are) supported by text-critical evidence. *Textual Criticism of the Hebrew Bible*, 313–49.

[14]Ibid., 258–85.

arguments made in the survey of scholarship in Chapter One above, the need for the full employment of this evidence is further demonstrated by J. Sanders's outline of the transmission history of the Hebrew Bible.[15] Sanders described four stages in the transmission history of the biblical text as revealed by twentieth century manuscript discoveries. Those stages are: (1) the stage of the *Urtext*, which was the stage of the composition of the text in its pre-literary and literary forms; (2) the stage of the *accepted texts*, reflected in the textual variety first suggested by the ancient versions and subsequently confirmed in the manuscripts from the Judean Desert; (3) the stage of the *received text* that resulted in the survival of a single, standardized textual tradition (proto-Masoretic or proto-rabbinic); and (4) the *Masoretic text*, including the Masoretic notations that insure the text's preservation in all its particularity.[16]

Sanders's four stages of textual transmission may be applied directly to the scholarship on the Book of the Twelve. The primary focus of previous scholarship has been on the stage of the *Urtext* or the stage of composition and redaction of the text. Each analysis of the composition of the Book of the Twelve, however, has been based on the text of the MT.[17] The history of textual transmission reveals the methodological error of this approach. By focusing exclusively on the MT of the Book of the Twelve, previous scholarship has compressed the history of transmission by reading the Masoretic text anachronistically as the *Urtext*. The MT is located incorrectly during the period of literary composition rather than at the terminal point of textual transmission and stabilization. Although the MT of the Book of the Twelve does not differ radically from the other extant

---

[15]Sanders, "Text and Canon: Concepts and Method," *JBL* 98 (1979): 8–11.

[16]For a different but not incompatible description of the transmission of the OT text, see Talmon, "The OT Text," *Cambridge History of the Bible*, Vol. I (Cambridge: Cambridge University Press, 1970), 164–70.

[17]Wolfe, as noted in Chapter One, did use the LXX as evidence for his proposed final redactional stage of the Book of the Twelve. See "The Editing of the Book of the Twelve," 29.

textual witnesses, the point to be made is that it is possibly only one text that has survived out of a plurality of texts that may have existed in the early periods of textual transmission.[18] Such an exclusive focus on the MT ignores the textual and literary evidence presented by the Greek versions and in effect buries anew the evidence available from the Qumran manuscripts.

Stage two in Sanders's reconstruction, the stage of the accepted texts, should therefore be the starting point for an investigation of the literary history of the Book of the Twelve. The evidence for this stage of textual transmission is represented primarily by (1) the text of the medieval MT manuscripts, whose antiquity and continuity with the proto-MT text is demonstrated by the Wadi Murabba'at and Naḥal Ḥever scrolls; (2) by the Hebrew *Vorlage* of the LXX of the Minor Prophets where this can be reliably reconstructed; and (3) by the Qumran fragments of the Book of the Twelve.[19]

Sequence Changes in Biblical Manuscripts and Their Implications for Literary Criticism

In his discussion of the use of textual evidence for the literary criticism of the Bible, Tov has isolated two primary indications of literary/editorial activity that are attested by textual

---

[18]This ancient plurality is true whether one accepts F. M. Cross's theory of three local texts or Talmon's proposal of an indefinite multiplicity of variant texts. See Cross, "The Evolution of a Theory of Local Texts," in *Qumran and the History of the Biblical Text*, 306–20, and Talmon, "The Textual Study of the Bible," 324–25.

[19]The evidence of other versions such as the Peshitta, the Targums, the Vulgate, and the so-called "daughter versions" such as the Old Latin and the Coptic translations, may also be used when this evidence impinges upon variants attested by the three textual sources cited above. The evidence from these versions, however, is greater in complexity and lesser in quantity than the three primary sources. A full treatment of the value of these witnesses for the formation of the Book of the Twelve therefore falls outside the limits of the present study.

evidence. These are: (1) quantitative differences between textual witnesses that give evidence of an identifiable editorial purpose; and (2) changes in the sequence of textual units within the respective textual witnesses.[20] Most often, the literary growth of a biblical text is attested by a significant difference in the size of the text among the extant witnesses. When these textual additions appear to manifest a shared purpose or tendency, they are designated as a separate redactional edition. Occasionally, differences in size are accompanied by changes in sequence within the same textual unit.[21]

The primary example of the concurrence of quantitative differences and differences in sequence is found in textual witnesses to the Book of Jeremiah. There the LXX text is far shorter than the MT and the position and internal arrangement of the oracles against the nations differ between the MT (chs. 46–51) and the LXX (chs. 25:13–31:44).[22] The lengthier text of the MT of Jeremiah has been convincingly argued to be the result of editorial expansions of an original shorter edition of the book which is preserved only in the LXX.[23] The textual expansions in

---

[20]Tov, *Textual Criticism of the Hebrew Bible*, 320–21.

[21]Ezekiel chapter 7 is one example. See Tov, "Recensional Differences Between the MT and LXX of Ezekiel," *ETL* 62 (1986): 89–91.

[22]For detailed discussion of the differences in the Oracles against the Nations between the LXX and the MT, see J. W. Watts, "Text and Redaction in Jeremiah's Oracles against the Nations," *CBQ* 54 (1992): 432–47.

[23]J. G. Janzen, *Studies in the Text of Jeremiah*, HSM 6 (Cambridge: Harvard University Press, 1973). I do not find the questions raised against Janzen's conclusions by S. Soderlund (*The Greek Text of Jeremiah: A Revised Hypothesis*, JSOTSup 47 [Sheffield: JSOT Press, 1985]) to be convincing, in part due to the limited scope of his study (ch. 29 only). See Janzen's rejoinder in "A Critique of Sven Soderlund's *The Greek Text of Jeremiah*," *BIOSCS* 22 (1989): 16–47.

the MT of Jeremiah appear to fit into an identifiable editorial scheme that was the result of a single redaction.[24]

Although some minor quantitative differences exist between the LXX and the MT texts of the Book of the Twelve, these are neither as extensive as those in the books of Ezekiel or Jeremiah, nor do they appear to fit into a unified pattern.[25] The textual witnesses to the Book of the Twelve attest primarily changes in the sequence of the material. Tov has argued, however, that even when unaccompanied by textual evidence of editorial expansion, changes in sequence within different manuscripts may be used as evidence for the literary history of the biblical text. Tov has compared a number of biblical texts that contain differences in sequence of material between the MT and the LXX.[26] He observed that each of the texts that have variant sequences has also been suspected by means of literary criticism as being secondary additions within their immediate context. Tov concluded that a sequence difference between the Hebrew *Vorlage* of the LXX and the MT may be considered as further indication of the secondary nature of such texts. He suggested that differences in sequence reflected either confusion or

---

[24]Tov, "L'incidence de la critique textuelle sur la critique littéraire dans le livre de Jérémie," *RB* 79 (1972): 189–99; idem, "Exegetical Notes on the Hebrew *Vorlage* of the LXX of Jeremiah 27 (34)," *ZAW* 91 (1979): 73–93.

[25]Most of the quantitative differences between the MT and the reconstructed Hebrew *Vorlage* of the Book of the Twelve appear to be dictated by the immediate context rather that by an overarching redactional scheme. They are significant, nevertheless, as examples of the kinds of textual and exegetical alterations that were introduced into at least one Hebrew manuscript tradition of the Book of the Twelve. The significance of these quantitative differences for the transmission history of the Book of the Twelve is treated at length in Chapter Three below.

[26]"Some Sequence Differences Between the MT and the LXX and Their Ramifications for the Literary Criticism of the Bible," *JNSL* 13 (1987): 151–60. The texts examined were Josh 8:30–35; 1 Kgs 8:12–13; Num 10:34–36; Jer 23:7–8; 1 Sam 2:1–10; Ezek 7:3–9; 1 Kings 20–21; Jeremiah 10; and Jeremiah 46–51.

uncertainty on the part of ancient scribes regarding the proper location of the presumed addition.

Tov does not fully elaborate upon his suggestion that a difference in sequence indicates the uncertainty of ancient scribes about the placement of a secondary text. I assume that he meant that the copyist, when copying a text with a secondary addition, would have had knowledge of the previous unexpanded text and, rather than interrupt the sequence with which he was familiar, incorporated the addition into a different place within the new text that he was copying. The motivations behind such a change in sequence are difficult to determine. The change in sequence of the new material may have been a form of scribal notation of the fact that the displaced text was a secondary addition. For example, one of the texts that Tov discusses is Num 10:34–36, which possesses the feature in the Masoretic tradition of being written with the "inverted *nuns*." The ancient scribal practice of enclosing vv. 35–36 within inverted *nuns* has been interpreted as kind of scribal notation that the verses were a secondary insertion within their context.[27] The variant sequence of the verses in the MT possibly serves the same function, since the sequence of the LXX is the more logical arrangement of the material.

Another possible explanation exists, however, for why a scribe would vary the sequence of textual material. It is possible that a scribe would move certain textual material for editorial or exegetical purposes. Again, the Book of Jeremiah provides a comparable example. Scholars have argued that the varying arrangements of the book are editorial in nature. P.-M. Bogaert, for example, explained the respective positions of the Oracles against the Nations within the LXX and the MT of Jeremiah as functions of the overarching redactional scheme of the two

---

[27]S. Liebermann, *Hellenism in Jewish Palestine* (New York: Jewish Theological Seminary, 1962), 178–81; see also *Sipre* 84 to Num 10:35–36; cited in Tov, "Some Sequence Differences," 155.

different editions of the book.[28] B. Gosse argued that the editor of the MT moved the Oracles against the Nations to the end of the book of Jeremiah in order to highlight the oracles against Babylon.[29] J. W. Watts extended the limited comments of Bogaert and Gosse by comparing the changes in the sequence and arrangement of the Oracles against the Nations with the other redactional changes attested by the MT edition of Jeremiah.[30] Watts concluded that the repositioning of the oracles was consistent with the editorial tendencies represented in the MT edition of the book. These studies in the Book of Jeremiah argue for the possibility that changes in sequence may be the result of either scribal or editorial interests. These two sets of interest, however, should not be considered as mutually exclusive.[31]

If the reasoning of Tov concerning the significance of sequence changes for literary criticism is applied to the Book of the Twelve, then those books whose positions in the LXX and 4QXII[a] differ from their respective positions in the MT would be suspected of being late additions to an earlier collection of prophetic books. The books of Joel, Obadiah, and Jonah all occur in at least two different positions within the manuscript witnesses to the Book of the Twelve, as illustrated by the following table.

---

[28]Bogaert, "De Baruch à Jérémie: Les deux rédactions conservées du livre de Jérémie," in *Le Livre de Jérémie*, ed. P.-M. Bogaert, BETL 54 (Leuven: Leuven University Press, 1981), 168–73.

[29]Gosse, "La malédiction contre Babylone de Jérémie 51, 59–64 et les rédactions du livre de Jérémie," *ZAW* 98 (1986): 383–99.

[30]Watts, "Text and Redaction in Jeremiah," 432–47.

[31]For a demonstration of the overlap of functions between copyists and authors, see Talmon, "The Textual Study of the Hebrew Bible—A New Outlook." See also the remarks of M. Fishbane, *Biblical Interpretation in Ancient Israel*, 31–32. For a discussion of the difficulty of finding an appropriate term for such persons, and the proposed term "author/scribe," see E. Tov, *Textual Criticism of the Hebrew Bible*, 314.

Table 2.1. Joel, Obadiah, and Jonah in Manuscripts of the Book of the Twelve.

MT Sequence	LXX Sequence	4QXII[a]
Hosea	Hosea	u
Joel	Amos	n
Amos	Micah	a
Obadiah	**Joel**	t
Jonah	**Obadiah**	t
Micah	**Jonah**	e
Nahum	Nahum	s
Habakkuk	Habakkuk	t
Zephaniah	Zephaniah	e
Haggai	Haggai	d
Zechariah	Zechariah	Zechariah
Malachi	Malachi	Malachi
		Jonah

The three different placements of the Book of Jonah suggest that this book enjoyed the most flexibility with regard to its position among the Twelve and therefore supports the possibility that it was the latest book to be added to the collection. Chapters Four and Five of the dissertation will attempt to support the hypothesis, derived from the manuscript evidence, that Joel and Obadiah, and then Jonah, were added to a previous collection of nine prophetic books comprised of Hosea, Amos, Micah, Nahum, Habakkuk, Zephaniah, Haggai, Zechariah, and Malachi.

Although a detailed treatment of this hypothesis will be given in the chapters below, it may be helpful to address some preliminary issues in the present context. First, it should be explained why Joel, Obadiah, and Jonah are the three books whose sequence is said to differ among manuscripts of the Twelve, when the books of Amos and Micah also have different positions in the LXX and the MT. Amos and Micah are treated separately from Joel, Obadiah, and Jonah because Schneider, Freedman, and Nogalski have all argued convincingly that the LXX sequence of Hosea-Amos-Micah reflects the sequence of the earliest collection of prophetic books that formed the germ of the Book of the Twelve.[32] The differing positions of Amos and Micah with respect to Joel and Obadiah in the MT would therefore be the result of the insertion of the latter two books into the sequence of the pre-existing collection. The internal sequence of Hosea, Amos, and Micah is the same in both the MT and the LXX.

A second argument in support of the hypothesis stated above is that previous scholarship has painted a convincing portrait of the nine books of the Minor Prophets excluding Joel, Obadiah, and Jonah as a grouping of three highly integrated literary compilations. Mention has already been made of the unifying features within Hosea, Amos, and Micah. Schneider and Nogalski have also illustrated the integrated character of the group Nahum-Habakkuk-Zephaniah. Beyond the identical title, *maśśāʾ* (Nah 1:1; Hab 1:1), Nahum and Habakkuk possess a high degree of chronological and literary complementarity. Nahum supplies the identity of the unidentified oppressors described in Habakkuk 1, namely, Assyria. Habakkuk identifies the agent of Nineveh/Assyria's destruction described in Nahum, namely, Babylon. Nahum begins with theophany; Habakkuk ends with theophany.[33] Nogalski has demonstrated that both books incorporate pre-existing theophanic hymns and adapt them not only to the internal context of their respective books, but also to the larger context of the prophetic collection.[34]

---

[32]Schneider, "The Unity of the Book of the Twelve," 36–38; Freedman, "Headings in the Books of the Eighth Century Prophets," *AUSS* 25 (1987): 9–26; Nogalski, *Literary Precursors to the Book of the Twelve*, 85–88. Each of these scholars cites (1) the overlapping chronological information in the superscriptions, and (2) the conscious use in Micah (1:2ff.) of the judgment of Samaria as predicted in Hosea and Amos as an example for the situation of Jerusalem in the late eighth century. These arguments and others (e.g., book size, literary parallels) are given as evidence that Hosea-Amos-Micah formed a unified literary corpus.

[33]Schneider, "The Unity of the Twelve," 52–54.

[34]Nogalski, *Redactional Processes in the Book of the Twelve*, 180–81.

Similar unifying features have been identified for the grouping of Haggai-Zechariah-Malachi. Haggai and Zechariah 1–8 form a highly integrated literary corpus that is unified by an overarching chronological framework and linguistic parallels.[35] A number of literary and structural parallels also unify Haggai-Zechariah 1–8 with the Book of Malachi.[36] Although it is difficult to determine the chronological relationship between Zechariah 9–14 and the rest of the Haggai-Zechariah-Malachi corpus, it is sufficient to note the literary connections between Zechariah 9–14 with Zechariah 1–8 on the on hand, and with Malachi on the other.[37]

A final argument for a "Book of the Nine" that preceded the addition of Joel, Obadiah, and Jonah is the clearly indicated chronological arrangement of the nine books whose positions are identical in the varying manuscript traditions. The chronological information in Hos 1:1 has been shown to provide an overarching framework for the books of Hosea, Amos, and Micah that extends from the reigns of Kings Uzziah and Jeroboam II (Hos 1:1; Amos 1:1) to the reign of King Hezekiah (Hos 1:1; Mic 1:1).[38] As stated above, the books of Nahum and Habakkuk

---

[35]C. L. Meyers and E. M. Meyers, *Haggai, Zechariah 1–8*, The Anchor Bible Vol. 25A (Garden City, NY: Doubleday, 1989), xliv–xlviii.

[36]Beyond the work of Schneider ("Unity of the Twelve," 144–45), see R. Pierce, "A Thematic Development of the Haggai-Zechariah-Malachi Corpus," *JETS* 27 (1984): 401–11; idem, "Literary Connectors and a Haggai-Zechariah-Malachi Corpus," *JETS* 27 (1984): 277–89; E. Bosshard and R. G. Kratz, "Maleachi im Zwölfprophetenbuch," *BN* 52 (1990): 27–46; and the comments of Nogalski, *Redactional Processes in the Book of the Twelve*, 201–203.

[37]For the ties between Zechariah 1–8 and 9–14, see R. Mason, "The Relation of Zech 9–14 to Proto–Zechariah," *ZAW* 88 (1976): 227–39. For the view that the *maśśā᾽* headings in Zech 9:1 and 12:1 are dependent upon Mal 1:1, see Nogalski, *Redactional Processes*, 187–89. For discussion of the literary ties between Zechariah 9–14 and Malachi, see Meyers and Meyers, *Zechariah 9–14*, Anchor Bible 25B (New York: Doubleday, 1993), 90–91.

[38]Freedman, "Headings in the Books of the Eighth Century Prophets," 24–26.

describe in complementary fashion the chronological transition from Assyrian to Babylonian hegemony. The Book of Zephaniah then takes up again the chronological framework of Hosea-Amos-Micah and makes the transition from reign of Hezekiah (Mic 1.1; Zeph 1:1) to Josiah.[39] Finally, the books of Haggai and Zechariah are dated very specifically to the time of the rededication of the Temple, the date of which serves as the central chronological feature in the structure of the Haggai-Zechariah corpus.[40] Malachi, although not marked chronologically, assumes the cultic operation of the Second Temple and thus follows the time period described in Haggai and Zechariah.

The chronological development of such a nine book corpus is therefore not only clearly indicated, but also corresponds somewhat to the chronological markers of the three major prophetic books. Freedman has argued for a parallel structuring of the Book of the Twelve and the collection of the Major Prophets Isaiah, Jeremiah, and Ezekiel.[41] In this parallel structure, Hosea, Amos, and Micah correspond to the chronological framework of Isaiah 1–39 (compare Isa 1:1 and Hos 1:1). Based upon internal chronological information alone, Nahum, Habakkuk and Zephaniah are depicted as being roughly contemporary with the events described in the Book of Jeremiah. Although the books of Haggai, Zechariah, and Malachi are later than the events described in the Book of Ezekiel, the use of similar dating formulas, similar language, and shared concerns for the priesthood and the Temple create parallels between these two corpora as well. Freedman argues that these parallels indicated a conscious effort during the exilic and restoration periods to collect and arrange Israel's sacred literature into a unified collection. His comparison of the Major and Minor prophetic collections breaks down, however, precisely at the

---

[39]As observed in Nogalski, *Literary Precursors to the Book of the Twelve*, 85–86.

[40]Meyers and Meyers, *Haggai, Zechariah 1–8*, xlvi.

[41]*The Unity of the Hebrew Bible* (Ann Arbor, MI: University of Michigan Press, 1991), 49–52.

points at which Joel, Obadiah, and Jonah occur in the collections
of the Book of the Twelve. If, however, one removes these three
books from the collection as later additions to a pre-existing
corpus, the chronological parallelism that Freedman describes is
restored without difficulty.

A great deal more evidence than is discussed above is
necessary to demonstrate the thesis that the manuscript evidence
for the Book of the Twelve may contribute new insights into its
formation. This evidence will be discussed in Chapters Four and
Five below. These chapters will discuss literary and textual
arguments for the coherence and unity of the arrangements of
the Twelve in both the LXX and 4QXII^a. An explanation will
also be sought for the differences between these arrangements of
the Book of the Twelve and the arrangement attested in the MT,
specifically as they relate to the books of Joel, Obadiah, and
Jonah. At this point in the dissertation, the hypothesis stated
above about the development of the Book of the Twelve may
appear to be no less speculative than the previous explanations
surveyed in Chapter One. I hope to demonstrate below,
however, that the hypothesis pursued here has the distinct
advantage of beginning from the more objective starting point of
the manuscript evidence. Although this starting point does not
guarantee that the arguments below will provide either the best
or most conclusive explanation of the history of the Book of the
Twelve, I hope nonetheless to establish the benefits of integrating
the extant manuscript evidence into the scholarly discussion of
this issue.

Before moving forward to a discussion of the variant
arrangements of the Book of the Twelve that are preserved in
ancient manuscripts, the preceding discussion of the benefits of
using textual evidence for the study of the literary history of the
Hebrew Bible provides an opportunity to address another issue
that is frequently related to the formation of the Book of the
Twelve. A relationship has often been posited between the
formation of the Book of the Twelve and the history of the
biblical canon. Recent scholarship has argued that textual
evidence is useful not only for the study of the literary history

of biblical books, but also for describing the process that eventually led to the formation of a canon of Hebrew Scriptures. It is important, therefore, to investigate the contribution that a study of the textual evidence for the Book of the Twelve may make toward understanding the relationship between this collection and the development of canonical literature in ancient Judaism.

Textual Evidence and the Canonical Process

Numerous claims have been made about the relationship between the formation of the Book of the Twelve and the history of the canon of Hebrew Scriptures. A survey of these claims in light of recent research into the development of the Hebrew canon will show that a new assessment of this relationship is needed. Recent studies in textual criticism have argued that textual evidence provides new insight into the process of canonization. The remainder of this chapter will seek to demonstrate the need for a new description of the relationship between the Book of the Twelve and the history of the canon and will also discuss how the textual evidence for the Book of the Twelve contributes to this new description.

The Book of the Twelve and the Canon in Previous Scholarship

Discussions of the canonical implications of the Book of the Twelve may be found throughout the modern period of biblical scholarship, with some continuity between recent scholarship and that of the early modern period. In the early nineteenth century, J. G. Eichhorn argued that the completion of the Book of the Twelve coincided with a post-exilic collection of sacred books. Eichhorn suggested that perhaps even the autograph of the Book of Malachi, which he judged to be the latest book, was included in this initial collection.[42] In his 1979 dissertation, Schneider proposed a similar, although more sophisticated theory. He argued that the Book of Malachi was instrumental in

---

[42]*Einleitung in das Alte Testament* (Göttingen: C. E. Rofenbusch, 1824), 470.

the reforms of Nehemiah and was therefore included in an archive that Nehemiah founded (cf. 2 Macc 2:13). Schneider argued that the founding of Nehemiah's archive was the occasion of the completion of the Book of the Twelve, created by the addition of Malachi, and was also the fundamental moment in the closure of the prophetic canon (i.e., the eight books of the Former and Latter Prophets—Joshua through Malachi).[43]

Nineteenth century scholars K. F. Keil[44] and F. Bleek[45] shared in common the view that a post-exilic collection of the prophetic section of the canon was the occasion for the compilation of the Book of the Twelve. Despite a lack of supporting external evidence for this thesis, it persisted and formed the basis for K. Budde's argument for a single, comprehensive redaction of the Minor Prophets that was intended to secure a place for the book in the prophetic canon.[46]

Other commentators who have posited a relationship between the formation or redaction of the Book of the Twelve and the development of the biblical canon have focused on the editing of the Book of Malachi. H. Ewald was perhaps the first to argue in print that the name "Malachi" in Mal 1:1 was an editorial addition intended to make the number of the Minor Prophets total the sacred number twelve, thereby creating the Book of the Twelve.[47] Accepting Ewald's analysis, J. Blenkinsopp commented

---

[43]Schneider, "The Unity of the Book of the Twelve," 148–51. Unfortunately, as Schneider admits, the evidence for Nehemiah's library comes from an unauthentic letter (2 Macc 1:1–2:18) containing a great deal of legendary material. Its historicity, therefore, is necessarily suspect.

[44]*Manual of Historico-Critical Introduction to the Canonical Scriptures of the OT*, Vol. I, tr. G. Douglas (1st ed. 1892; reprinted Grand Rapids, MI: Eerdmans, 1952), 364.

[45]J. Bleek and A. Kampenhausen (eds.), *Einleitung in das Alte Testament von Friedrich Bleek*, 3rd ed. (Berlin: Georg Reiner, 1870), 517.

[46]"Eine folgenschwere Redaction des Zwölfprophetenbuchs," *ZAW* 39 (1922): 221.

[47]*Die Propheten des Alten Bundes*, Vol. I. (Göttingen: Vandenhoeck and Ruprecht, 1867), 81. See the arguments against this view by Childs,

on the canonical implications of this interpolation when combined with the two proposed appendices found in Mal 3:22–24.[48] He argued that 3:23–24 was appended to 3:22 in order to change the ending of the prophetic canon from one of Torah piety to one of eschatological hope for the restoration of all Israel. The eschatological-prophetic ending that resulted from the addition of Mal 3:24 created, according to Blenkinsopp, a counter-claim to the retrospective "no prophet like Moses" ending of the Pentateuch (Deut 34:10–12).[49]

Even the emphasis on the implications of the ending of the Book of the Twelve for the larger context of the canon is not a twentieth century innovation. In 1891, G. Wildeboer argued that Malachi ended the Book of the Twelve not necessarily because it was the latest book but rather because its ending formed an appropriate conclusion to the Latter Prophets as a whole.[50] A similar argument was made by W. Rudolph in his 1976 commentary on Malachi in the *Kommentar zum Alten Testament* series. He concluded that Mal 3:22–24 formed not only the end to the Book of Malachi or the Book of the Twelve, but also the end of the prophetic canon.[51] Citing parallels between Mal 3:22–

Introduction to the Old Testament as Scripture (Philadelphia: Fortress Press, 1979), 491–94.

[48]*Prophecy and Canon* (Notre Dame and London: University of Notre Dame Press, 1977), 120–23. Two recent dissertations on Malachi have defended the authenticity of 3:22–24. See B. Glazier-MacDonald, *Malachi: The Divine Messenger* (Atlanta: Scholars Press, 1987); and J. O'Brien, *Priest and Levite in Malachi* (Atlanta: Scholars Press, 1990), 79.

[49]See the further discussion of this text in Chapter Three below.

[50]*Die Entstehung des Alttestamentlichen Kanons* (Gotha: Friedrich Andreas Perthes, 1891), 123.

[51]*Haggai-Sacharja 1–8–Sacharja 9–14–Maleachi* (Gütersloh: Gerd Mohn, 1976), 291. Like Wildeboer, Rudolph did not think that Malachi was the latest book among the Twelve. He argued that Joel, Jonah, and Zech 9–14 were all later than Malachi. The variant orders of the prophetic books in the LXX codices, most of which have the Twelve at the beginning and not at the end of the Latter Prophets, is clearly a problem for Rudolph's argument.

24 and Josh 1:2,7, Rudolph argued that these texts formed an *inclusio* encompassing the entirety of Israelite prophetic literature. O. Steck expanded Rudolph's argument to include the final redactional stages of Isaiah, Zechariah 9–14, and Malachi. Steck argued that these redactional stages were intended to unify the entire prophetic corpus through the use of verbal cross references.[52]

A general degree of agreement holds together the various proposals about the Book of the Twelve and the history of the canon. The consensus view is that the completion of the Book of the Twelve as a single volume was related in some way to the closing of the prophetic canon and that this closure occurred no later than 250–225 BCE. The reasons for this agreement appear to be quite sound. First, "the Praise of the Fathers" in Sirach 44–50, which contains the earliest reference to the Book of the Twelve, also provides the earliest external evidence for the authoritative status of all the books of the Former and Latter Prophets. The minimum date of 250 BCE for the completion of the prophetic canon is extrapolated from the probable date of Sirach, ca. 200–180 BCE. Second, the text of Mal 3:22–24, with references to the Mosaic Torah and to Elijah, who is representative of the prophetic *typos*, certainly forms an appropriate conclusion to the corpus of books that have been transmitted in the Masoretic tradition as the Torah and the Prophets. Third, traditions about the cessation of prophecy following the time of Haggai, Zechariah, and Malachi support the conclusion that the addition of these prophets to the Book of the Twelve brought to completion the prophetic canon.[53] Texts such as I Macc 9:27,

---

[52]*Der Abschluss der Prophetie im Alten Testament* (Neukirchen: Neukirchener Verlag, 1991). Although Steck consciously treats the issue of the "prophetic corpus" and not the "prophetic canon," the two issues are for all purposes identical in his discussion.

[53]For an example of this argument, see Schneider, "Unity of the Book of the Twelve," 232–33. For a full listing and discussion of ancient references to this tradition, see F. Greenspahn, "Why Prophecy Ceased," *JBL* 108 (1989): 37–49.

which refers to a time long ago when prophets ceased to appear, fit well with the conclusion that the canon of prophetic books was an accomplished fact by at least the middle of the third century BCE.

The compelling evidence for the relationship between the completion of the Book of the Twelve and the closing of the prophetic canon, however, is not incontrovertible. Scholars in both the early and latter parts of the twentieth century have rejected the intuitive appeal of the consensus opinion. A review of the arguments against the consensus view of the relationship between the formation of the Book of the Twelve and the development of the Hebrew canon will demonstrate the weaknesses of that view.

The Question of a Prophetic Canon

An extended argument against a closed prophetic canon prior to the end of the first century CE was made by T. N. Swanson.[54] Swanson argued that the term "canonical" should not be applied to any stage of the literature prior to the introduction of a closed list of Scripture, i.e., before the canon proper existed. According to Swanson, there was no closed *prophetic* canon prior to the final collection of Scriptures and the term "the Prophets" in ancient Jewish literature was applied freely to any scriptural books outside of the Torah.

The Book of Sirach, particularly the Praise of the Fathers in chapters 44–50, presents the most significant evidence for the "prophetic canon" theory. Ben Sira's familiarity with nearly all of the books of the Hebrew canon is obvious from his numerous citations and allusions to biblical texts.[55] Nevertheless, Ben Sira

---

[54]Swanson, "The Closing of the Collection of Holy Scriptures" (Ph.D. dissertation, Vanderbilt University, 1970), 1–5.

[55]See the discussions by J. L. Koole ("Die Bibel des Ben Sira," *OTS* 14 [1965] 382–83), who argues that Ben Sira knew every book except Daniel and Esther, and H. P. Rüger ("Le Siracide: un livre à la frontière du canon," in *Le Canon de l'Ancien Testament: Sa formation et son histoire*, eds. J.-D. Kaestli

gives no indication that the number of scriptural books is a determined fact, or that the Scriptures that he cites form an exclusive collection.[56] Although the closure of the prophetic section of the subsequent Hebrew canon is often assumed from the text of Ben Sira, it is not explicitly stated and a number of factors argue against it. Swanson gives a detailed treatment of these arguments, such as: (1) Ben Sira's use of Chronicles without distinguishing it from the Former Prophets; (2) his listing of Job with the prophet Ezekiel (49:9); (3) the lack of any notable distinction between the events of the "prophetic era" and Ben Sira's own time; and (4) Ben Sira's own prophetic aspirations (24:33).[57]

The Prologue to the Greek translation of Sirach by Ben Sira's grandson has also been interpreted as evidence for a closed prophetic canon. Ben Sira's grandson makes three references to Israel's sacred literature. He mentions in lines 1–2 "the Law and the Prophets and the others that followed them," in line 10 "the Law and the Prophets and the other books of the ancestors," and finally in lines 24–25, "the Law itself, the prophecies and the rest of the books." These references have been interpreted as evidence of a pre-Christian date for a closed tripartite Hebrew

---

and O. Wermelinger [Genève: Labor et Fides, 1984], 60–65), who lists references to every book except Daniel, Esther, Ruth, and Song of Songs.

[56]Koole, "Die Bibel des Ben Sira," 283–4; Rüger, "Le Siracide," 66.

[57]Swanson, "The Closing of the Collection of Holy Scriptures," 115–21. Some of those who have questioned the canonicity of the prophets for Ben Sira have been G. Wildeboer, *Entstehung des alttestamentlichen Kanons*, 17–19; G. Hölscher, *Kanonisch und Apokryph: Ein Kapital zu der Geschichte des alttestamentlichen Kanons* (Leipzig: A. Deichert, 1905) 19–21; and R. Meyer, "The Canon and the Apocrypha in Judaism," *TDNT* Vol. 3, 979. Koole also raises this possibility ("Die Bibel des Ben Sira," 283). For the view that Ben Sira used an arrangement of scriptures based on the idea of prophetic succession and therefore including such "non-prophetic" works as Chronicles and Ezra-Nehemiah, see J. C. H. Lebram, "Aspekte der alttestamentlichen Kanonbildung," *VT* 18 (1968): 183.

canon.[58] The Prologue offers no evidence, however, of an exclusive number of books for either "the Prophets," or the "rest of the books." There is no indication that some form of the Book of Enoch, for example, or Sirach itself, would be excluded from the "other books of the ancestors."[59] Rüger has argued that the variety of terminology for the third category of books after the Law and the Prophets suggests that the specific content and limits of this category were undetermined.[60]

While Sirach and its Prologue are silent on the contents and limits of "the Prophets," other evidence argues directly against a closed collection of prophetic literature prior to the introduction of a closed canon. Reference has already been made to Ben Sira's mention of Job in his discussion of the major prophets. Job is also counted among the prophets in Josephus's enumeration of the Scriptures.[61] These Scriptures included the five books of Moses, thirteen books of the prophets, and four books containing "hymns to God and precepts for the conduct of human life." Josephus's prophetic books would have included not only Job but also Daniel, Chronicles, Ezra-Nehemiah, and

---

[58]Most recently by R. T. Beckwith, *The Old Testament Canon of the New Testament Church* (Grand Rapids, MI: Eerdmans, 1985), 111. Beckwith's treatment of the issue appears to be determined by the *a priori* theological claim that the Hebrew Bible was the canon of Jesus and the apostles. His arguments therefore appeal primarily to this "apostolic" authority. See the reviews of Sundberg, "Reexamining the Formation of the Old Testament Canon," *Interpretation* 42 (1988): 78–82; and Barton, *Theology* 90 (1987): 63–65.

[59]In lines 24–25, for example, the Greek translation of Sirach is explicitly compared with that of the Torah and other scriptural works. For a discussion of Ben Sira's use of pseudepigraphal traditions, see J. Marböck, "Henoch-Adam-Der Thronwagen. "Zu frühjüdischen pseudepigraphischen Traditionen bei Ben Sira," *BZ* 25 (1981): 103–11.

[60]"Le Siracide," 66.

[61]See *Against Apion* I.37–43. On this issue see also H. Bartdke, "Prophetische Züge im Buche Hiob," in *Das Ferne und Nahe Wort: Festschrift Leonhard Rost*, BZAW 105 (Berlin: Walter de Gruyter, 1967), 1–10.

Esther.[62] If Josephus counted the Book of Ruth with Judges as a single volume, similar to the order of the LXX manuscripts, and likewise the Book of Lamentations with Jeremiah, then these two works were included among the prophets also.[63]

Other evidence also demonstrates the shifting place of the Book of Daniel in ancient classifications of scriptural books. K. Koch has marshalled this evidence into a convincing argument for the original prophetic status of the book in the early centuries of the Common Era.[64] The evidence includes references to Daniel as a prophet in the NT (Matt 24:15), the literature of the Qumran community (4Q174), the manuscripts of the LXX, and Josephus.[65] Such references directly contradict the argument that the inclusion of Daniel among the Writings proves that the prophetic canon was already closed by the time of Daniel's composition.

The most thorough argument since Swanson against the existence of a closed prophetic canon before the first century CE

---

[62]See G. Wanke, "Die Entstehung des Alten Testaments als Kanon," *TRE* Bd. VI (1980), 5. With regard to the objection that Josephus's arrangement reflects his historical interests, see Lebram's argument that such a historical scheme formed the structure of Ben Sira's Praise of the Fathers some three centuries prior to Josephus ("Aspekte des Alttestamentlichen Kanonbildung," 181–83).

[63]For an argument for the fluidity of the prophetic and hagiographic sections of the canon in the first two centuries CE as based upon the evidence of the Book of Ruth, see L. B. Wolfenson, "Implications of the Place of the Book of Ruth in Editions, Manuscripts, and Canon of the OT," *HUCA* 1 (1924): 151–78.

[64]Koch, "Is Daniel also among the Prophets?" *Interpretation* 39 (1985): 117–30. Koch argued that following the disastrous results of the Bar Kokhba revolt, the rabbis relegated Daniel to the Writings for fear of its apocalyptic message. It was retained among the Scriptures, however, possibly because of the reinterpretation of Rome as the fourth kingdom of Daniel chs. 2 and 7.

[65]Besides *Against Apion* I.37–43, see *Jewish Antiquities* 9.267–69.

is found in the work of J. Barton.[66] He argues that until at least the end of the second century CE, the Hebrew Scriptures consisted of a two part division: (1) the Torah, and (2) an undetermined number of other works that were considered prophetic in nature. Like Swanson, Barton interpreted the term "the Prophets" in the title "the Law and the Prophets" to refer to any authoritative book outside of the Pentateuch. Since all Scripture was thought to have originated during a "prophetic age" and to have been written by prophetic figures,[67] the term "the Prophets" was used to include all such authoritative writings.

The usage of the NT, for example, is best understood as reflecting this fluid concept of prophetic books. The most common designation of the Scriptures in the NT is the term "Law and Prophets."[68] Luke 24:44 ("the Law of Moses and the Prophets and the Psalms") is the only exception to this bipartite scheme.[69] Once the assumption of the traditional tripartite development of the canon is suspended, a bipartite classification of Torah and prophetical books provides an equally if not more satisfying explanation of such usage.

The post-biblical traditions about the end of prophecy have also been cited as evidence for the closure of the prophetic canon by the end of the third century BCE. These traditions,

---

[66]Barton, "'The Law and the Prophets': Who are the Prophets?" *OTS* 23 (1984): 1–18; idem, *Oracles of God: Perceptions of Ancient Prophecy in Israel after the Exile* (London: Blackwell, 1986), 35–44. For examples of this view in scholarship prior to Swanson, see G. Wildeboer, *Entstehung des Alttestamentlichen Kanons*, 13, 17–20; N. Schmidt, "Biblical Canon: Untraditional View," *The Jewish Encyclopaedia*, Vol. III (1902), 150–54; and Wolfenson, "Implications of the Place of the Book of Ruth," 172–73.

[67]This is one of the criteria for canonicity in Josephus, *Against Apion*, I.37–43.

[68]Matt 5:17; 7:12; 22:40; Luke 16:16; John 1:45; and Rom 3:21. See also Luke 16:29, 31 ("Moses and the Prophets").

[69]Barton *(Oracles of God,* 35) argues convincingly against interpreting "the Psalms" as a synecdoche for the *Kethubim.*

however, do not necessarily prove an early date for the existence of a prophetic canon. The idea that all great truths arose originally in a "classical age" in the past has parallels in ancient Near Eastern thought.[70] As Barton points out, however, this idea does not eliminate the possibility that "classical" works may be "discovered" by subsequent generations.[71] The phenomenon of pseudepigraphy is based on such an assumption. It may indeed be argued that Josephus's limitation of the beginning of the prophetic age to the time of Moses was motivated by a desire to exclude pseudepigraphal literature that made claims to prediluvian origins. The idea of a prophetic age, therefore, does not require the notion of a closed canon.

The Meaning of "Canon"

The question of a prophetic canon as discussed above raises the issue of the meaning and usage of the term "canon" itself. Those who focus upon the authoritative status of biblical texts in antiquity would identify a text as canonical at the time of the earliest appeal to the text's authority, which for many texts would mean a time long before the Hebrew Bible itself was completed. Those who define canon as a final, closed list of authoritative works would date the origin of such a narrowly defined canon to a time much later than the composition of the majority of biblical texts.

The ambiguity of the meaning of the terms "canon" and "canonical" stems not only from their varied modern usage, but from the philological history of the terms as well. The philological evidence for the term canon supports the two primary meanings described above. Originally, the Greek word *kanōn* was construed very broadly in classical literature to mean a standard or a norm, a meaning derived from the well known etymology of the Semitic word for reed or rod (cf. Hebrew

----

[70]See for example, W. G. Lambert, "Ancestors, Authors, and Canonicity," *JCS* 2 (1957): 9.

[71]Barton, *Oracles of God*, 42–44.

qāneh).[72] The derivative and more narrow meaning of canon as a fixed list is not attested before the beginning of the fourth century CE. The earliest attestation of its use as a reference to the definitive list of scriptural books occurred in the latter half of the fourth century.[73] Metzger characterizes these two primary meanings of the term not only as being either broad or narrow, but also as either active or passive meanings. The broad, active sense of canon as a standard or a norm (Latin *norma normans*) describes the *function* of canons in their respective communities. The narrow, passive sense (*norma normata*) describes the *limits* of canons as determined, fixed lists of items.[74]

The present treatment of the history of the Hebrew canon is based upon a determination that the narrow meaning of canon as a closed list of books is technically more precise and therefore preferable to the broader sense of canon as an authoritative text or texts.[75] If the definition of canon is limited to a closed list of scriptural books, then direct historical evidence for the closed canon of Scriptures does not exist prior to the end of the first century CE.[76] This evidence is found in Josephus's remarks about the Jewish Scriptures in *Against Apion*, I.8, 37–43 and in 4 Ezra

---

[72]Numerous treatments of the philology of the term "canon" are available in scholarly literature. The following description is based on the article by H. W. Beyer,"*kanon*," *TDNT*, Vol. 3, 596–602; and the recent treatment of B. Metzger, "History of the Word *KANON*," Appendix I to *The Canon of the New Testament* (Oxford: Clarendon Press, 1987), 289–93.

[73]Metzger, *Canon of the New Testament*, 292.

[74]Ibid., 283.

[75]See the arguments for this definition in E. Urlich, "The Canonical Process," 268–71; and J. Barr, *Holy Scripture: Canon, Authority, Criticism* (Philadelphia: Westminster Press, 1983), 50–51.

[76]For a date for the canon in the first century BCE that is based upon the stabilization of the consonantal Hebrew text, see D. Barthélemy, "L'Etat de la Bible juive depuis le début de notre ère jusqu'à la deuxième révolte contre Rome (131–135)," in *Le Canon de l'Ancien Testament*, 9–45.

14:44–46.[77] Both texts originated ca. 90–100 CE and both show the Scriptures of Judaism to be limited to a fixed number of books.[78]

The narrow definition of canon as a closed list of books has the advantage of avoiding the anachronism of reading the authority of the final, closed collection of Scripture back into the earliest identifiable stage of composition.[79] This being said,

---

[77]For Josephus, see the discussion in R. Meyer, "The Canon and the Apocrypha in Judaism," 985; and idem, "Bermerkungen zum literargeschichtlichen Hintergrund der Kanontheorie des Josephus," in *Josephus-Studien. Untersuchungen zu Josephus, dem antiken Judentum und dem Neuen Testament,* ed. O. Betz, K. Haacker, and M. Hengel (Göttingen: Vandenhoeck and Ruprecht, 1974), 285–99. Meyer discusses Josephus's criteria of canonicity and argues that Josephus was attempting to promulgate the post-70 CE Pharisaic canon.

For 4 Ezra 14, see J.-D. Kaestli, "Le récit de IV Esdras 14 et sa valeur pour l'histoire du canon de l'Ancien Testament," in *Le Canon de l'Ancien Testament,* 71–97. Kaestli argues that the 24 books of Scripture dictated by Ezra in 4 Ezra 14:44 represent the post-70 CE Pharisaic canon. He concludes that the claim in 4 Ezra 14:46 for the superior status of the 70 esoteric books was an effort to assert the value of apocalyptic writings in response to their exclusion by the Pharisees.

[78]Josephus sets the number of books at 22; 4 Ezra 14 at 24. The difference in numbering is often attributed to counting Ruth with Judges and Lamentations with Jeremiah although dissenting opinions exist. See the discussion and bibliography in Swanson, "The Closing of the Collection of Holy Scriptures," 269–71.

[79]This is precisely the difficulty with the treatment of canon by S. Leiman (*The Canonization of Hebrew Scripture* [Camden, CT: Arcon Press, 1976]). Leiman makes no distinction between the early authority of a biblical book and the final, closed list of scriptural works. He thus collapses the distinction between the two meanings of canon. He also includes the element of inspiration within his definition of canon, which in essence makes a work "canonical" at the very moment of its "inspired" composition. See the criticism of Leiman in J. N. Lightstone, "The formation of the biblical canon in Judaism of late antiquity: Prolegomenon to a general reassessment," *SR* 8 (1979): 141.

however, much evidence exists for the authoritative use of numerous biblical texts within the biblical period itself. The evidence for the antiquity of the "canon" in its broader sense is best seen in D. N. Freedman's work on the canonization of the Hebrew Bible.[80]

For Freedman, canonization involves an official act of publication by an authoritative body. Such official collections or publications function to meet the religious and institutional needs of specific groups in concrete historical situations. Because of their functional nature, Freedman concludes that such editions originated near the time of the latest historical events referred to in the text.[81] Subsequent publications may extend the contents of the collection if events and circumstances necessitate such expansion. Freedman argues that the earliest identifiable collection to function in this manner was published in the middle of the sixth century BCE. This collection included the Primary History (Genesis-2 Kings) and a supplement of prophetic books (Isaiah 1–39, Jeremiah, Ezekiel, and a group of from six to nine of the Minor Prophets).[82]

Freedman is flexible in his use of the term "canon," qualifying his proposed earliest Bible as "a quasi-canonical work"[83] having received "some kind of canonization."[84] Such qualifications demonstrate his awareness that canon in its strictest sense means the final, closed list of Hebrew Scriptures. A careful

---

[80]Freedman's works on the early stages of the canon include the following: "The Law and the Prophets," *VTSup* 9 (1963): 250–65; "Canon of the OT," *IDBS* (Nashville, Abingdon Press, 1976), 130–36; "The Earliest Bible," *MQR* 22 (1983): 167–75; "Formation of the Canon of the Old Testament," in *Religion and Law: Biblical-Judaic and Islamic Perspectives*, ed. E. B. Firmage and B. G. Weiss (Winona Lake, IN: Eisenbrauns, 1990), 315–31; and *The Unity of the Hebrew Bible*.

[81]Freedman, "The Law and the Prophets," 251; "Canon of the OT," 132, 135; "The Earliest Bible," 167.

[82]Freedman, "Canon of the OT," 132.

[83]Freedman, "The Earliest Bible," 167.

[84]Freedman, "Canon of the OT," 132.

reading of his work shows that his interest is primarily to understand the early history of the final Hebrew canon rather than to read that final canon back into a far earlier period.[85]

Freedman's primary contribution is his argument that numerous texts of the Hebrew Bible were already functioning authoritatively for the religious communities of the exilic and early post-exilic periods. The extensive evidence for the phenomenon of inner-biblical exegesis, as demonstrated by M. Fishbane,[86] corroborates Freedman's argument. Even J. Barr, who argues that the idea of a biblical canon did not fully emerge in Judaism or Christianity until after the NT period, is willing to recognize the existence of a "pre-canon," a predecessor to the final canon that is essentially in agreement with Freedman's proposed Primary History and Prophetic Supplement.[87]

The Canonical Process

Despite the historical arguments and the terminological advantages of assigning the origin of the canon as strictly defined to the late first or early second century CE, the question remains of how to give proper acknowledgement to the significant evidence for the authoritative status of much of biblical literature at times far earlier than the closing of the Hebrew

---

[85]A weakness of Freedman's theories is that, in his most recent writings, he demonstrates a rather rigid stance on overly specific early dates for the completion and canonization of certain biblical books. In his earlier essays, for example, he expressed caution on the dates of Joel, Jonah, and Zechariah 9–14, giving a range of dates between 520 and 450 BCE ("Law and Prophets," 264; "Canon of the OT," 133). Recently, however, he has dated Joel and Jonah prior to 540 BCE and Zechariah 9–14 and Malachi to no later than 515 BCE ("Formation of the Canon of the Old Testament," 283).

[86]*Biblical Interpretation in Ancient Israel* (Oxford: Clarendon Press, 1985).

[87]Barr, *Holy Scripture: Canon, Authority, Criticism* (Philadelphia: Westminster Press, 1983), 53, 83. Barr is willing to concede the existence of a "pre-canon" that functioned authoritatively in the exilic period because the identification of such relies precisely on the kind of historical criticism that B. Childs overtly criticizes in his canonical approach.

canon. Although the strict definition of canon is preferable, it is necessary to recognize the antiquity of what Barr has called the "pre-canonical" authority of the Scriptures of ancient Israel and early Judaism. Ulrich has suggested a way out of this terminological impasse by advocating the use of the term "canonical process" to describe what Freedman and others mean by their broadly-defined use of the term canon. According to Ulrich, the canonical process includes all of the literary, editorial, and scribal activities that led to the production, transmission, and recognition of biblical texts as the exclusively authoritative religious literature of ancient Judaism.[88] "Canonical process," therefore, is a mediating term that recognizes both the post-biblical origin of the Hebrew canon and its lengthy, dynamic, and complex history of development prior to its final canonization.

Although Ulrich has recently advocated the use of the term "canonical process" to describe the complex history of ancient Israel's sacred literature, the dissemination of the term, if not also its coinage, is the result of the work of J. Sanders. In numerous published works on the history and development of the biblical canon, Sanders has described the canonical process as the growth of biblical literature "from sacred story to sacred text."[89] Such growth includes the text's literary and pre-literary history (sacred story) as well as its transmission history (sacred text). At first glance, Sanders's portrayal of the canonical process appears to be too general. His descriptions of the growth of the canon are usually sweeping summaries of the literary history of the Hebrew Bible from the time of Moses to the end of the Second Temple period. Nevertheless, his work does offer a methodological foundation from which to describe the canonical

---

[88]"The Canonical Process," 272.

[89]Sanders, "Text and Canon: Concepts and Method," *JBL* 98 (1979): 19. See also *Canon and Community: A Guide to Canonical Criticism* (Philadelphia: Fortress Press, 1984); the collected essays in *From Sacred Story to Sacred Text* (Philadelphia: Fortress Press, 1987); and "Canon. Hebrew Bible," *Anchor Bible Dictionary*, Vol. 1 (New York: Doubleday, 1992), 837–52.

process with some degree of specificity and as based upon reliable evidence.

Sanders's reconstruction of the history of the Hebrew Bible from sacred story to sacred text is based primarily on his studies in textual criticism.[90] Sanders recognizes an essential continuity between the following three kinds of intentional literary adaptations: (1) intentional textual changes attested in ancient manuscripts; (2) ancient adaptations of sacred traditions by biblical authors and redactors attested by the tools of literary criticism; and (3) hermeneutical adaptations of biblical texts as seen in post-biblical exegesis.[91] The tangible evidence of textual criticism serves as an objective point of reference for Sanders's comparisons of these three levels of literary development.[92]

Based upon such a comparison, Sanders identifies the essential elements of the canonical process as "selectivity" and "repetition."[93] "Selectivity" refers to the decisions of ancient communities to value certain traditions or texts and to pass them on to succeeding generations. Moreover, it denotes a tendency within the canonical process to limit the number of authoritative texts and traditions. "Repetition" refers to the hermeneutical

---

[90]See "Cave 11 Surprises and the Question of Canon," *McCormick Quarterly* 21 (1968) 284–98; "Text and Canon," passim; "Hebrew Bible *and* Old Testament: Textual Criticism in Service of Biblical Studies," in *Hebrew Bible or Old Testament: Studying the Bible in Judaism and Christianity,* R. Brooks and J. J. Collins, eds. (Notre Dame: University of Notre Dame Press, 1990) 41–68; and "Stability and Fluidity in Text and Canon," in *Tradition of the Text,* ed. G. Norton and S. Pisano, OBO 109 (Freiburg/Göttingen: Freiburg University Press/Vandenhoeck and Ruprecht, 1991), 203–17.

[91]*Torah and Canon,* xii–xiv.

[92]For a description of the canonical process based upon the methodology of a highly-refined literary criticism, and which bears the limitations of this methodology, see Steck, "Der Kanon des hebräischen Alten Testaments" in *Vernunft des Glaubens: Festschrift zum 60 Geburstag von Wolfhart Pannenberg* (Göttingen: Vandenhoeck and Ruprecht, 1988), 231–52.

[93]Sanders, *Canon and Community,* 32–33. For the text-critical basis for this description, see idem, "Text and Canon."

adaptations required to overcome the temporal or thematic limitations of the selected sacred traditions and to make the traditions or texts relevant or meaningful to their new historical context.

M. Smith gives a description of the canonical process that is similar to that of Sanders.[94] Smith points out that the processes of selection and repetition that Sanders describes are necessary results of the physical realities of textual reproduction in the ancient world. His succinct description of this process merits full quotation.

> Except for archaeological finds, ancient texts have never simply "survived." Those which survive have always been preserved by copying, and copying a text is a long, tedious job which is not done without some strong motive. Therefore, of the texts produced by any one generation, only a few were copied by the next, and the motives for copying those few were also the motives for editing or "correcting" them. The primary *Sitz im Leben* of the books of the Old Testament therefore is their role in the life of those who wrote, copied, and corrected them.[95]

Like Sanders, Smith recognized that the practice of textual transmission is necessarily a selective, delimiting process. The necessary complement to the limiting process of textual transmission is a means of interpreting the selected tradition so that it remains meaningful for its tradents and for succeeding generations. These interpretations, as Smith and Sanders note, may take many forms, including textual expansions, emendations, interpolations, as well as extra-textual oral traditions of interpretation. Regardless of the form such activities take, the dynamics of limited textual transmission and flexible interpretation remain constant throughout the canonical process.

---

[94]*Palestinian Parties and Politics That Shaped the Old Testament* (London and New York: Columbia University Press, 1971), 1–8.

[95]Ibid., 7.

Implications for the Study of the Book of the Twelve

The evidence for the role of the Book of the Twelve in the history of the Hebrew canon points in two contradictory directions. First, there is evidence that the Book of the Twelve was an authoritative collection at least as early as 250 BCE, and that many of its books were authoritative for some communities at least as early as the exilic period. At the same time, there is no direct evidence of a closed, fixed canon of Hebrew Scriptures until the end of the first century CE. Prior to that time, it is only possible to speak of a "canonical process," a process of selective transmission and actualizing interpretation that includes every aspect of textual production from its composition to the stabilization of the biblical text. Although literary and redactional analyses attempt to illuminate this greatly complex process, textual evidence of interpretative alterations and adaptations provides a more concrete starting place for investigating and illustrating the dynamics of the canonical process.

Scholars have often questioned whether the Book of the Twelve was the result of a bibliographic technique developed primarily in order to preserve relatively short texts, or the result of interpretative techniques that sought to unify diverse prophetic traditions into a single literary work. Within the canonical process as described above, however, scribal techniques and interpretative techniques serve the identical function of transmitting the text to successive generations of readers and hearers. Such techniques facilitated the preservation of the Book of the Twelve from its earliest literary stages until such time when the sacred literature of Judaism became limited to a fixed number of volumes. The activities of unnamed tradents and interpreting communities helped to insure a place for the Book of the Twelve within that delimited collection.

As is the case with the literary history of the Book of the Twelve, a description of the canonical process as it applies to this text finds its most promising beginning point in the textual evidence for the book. Chapter Three will attempt to demonstrate that the Hebrew text lying behind the LXX Book of the Twelve, where this can be reasonably reconstructed, offers evidence of textual adaptations that are illustrative of the kind of interpretative techniques that facilitated the text's transmission and appropriation by successive generations. Such textual evidence should therefore provide a reliable starting point for a description of the canonical process as it applies to the Book of the Twelve. In light of Talmon's demonstration of the continuity between the literary techniques of ancient authors and the stylistic techniques of ancient copyists, a study of alterations to the text of the Book of the Twelve should also provide concrete examples of the kind of exegetical and editorial changes that have been proposed by the tools of literary criticism. The proposals of literary analyses such as those of Steck and Nogalski may therefore be evaluated by comparison with the adaptations attested by textual evidence.

Conclusion

This chapter has attempted to set forth a methodology for incorporating the manuscript evidence of variant arrangements of the Book of the Twelve into the scholarly research on the history and significance of this compilation. Recent research in textual criticism has indicated that such textual evidence may be useful for investigating two issues that are recurrent within scholarship on the Book of the Twelve: the literary history of the book, and its relationship to the growth of the Hebrew canon. Chapters Four and Five below will address the variant arrangements of the Book of the Twelve that are preserved within 4QXII[a] and in the LXX manuscript tradition. These arrangements of the Twelve will be investigated for the information that they may yield on the formation of the Book of the Twelve. Chapter Three below will address the contribution of textual evidence to the issue of the Book of the Twelve and the canonical process by examining examples of interpretative activities that are attested within the textual transmission of the book. The aim will be to identify ancient interpretations of the

Minor Prophets by which their scribal tradents appropriated the texts for their own and for subsequent communities.

CHAPTER 3

INTERPRETATIVE TECHNIQUES IN THE TEXTUAL TRANSMISSION OF THE BOOK OF THE TWELVE

Just as scholars have often disregarded the literary unity of the Book of the Twelve in favor of its smaller constitutive units, so also the form of the Book of the Twelve preserved in the Old Greek translation has received little attention as a unified collection. Commentators on the Book of the Twelve most often treat the LXX version as merely a thesaurus of possible textual emendations for occasionally problematic readings. The present study is an attempt to use the textual and literary evidence preserved in the LXX to address two important issues within the scholarly literature on the Book of the Twelve. Chapter Five will examine the LXX arrangement of the Minor Prophets as a literary unity and will compare this arrangement with that of the MT. The present chapter will seek to illustrate the dynamics of the canonical process that were at work in the transmission of the Book of the Twelve by examining the interpretative textual alterations that are attested by a comparison of the texts of the LXX and the MT manuscript witnesses.

Recent scholars have argued that the LXX Book of the Twelve should be studied for its own sake as a literary creation that offers a presentation of the text that is distinct from the Hebrew text of the Minor Prophets.[1] Although I fully agree with such an approach, the present study looks beyond the LXX *translation* of the Minor Prophets to address the distinct text and unique literary form of its Hebrew *Vorlage*. The use of the LXX as evidence for a reconstruction of its Hebrew *Vorlage* will require a preliminary discussion of some critical methodological questions involved in such an enterprise. Following a treatment of these methodological issues, the chapter will describe, where possible, the unique features of the Hebrew text of the Book of the Twelve underlying the LXX version. A demonstration of the distinct textual history of the Hebrew source text of the LXX Book of the Twelve will reveal various ancient strategies for preserving and interpreting these texts and will also serve as a preface to the discussion in Chapter Five of the coherence and unity of this alternative version of the Book of the Twelve.

A Methodology for the Text-Critical Use of the LXX

Preliminary Considerations

A translation document such as the LXX of the Book of the Twelve can be used as evidence for its source text only by cautiously following a carefully delineated set of methodological guidelines. A number of previous studies have dealt with the

---

[1] J. Sasson, *Jonah*, The Anchor Bible Vol. 24B (New York: Doubleday, 1990), 13; D. Barthélemy, *Critique Textuelle de l'Ancien Testament, Tome 3. Ezéchiel, Daniel et les 12 Prophètes*, OBO 50/3 (Göttingen: Vandenhoeck and Ruprecht, 1992), ccxxi–ccxxvii. Examples of the results of such a study are provided in S. Pisano, "'Egypt' in the Septuagint Text of Hosea," in *Tradition of the Text*, ed. G. J. Norton and S. Pisano, OBO 109 (Freiburg–Schwerz/Göttingen: Universitätsverlage/Vandenhoeck and Ruprecht, 1991), 301–308; and L. Perkins, "The Septuagint of Jonah: Aspects of Literary Analysis Applied to Biblical Translation," *BIOSCS* 20 (1987): 43–53. With regard to the LXX as a whole, see also M. K. H. Peters, "Why Study the Septuagint?" *BA* 49 (1986): 174–81.

methodological issues related to the text-critical use of the LXX.[2] It will therefore be necessary only to survey briefly the difficulties in using the LXX for text-critical research and the manner in which these difficulties may be overcome.

The initial difficulty to be overcome in the use of the LXX in the textual criticism of the Hebrew Bible is the textual variety found in the extant manuscripts of the Greek versions. In order to say something about the *Vorlage* of the LXX, it is necessary to isolate the text of the presumed original Greek translation from the variety of readings contained in existing Greek manuscripts. This requirement, however, has been greatly simplified for those books whose critical editions have been published by the *Göttingen Septuaginta-Unternehmen*. The critical editions of the Göttingen Septuagint project provide a reliable source for the original text of the LXX translation.[3] Although in theory it is possible to question individual textual decisions of the editors of the critical editions of the LXX, in practice the monumental task of evaluating the numerous variants of the various Greek and versional manuscripts gives the critical editions a distinct authority for all but the most highly specialized scholars in the field of the textual criticism of the LXX.

A more serious difficulty in using the LXX as evidence for the history of the Hebrew text is the fact that deviations between the received Hebrew text and the LXX do not

---

[2]Thorough discussions of these issues, along with bibliographical data, are found in E. Tov, *The Use of the Septuagint in Text-Critical Research* (Jerusalem: Simor Ltd., 1981); idem, *Textual Criticism of the Hebrew Bible* (Minneapolis/Assen/Maastricht: Fortress Press/Van Gorcum, 1992), 121ff.; and S. Olofsson, *The LXX Version: A Guide to the Translation Technique of the Septuagint*, ConBOT 30 (Stockholm: Almqvist & Wiksell, 1990). For a brief but helpful treatment of these issues, see A. Aejmelaeus, "What Can We Know about the Hebrew *Vorlage* of the Septuagint?" *ZAW* 99 (1987): 58–89.

[3]Aejmelaeus, "The Hebrew *Vorlage* of the Septuagint," 61–62. For the critical edition of the Book of the Twelve, see J. Ziegler, ed. *Septuaginta. Vetus Testamentum Graecum*, Vol. XIII, *Duodecim prophetae*, 3rd ed. (Göttingen: Vandenhoeck and Ruprecht, 1984).

necessarily indicate the existence of a variant reading in LXX translator's the Hebrew *Vorlage*. Textual deviations could have plausibly arisen from one of three possible sources. These sources are: (1) deviations arising during the transmission of the Greek text of the LXX; (2) deviations attributable to the process of translation; or (3) deviations that were present in the translator's Hebrew source text. With the exception of variants whose presumed Hebrew source texts are verified by ancient Hebrew manuscripts such as the texts discovered at Qumran, reconstructions of a supposed Hebrew text lying behind the text of the LXX are unavoidably hypothetical in nature.[4] Therefore, methodological caution dictates that proposals for reconstructing a Hebrew *Vorlage* that differs from the received text should be made only after all other possible explanations for the variant reading have been exhausted.[5]

Fortunately, variants arising from inner-Greek textual transmission are most often identified by the tools of the textual criticism of the LXX and fall under the purview of the editors of the respective critical editions. The task of distinguishing between variants that arose from the work of the Greek translator and variants that were present in the translator's source text is a more difficult one. Many deviations from the received Hebrew text are the result of the translation process and may be explained without recourse to a reconstructed Hebrew variant.[6] In order to arrive at such a conclusion, however, a thorough analysis of the translation tendencies

---

[4]M. H. Goshen-Gottstein, "Theory and Practice of Textual Criticism—The Text-Critical Use of the Septuagint," *Textus* 3 (1963): 131–32.

[5]Tov, *The Text-Critical Use of the Septuagint,* 74.

[6]Examples of variants arising at the stage of the translation are discussed in J. Barr, *Comparative Philology and the Text of the Old Testament* (Oxford: Clarendon Press, 1968), 238–72; and C. Rabin, "The Translation Process and the Character of the Septuagint," *Textus* 6 (1968): 1–26.

employed within the entire translational unit under consideration is an absolute prerequisite.[7]

Translation Technique in the LXX Minor Prophets

The probability of making reliable judgments about the source text of a given unit of the LXX is directly related to the translator's attitude toward literal representation of the source text. The more literal the translation, the easier it is to recreate reliably the details of the source text. Conversely, the more freedom employed by the translator in rendering the source text, the less one is able to say about that text. As Barr has shown, however, most ancient translations, including even the most "free" renderings within the LXX, exhibit literalistic tendencies.[8] Therefore, the characterization of translations of individual blocks of material within the LXX actually concerns varying degrees of literalness rather than a true polarity between literal and non-literal translations.

A thorough description of the translation technique of the LXX Minor Prophets, although an important endeavor, is not the aim of this dissertation and would in any case exceed the limitations of the present study. Nevertheless, the translation technique employed in the LXX Minor Prophets may accurately be described as being characterized by a high degree of literalness accompanied by a limited range of flexibility and inconsistency. The relatively high degree of literalness in the LXX Minor Prophets may be observed by comparing it with translations of other textual units within the LXX. The LXX Minor Prophets occupies a median position of literalness between the extremely wooden and mechanical translation of

---

[7]Tov, *Text-Critical Use of the Septuagint*, 50; Aejmelaeus, "The Hebrew *Vorlage* of the Septuagint," 61.

[8]Barr, *The Typology of Literalism in Ancient Biblical Translations*, NAWG, I. Phil.-Hist. Kl., MSU 15 (Göttingen: Vandenhoeck and Ruprecht, 1979), 279–325. See also S. P. Brock, "Translating the Old Testament," in *It Is Written: Essays in Honour of Barnabas Lindars, SSF*, ed. D. A. Carson and H. G. M. Williamson (Cambridge: Cambridge University Press, 1988), 87–98.

Ecclesiastes attributed to Aquila, for example, and the more "free" translations of books such as Job, Proverbs, Isaiah, and the Old Greek of Daniel.[9] The LXX of the Book of the Twelve is most comparable to other fairly literal translations such as the LXX of Jeremiah and Ezekiel. In fact, Thackeray argued that the translations of the Book of the Twelve, Jeremiah 1–28, and Ezekiel were so similar that they were likely the products of the same translator, an argument repeated more recently by Tov.[10]

A more precise method of describing the literalness of the LXX translations has been described by Tov, who lists five criteria for measuring the relative freedom or literalness of a translation.[11] First, a literal translation is one that consistently renders a given Hebrew element by the same Greek equivalent, a technique referred to as "stereotyping." Second, a literal translation tends to represent each grammatical element of a Hebrew word by a corresponding Greek equivalent. Third, literal translations tend to follow the word order and sequence of their source text. Fourth, literalness is characterized by a quantitative representation of Hebrew elements that is as close as possible to a one-to-one ratio of elements in the source language and the target language. Fifth, literal translations strive for renderings of their source text that are linguistically precise.

By using Tov's criteria of literalness, it is possible to illustrate the high degree of literalness of the LXX translation of the Book of the Twelve and to expose instances in which the translation falls short of the strictest expressions of literalism. With regard to

---

[9]This was already the assessment of H. St. J. Thackeray in *A Grammar of the Old Testament in Greek according to the Septuagint* (Cambridge: Cambridge University Press, 1909), 13.

[10]Thackeray, "The Greek Translators of the Prophetical Books," *JTS* 4 (1902–3): 78–85; idem, *The Septuagint and Jewish Worship: A Study in Origins* (London: Oxford University Press, 1920), 28; and Tov, *The Septuagint Translation of Jeremiah and Baruch—A Discussion of an Early Revision of Jeremiah 29–52 and Baruch 1:1–3:8,* HSM 8 (Missoula, MT: Scholars Press, 1976), 135–37.

[11]Tov, *The Text-Critical Use of the Septuagint,* 54–60.

the first criterion, for example, the LXX Book of the Twelve contains a large number of stereotyped equivalents. For example, the word *ḥereb* "sword" is translated by the Greek word *rhomphaia* in twenty-five of its twenty-six occurrences in the Minor Prophets. The exceptional rendering of *ḥereb* (Zech 11:17) uses the word *maxaira*, which is the primary equivalent of this term employed in the LXX of Isaiah. Other examples of the tendency toward consistent use of Hebrew-Greek equivalents may be taken from the vocabulary of sin in the LXX Minor Prophets. The Hebrew root *ḥṭʾ* is rendered in all twenty occurrences in the Minor Prophets by the Greek root *hamartanein/hamartia*. The twenty-six occurrences of the Hebrew root *pšʿ* are rendered consistently by the Greek root *asebein/asebeia*. The Hebrew word *ʿāwōn* is rendered fifteen times by the Greek word *adikia*, once by the word *hamartia* (Amos 3:2), and once by *anomia* (Zech 3:4). The exceptional renderings of *ḥereb* and *ʿāwōn* illustrate the fact that in spite of the LXX's general consistency in the use of Hebrew-Greek equivalences, it nevertheless displayed a slight degree of occasional flexibility or inconsistency in the choice of equivalents.[12]

Several examples may be offered to demonstrate the limited flexibility of the translator of the LXX Minor Prophets in selecting equivalents.[13] For example, the translator did not choose to repeat the same Greek equivalent for the two uses of the Hebrew word *šōd* in Amos 5:9. The first occurrence was rendered by *syntrimmon* and the second by *talaipōrian*, apparently

---

[12]Recently, Aejmelaeus has expressed dissatisfaction with the term "translation technique" because it implies a thoroughness and consistency of method that should not be expected of an ancient translator. See "Translation Technique and the Intention of the Translator," in *Proceedings of the VIIth Congress of the International Organization of Septuagint and Cognate Studies*, ed. C. Cox (Atlanta: Scholars Press, 1989), 23–36.

[13]An extensive list of examples is given in J. Ziegler, "Die Einheit der Septuaginta zum Zwölfprophetenbuch," *Beelage zum Vorlesungsverzeichnis der Staatl. Akademie zu Braunsberg* (Göttingen: Vandenhoeck and Ruprecht, 1934–35), 1–16.

on stylistic grounds.[14] Another stylistic variation of Greek equivalents is found in the translation of the five occurrences in the Book of Haggai of the idiom *śîmû lĕbabkem* "set your heart (upon your ways)." This phrase occurs at Hag 1:5, 7; and 2:18, and in the form *śîmû-nā᾽ lĕbabkem* at 2:15, 18. The five occurrences of this idiom are rendered in five different ways by the LXX. These renderings are:

1:5 *taxate dē tas kardias hymōn*
1:7 *thesthe tas kardias hymōn*
2:18 *hypotaxate dē tas kardias hymōn*
2:15 *thesthe dē eis tas kardias hymōn*
2:18 *thesthe en tais kardias hymōn*

The characteristics of a general literalness of translation marked by limited flexibility or occasional inconsistency hold also for the other four criteria described by Tov. With regard to Tov's second criterion, for example, the LXX Minor Prophets generally analyzed the various elements of Hebrew words and represented them by their individual Greek equivalents. Exceptions to this tendency may be seen by comparing the LXX to the text of the Greek translation of the Minor Prophets attested in 8Ḥev GrXII. This translation, designated as "R" by Barthélemy, is a recension of the Old Greek translation corrected in the direction of the proto-MT text.[15] Easy comparison of these two texts is facilitated by the critical edition of Tov, which underlines those places where R differs from the LXX.[16] Jonah 2:5 provides an example of an exception to the practice of representing each individual Hebrew element by a

---

[14]J. de Waard, "Translation Techniques Used by the Greek Translators of Amos," *Biblica* 59 (1978): 347. De Waard also cites the variations employed in the translation of the fivefold phrase *wĕlō᾽ šabtem ῾āday* in Amos 4:6–11.

[15]Barthélemy, "Redécouverte d'un chaînon manquant de l'histoire de la Septante," *RB* 60 (1953): 18–29; idem, *Devanciers d'Aquila*, VTSup 10 (Leiden: E. J. Brill, 1963).

[16]Tov, *The Greek Minor Prophets Scroll from Naḥal Ḥever*, DJD VIII (Oxford: Oxford University Press, 1990).

corresponding Greek one. The MT of Jonah 2:5 reads *nigraštî minneged ʿênekā* ("I was driven out from before your eyes"). This phrase is rendered by the LXX as *apōsmai ex ophthalmōn sou*. R renders the Hebrew text more literally, however, as *apōsmai ex enantias ophthalmōn sou*, thus representing each individual Hebrew element.

With regard to Tov's third criterion of word order, the LXX Book of the Twelve is extremely literal in following the word order found in the MT. The number of exceptions to this practice compared with the number of words in the Minor Prophets is extremely small.[17] The same description applies to the quantitative representation of Hebrew elements by the LXX. The LXX generally follows a one-to-one ratio of Hebrew to Greek elements. One exception to this tendency is the translation of the Hebrew word *lapîd* "flame." At Nah 2:4(5) and Zech 12:6, this word is translated by the Greek words *lampades pyros* "flame of fire."[18]

Tov's fifth criterion of literalness, that of qualitative representation, is the most difficult of the five criteria to assess because of its subjective nature. Although on numerous occasions the translator mistakenly translated the source text, the test of literalness is whether or not the translator intended to render the *Vorlage* as accurately as possible. One way to make such a judgment is to examine how the translator rendered those words most difficult to translate, namely, *hapax legomena*. J. Arieti has made such an examination for the *hapax legomena* within the Book of Amos.[19] In such cases, where little if any philological information was available, the translator's tendency was to render the given word as accurately as possible based upon the

---

[17]Deviations in the order of two or more words may be found at Hos 8:13; Joel 2:22; Amos 5:14, 26; 7:7; 8:9; Micah 2:12; 4:13; Nah 3:8; and Hag 2:4.

[18]R. Harrison notes that this rendering is also found at Dan 10:6 and Gen 15:7 and suggests that the translator was simply following convention. See "The Unity of the Minor Prophets in the LXX: A Reexamination of the Question," *BIOSCS* 21 (1988): 66, n. 11.

[19]J. Arieti, "The Vocabulary of Septuagint Amos," *JBL* 93 (1974): 343–45.

surrounding context rather than to use the lack of philological information as license to introduce innovations into the text.

[*Excursus: The Translational Unity of the LXX Minor Prophets.* The general description of the translation technique given above relates directly to an issue that has been raised at various times concerning the so-called "unity of the LXX Minor Prophets," or the question of whether a single translator is responsible for the entire translation. A single translator was generally assumed for the LXX Minor Prophets until 1923, when J. Hermann and F. Baumgärtel argued that it was instead the work of two translators.[20] Hermann and Baumgärtel worked from the assumption that each translator used a consistent set of Hebrew/Greek equivalences and that a variation in the translation of a Hebrew word was an indication of a different translator. This reasoning was refuted by J. Ziegler in an article appearing in 1934.[21] Ziegler argued that only the most mechanical translation style would repeatedly employ the same Greek equivalents in translating as large a document as the Book of the Twelve. He illustrated the limited variation of equivalents employed by the translator of the LXX Minor Prophets by citing numerous examples of Hebrew words that were translated by different Greek equivalents in both of Hermann and Baumgärter's proposed translation units. Ziegler also listed forty-five examples of preferred Greek words which the LXX translator used to render several different Hebrew words. Finally, Ziegler listed twenty-three examples of uncommon Hebrew words that were rendered consistently in Greek throughout the LXX Minor Prophets. Ziegler's description of the unity of the LXX Minor Prophets agrees with the general consistency and limited flexibility of translation technique described in the present study.

In spite of Ziegler's strong case for a single translator, the question of multiple translators has twice been raised since his essay. First, G. Howard noted differences between the translation of the majority of the Book of Amos and a small unit of the book comprised of Amos 8:12–9:10.[22] Howard's

---

[20]Hermann and Baumgärtel, *Beiträge zur Entstehungsgeschichte der Septuaginta* (Berlin/ Stuttgart/Leipzig: Kohlhammer, 1923).

[21]Ziegler, "Die Einheit der Septuaginta zum Zwölfprophetenbuch."

[22]G. Howard, "Some Notes on the Septuagint of Amos," *VT* 20 (1970): 108–12.

suggestion of a separate translator for this small unit was refuted by T. Muraoka.[23] Muraoka argued that the differences in translation described by Howard could be explained by factors in the immediate context of the texts cited and also by the flexibility of the translator described by Ziegler. What could not be explained by Howard, however, was why such a small unit with no discernable structural distinctions would be assigned to a second translator.

Recently, R. Harrison[24] has questioned the merits of Ziegler's arguments as well as the supporting evidence offered subsequent to Ziegler's essay by E. Tov.[25] Harrison disputed Ziegler's one-translator theory on the basis of methodological questions and on the basis of a study of the LXX of Joel and Nahum. He argued that Ziegler and Tov's methodology, although suggestive, was not sufficient to prove the unity of the translation. Harrison suggested that the differences between the translations of Joel and Nahum were inconsistent with the assumption of a single translator.

Again it was Muraoka who wrote "in defense of the unity of the LXX Minor Prophets."[26] Muraoka admitted that Harrison had raised some important methodological questions, but denied that these questions were sufficient to counter the assumption of a single translator. The distinctions drawn by Harrison between the translation of Joel and Nahum could be explained by the circumstances of literary context and by the common inconsistencies accompanying most translation units of the LXX.

My own study of the translation technique of the LXX Minor Prophets finds the theory of a single translator to be the most acceptable hypothesis. Although translational consistency is to be expected of a single translator, one should not assume that the translator of so large a textual unit as the Minor Prophets would remember the precise equivalent previously used for every Hebrew word, or that such a translator would not be influenced more by the immediate context of the passage at hand than by a previously established equivalence. The inconsistencies in the translation of the LXX

---

[23]T. Muraoka, "Is the Septuagint of Amos viii 12–ix 10 a Separate Unit?" *VT* 20 (1970): 496–500.

[24]Harrison, "The Unity of the Minor Prophets in the LXX."

[25]Tov, *The Septuagint Translation of Jeremiah and Baruch.*

[26]Muraoka, "In Defense of the Unity of the LXX Minor Prophets," *AJBI* 15 (1989): 25–36.

Minor Prophets may be more than would be expected of a mechanically literal rendering, but do not exceed the normal range of inconsistency to be expected of a single translator who worked on an extensive literary corpus over an extended period of time.

Furthermore, a number of consistent renderings of identical phrases within the Minor Prophets are difficult to explain except by a theory of a single translator. The identical rendering of the enigmatic Hebrew phrase *qibbĕṣû pāʾrûr* in both Joel 2:6 and Nah 2:11 as *hōs proskauma chytras* "like blackened pots" is one example of such consistent renderings. Another example is the consistent rendering of *yādad gôrāl* "to cast lots," by the Greek *ballein klērous* in the only three occurrences of this phrase in the Hebrew Bible in Joel 4:3, Obad 11, and Nah 3:10. The mistaken rendering of the word *lāʿad* "for eternity" by the phrase *eis martyrion* "for a witness" (= Heb. *lĕʿēd*) in Amos 1:11 and Mic 7:18 is further evidence that suggests the work of a single translator. Although Harrison is correct that a single translator for the LXX Minor Prophets, like much in biblical studies, has not been conclusively proven, it remains the best working assumption among the available possibilities.]

The literal tendencies of the LXX Book of the Twelve are very helpful for deciding whether a particular variant originated from the translation process or from the translator's source text. One may assume that a translator who took pains to be faithful to the *wording* of the source text, even to the point of creating an awkward or even incomprehensible Greek text, would be less likely to alter the source text intentionally. The limited flexibility and occasional unevenness of the LXX Minor Prophets, however, also advises caution in moving too easily from the text of the version to the presumed text of its *Vorlage*.

Another benefit of the literal translation technique of the LXX Minor Prophets is the fact that it gives evidence of the high degree of agreement between the text of the LXX *Vorlage* and the consonantal text of the MT Book of the Twelve. Tov has noted the often overlooked fact that the majority of linguistic elements present in the MT are indeed reflected in the LXX.[27] The degree

---

[27]Tov, *The Text-Critical Use of the Septuagint*, 99.

of agreement between the texts of the MT and the LXX should not be neglected or overlooked, especially since such widespread agreement highlights the significance of their textual differences.

Variant Readings in the Hebrew Vorlage of the LXX Book of the Twelve

In spite of the difficulty of reconstructing the Hebrew source text behind the LXX translation, a number of textual variants within the Hebrew *Vorlage* of the LXX can be reconstructed with a relative degree of certainty. The remainder of the chapter will describe the most compelling cases of textual variation between the Hebrew *Vorlage* of the LXX and the MT of the Book of the Twelve. As I shall argue below, these variants demonstrate not only the somewhat distinct transmission histories of the Hebrew source text of the LXX and the MT, but they also illustrate the dual roles of ancient scribes as both copyists and interpreters of their source texts. To the extent that interpretative activities may be demonstrated in the textual transmission of the Book of the Twelve, such activities illustrate the dynamics of the canonical process.

Even given the high degree of literalness in the translation of the LXX Minor Prophets, the examples of unevenness in the translation cited above make it impossible to determine with certainty the exact origin of many of the variants in the LXX. One type of textual variant, however, does lend itself to reliable conclusions about the presence of the versional text in the Hebrew *Vorlage* of the LXX. Variants based on quantitative differences between the MT and the LXX, i.e., pluses and minuses, may often be convincingly argued to have existed in the *Vorlage* of the LXX translator. Several factors affect the probability that a plus or a minus in the LXX originated in the Hebrew *Vorlage*.[28] Obviously, a quantitative difference in the

---

[28]Tov (Ibid.) makes a distinction between (1) minor elements that translators either added or omitted for purposes of readability (83–86); and (2)

LXX that is also attested in an ancient Hebrew manuscript has the highest probability of having originated in the translator's source text. The discoveries at Qumran have provided numerous examples of variants in the LXX that are attested by external manuscript evidence.[29]

The majority of quantitative differences between the MT and the LXX, however, do not have textual attestation in Hebrew manuscripts and therefore must be evaluated by other means. A prerequisite to attributing an addition in the LXX to its Hebrew *Vorlage* is that the additional text must have a plausibly reconstructed Hebrew source text based on known Greek-Hebrew equivalences. Greek readings that cannot be expressed in Hebrew originated either with the translator or during the transmission of the Greek text.[30]

Tov has argued that the translation technique of the unit of the LXX containing the addition is also a factor in deciding the textual significance of such variants. Quantitative differences that are found in more literal translation units are more likely to have been in the *Vorlage* of the LXX.[31] Aejmelaeus has argued against Tov, however, that even translators who were relatively free in their translation technique, such as the LXX translator of Exodus, have demonstrated no tendency to add or subtract substantively from the content of their source text.[32] Aejmelaeus concluded that *quantitative differences between the LXX and the MT, particularly those that create parallelism or harmonization with the immediate context, should be assumed to have been present in the translator's source text.* The harmonization of one text with another text in the immediate context, according to Aejmelaeus, is characteristic of the activities of copyists rather than the activities of translators, who generally considered only the

---

pluses and minuses which alter the content of the text and may be reconstructed as the reading of the *Vorlage* (186–90).

[29]Ibid., 111, 126–27.

[30]Ibid., 101.

[31]Ibid., 186–7.

[32]Aejmelaeus, "The Hebrew *Vorlage* of the Septuagint," 86–87.

immediate contexts of individual words and phrases.[33] The burden of proof, therefore, belongs to those who would attribute harmonizing additions and deliberate textual alterations to the translator rather than to a copyist of the Hebrew text.[34]

LXX Variants Attested by Manuscript Evidence

The LXX of the Book of the Twelve contains a number of lengthier textual readings compared to the text of the MT. Many of these lengthier texts appear to be the result of harmonization with language found in the immediate context. Two such harmonizing additions have been attested in manuscript remains from Qumran. These two examples are important because they speak to the probability that other textual additions in the LXX Minor Prophets were also present in its Hebrew source text.

Hosea 13:4. The MT of Hos 13:4 reads as follows:

wĕ'ānōkî yhwh 'ĕlōhêkā mē'ereṣ miṣrāyim

I am Yahweh your God from the land of Egypt.

The LXX of Hos 13:4 contains a significant addition, however. It reads:

---

[33]For a discussion of the phenomenon of textual harmonization, see E. Tov, "The Nature and Background of Harmonizations in Biblical Manuscripts," *JSOT* 31 (1985): 3–29. For a description of the methodology of ancient translators, see I. Soisalon-Soininen, "Beobachtungen zur Arbeitsweise der Septuaginta-Ubersetzer," in *Isac Leo Seeligman Volume: Essays on the Bible and the Ancient World III.*, ed. A. Rofé and Y. Zakovitch (Jerusalem: E. Rubenstein, 1983), 319–29.

[34]The same methodological argument has been made recently by E. Ulrich, "The Canonical Process, Textual Criticism and latter Stages in the Composition of the Bible," in *"Sha'arei Talmon,"* ed. M. Fishbane and E. Tov (Winona Lake, IN: Eisenbrauns, 1992), 286.

[egō dē kyrios ho theos sou] stereōn ouranon kai ktizōn gēn, ou hai cheires ektiasan pasan tēn stratian tou ouranou, kai ou paredeixa soi auta tou poreuesthai opisō autōn. kai egō anēgagon se [ek gēs Aigyptou]

[I am Yahweh your God] who stretched out the heavens and created the earth, whose hands made all the hosts of heaven, yet I did not reveal them for you to walk after them. And I brought you up [from the land of Egypt].

The LXX addition is the only description of Yahweh as creator of the universe in the Book of Hosea.[35] The language is closer to texts in Isaiah, Jeremiah, and the doxologies of Amos than any other language in Hosea.[36] It appears clearly to be secondary to the wording of the MT. The evaluation of such textual variants as original or secondary, however, is a separate undertaking from the reconstruction of the Hebrew *Vorlage* of the LXX. The reconstruction would ordinarily require a text-critical decision on whether the addition was added by a copyist transmitting the Greek text, by the Greek translator, or by a copyist of the Hebrew *Vorlage*. In this case, however, the text of 4QXII^c provides a ready answer.[37] For Hos 13:4, this Qumran fragment inserts after the phrase "I am Yahweh your God" the words *[n]ōteh šāmayim* "who stretches out the heavens," and, following a lacuna large enough for approximately sixty letters, the words *[wĕ]ʾānōkî haʿălîtîkâ* "and I brought you up (from the land of Egypt)." These additions and the size of the gap between them

---

[35]Barthélemy, *Critique Textuelle de l'Ancien Testament*, ccxxiv.

[36]The phrase "stretching out the heavens" appears in Isa 45:12; and 48:13. "All the hosts of the heavens" occurs in Jer 8:2 and 19:13. The verb pair *stereōn . . . kai ktizōn* occurs only in LXX Amos 4:13. Only the phrase "to walk after him" is common to the Book of Hosea (Hos 2:7, 15; 5:11; and 11:10). Barthélemy, *Critique Textuelle de l'Ancien Testament*, ccxxiv.

[37]Barthélemy, *Critique Textuelle de l'Ancien Testament*, cxvi, and ccxxiii, n. 13; M. Textuz, "Deux fragments inedits der manuscripts de la Mer Morte," *Semitica* 5 (1955): 38–39. The fragment has been edited for publication by R. Fuller for a forthcoming volume in *Discoveries in the Judean Desert*.

correspond to the reading of the LXX and confirm that the expansion existed in the translator's Hebrew source text.

Amos 1:3. LXX Hos 13:4 contains a lengthy addition that would be out of character with the conservative and literal approach of the LXX translator. The manuscript remains from Qumran also provide an example, however, of a much smaller addition found in the LXX that was also present in the translator's *Vorlage.* The MT of Amos 1:3 describes the sin of Damascus as follows:

ʿal dûšām baḥărūsôt habbarzel ʾet haggilʿād

because they threshed Gilead with sledges of iron

The LXX rendering of this text reflects a different understanding of the offense of Damascus. It reads:

*anth' hōn eprizon priosi sidērois **tas en gastri echousas** tōn en Galaad*

because they have cut with iron saws *those who were pregnant* in Gilead.

The phrase *tas en gastri echousas* is an intrusion into the text that is obviously intended to specify the vague offense of Damascus by means of harmonization with Amos 1:13. There Ammon is condemned "because they have ripped open the pregnant women in Gilead" (Heb. *ʿal biqʿām hārôt haggilʿād*; Gr. *anth' hōn aneschizon tas en gastri exousas tōn Galaaditōn*). The Hebrew verb *dwš* of Amos 1:3 ("to tread or thresh") was read in light of the verb *bqʿ* "to split" in 1:13 and the vague offense of Damascus was clarified as an act of brutality by the insertion of the phrase "those who were pregnant." A fragment of Amos 1:3–5 from Qumran Cave V, however, demonstrates that this harmonizing interpretation was present in a Hebrew text and not only in the translation of the LXX. 5QAmos shows that the suggested parallel with Amos 1:13 was created by the insertion of the single Hebrew word *hrwt* "those who are pregnant."[38]

The textual additions found in LXX Hos 13:4, LXX Amos 1:3, and their respective Qumran manuscripts support Aejmelaeus's argument that substantive alterations in the content of the source text is contrary to the nature of ancient translations, particularly literal translations, and that quantitative differences should be assumed to have originated in the translator's *Vorlage* unless there is clear evidence to the contrary. LXX Amos 1:3, for example, might appear to be a slight alteration by a translator attempting to understand a difficult expression by reference to a text in the immediate context. Nevertheless, the Qumran fragment and the translation technique of the entire unit confirm that the variant reading was created by the addition of a single word in the Hebrew text translated by the LXX, thus demonstrating that even small additions in the text of the LXX were likely to have been present in its Hebrew *Vorlage*.

A number of quantitative differences of varying size exist between the LXX and the MT of the Book of the Twelve. Many of these are harmonizations similar to Amos 1:3. Although they are not attested by manuscript evidence as are Hos 13:4 and Amos 1:3, based on the methodological arguments given above and the translation tendencies of the LXX Minor Prophets, I conclude that the examples listed below were present in the translator's source text. I have grouped the variants into categories that are related to the kinds of textual alterations that they reveal. These categories are: (1) harmonizations with common phrases or formulaic language; (2) harmonizations that create a parallelism with a text within the immediate context; (3) exegetical harmonizations that attempt to explicate the text by adopting language from other biblical texts; (4) lengthy textual expansions that are either imitations or combinations of

---

[38]F. Andersen and D. N. Freedman, *Amos*, The Anchor Bible Vol. 24A (New York: Doubleday, 1989) 238. For the text of 5QAmos, see M. Baillet, J. T. Milik, and R. de Vaux, *Les 'Petites Grottes' de Qumran*, DJD III (Oxford: Clarendon Press, 1962), 173.

"biblical" language; and (5) one example of a textual expansion that is indicated by a difference in sequence between the LXX and the MT.

The variants to be discussed below are of a diverse nature, and range in character from minor textual changes to changes of an interpretative and even editorial nature. These textual variants are significant for three reasons. First, they demonstrate that the Hebrew text underlying the LXX, although very similar to that of the MT, nevertheless possessed a history of transmission independent of the MT. Secondly, many of these textual alterations are similar in appearance to texts in the MT that are thought to be either redactional insertions or interpretative glosses. They therefore demonstrate a degree of continuity between textual alterations on the one hand and redactional activity on the other. Thirdly, and relatedly, they offer concrete textual examples of the kind of literary and exegetical processes by which the Hebrew text of the Book of the Twelve developed into its present canonical form.

Textual Harmonizations with Formulaic Language

Some of the textual variants in the Hebrew *Vorlage* of the LXX are the result of changes that conform that text to more common biblical phrases or formulas. Although these changes hardly alter the interpretation of the text, they are worthy of mention because they may be reconstructed with a high degree of certainty. They therefore serve as a helpful introduction to the other reconstructed Hebrew variants to be discussed below.

Hosea 2:14; 4:3. These verses contain additions that bring them into conformity with the familiar three-part phrase "the beasts of the field, the birds of the heavens, and the creeping things of the ground."[39] All three elements occur in Hos 2:20 (LXX v. 18). In the MT of Hos 2:14 (LXX v. 12), the phrase "beasts of the field" occurs alone ("the beasts of the field shall devour them"). The LXX, however, adds the other two parts of

---

[39]Barthélemy, *Critique Textuelle de l'Ancien Testament*, ccxxv.

the trio in parallel to Hos 2:20(18). Again in Hos 4:3, where the MT mentions only beasts and birds, the LXX adds "the creeping things of the ground."

Haggai 1:1, 12; 2:4, 20, 21. The Book of Haggai has by far the greatest number of textual additions in the LXX in proportion to the size of the book. Many of these additions may be explained, however, by a degree of verbal repetition within the book that is almost formulaic in character. For example, four times in the Book of Haggai, Zerubbabel ben Shealtiel is referred to as *paḥat yĕhûdâ* "governor of Judah" (1:1, 14; 2:2; 21). The only exception to this pattern is 1:12, where the title is omitted. The title is present, however, in LXX 1:12, in harmony with the other occurrences in the book. Similarly, Hag 2:4 and 2:21 are the only two of the seven occurrences of Zerubbabel's name in the book that omit his patronymic "son of Shealtiel." The LXX of 2:21, however, includes the patronymic in harmony with the five previous occurrences. Other examples of harmonizations with formulaic language in Haggai include: (1) LXX Hag 2:20, where the title *hannābîʾ* "the prophet" is added after Haggai's name, in harmony with Hag 1:1, 12; 2:1; and 2:10; and (2) LXX Hag 1:1, which adds the words *legōn eipōn* "(the word of Yahweh came by way of Haggai ...) *saying, 'Speak* (to Zerubbabel ...).'" This addition harmonizes the oracular formula of 1:1 with that of 2:1–2, where these two words are present in the MT. Each of these textual harmonizations is more appropriately attributed to the leveling tendencies of a copyist of the Hebrew text than to the activities of a translator.

Zechariah 1:17. A final example of a textual addition that employs formulaic language is found in LXX Zech 1:17. Zechariah's dialogues with the interpreting angel are often reported in a highly repetitive manner.[40] Part of this formulaic repetition is the recurrence of the phrase "the angel who spoke

---

[40]See the chart of formulaic language in the visions of Zechariah in C. L. Meyers and E. M. Meyers, *Haggai, Zechariah 1–8,* The Anchor Bible, Vol. 25B (Garden City, NY: Doubleday, 1987), lvii.

with me" (Zech 1:9, 14; 2:2, 8; 4:1, 5; 5:5; 6:4). Zech 1:17 repeats the imperative "Proclaim" which the interpreting angel addressed to Zechariah in 1:14. The LXX of Zech 1:17, however, contains the addition *kai eipe pros me ho aggelos ho lalōn en emoi* "and the angel who spoke with me said ('Proclaim . . .).'" This addition makes explicit that the identity of the speaker and the addressee is the same in 1:17 as it is in 1:14 by supplying a formulaic introduction from that context.

Parallelistic Harmonizations with the Immediate Context

A different kind of textual addition in the presumed Hebrew *Vorlage* of the LXX harmonizes the text with a similar phrase in the immediate context in such a way as to create parallelism. Parallelism of members is perhaps the most easily recognized stylistic feature of ancient Hebrew literature. The following examples show that this stylistic technique was employed by ancient copyists as well as ancient authors. They also support the argument of S. Talmon that the roles of scribe and author in antiquity were often embodied in *unio personalis.*[41]

Hosea 8:13. The MT of Hos 8:13 ends with the pronouncement "they (Israel) shall return to Egypt." The LXX adds after this statement the words *kai en Assyrois akatharta phagontai* "and in Assyria they shall eat unclean food." The parallel construction "they shall return to Egypt and in Assyria they shall eat unclean food" occurs in both the MT and LXX of Hos 9:3, which is undoubtedly the source of the addition in 8:13. The fact that the LXX translates the verb *šwb* differently in 8:13 (*apestrepsan*) and 9:3 (*katoikēsen=* Heb. *yšb*) confirms the assumption that the harmonization between these two verses originated with the Hebrew *Vorlage* of the LXX rather than with the translator. It would be inconsistent to conclude that the translator inserted a phrase into Hos 8:13 in order to create a

---

[41]Talmon, "The Textual Study of the Bible—A New Outlook," in *Qumran and the History of the Biblical Text*, ed. Cross and Talmon (Cambridge: Harvard University Press, 1975), 336–43.

parallelism with 9:3, only to translate the main verb of the two verses by different equivalents.

Micah 5:7. A similar harmonization is found in LXX Mic 5:7 (MT v. 6). The MT contains the text "And the remnant of Jacob shall be in the midst of many peoples." The LXX, however, inserts the additional phrase *en tois ethnesin* "among the nations" (Heb. *baggôyim*) prior to "in the midst of many peoples." The parallelism of "nations" and "peoples" in LXX 5:7 is presumably the result of an addition in the Hebrew source text, under the influence of the following verse, which reads in both the MT and the LXX "and the remnant of Jacob shall be among the nations, in the midst of many peoples."[42]

Haggai 2:21. The MT of Hag 2:6 contains the statement that Yahweh "will shake the heavens and the earth, the sea and the dry land." Hag 2:21 has the similar statement "I am about to shake the heavens and the earth." The LXX of Hag 2:21 adds the phrase "the sea and the dry land" to complete the parallel expression as found in Hag 2:6.

Malachi 1:7. Mal 1:7 reports Yahweh's complaint against the priests who say, "The table of Yahweh has been desecrated." The LXX adds, at the end of the verse, the synonymous phrase *kai ta epitithemena brōmata exoudenōmena* "and the food that is placed upon it is desecrated." This addition harmonizes Mal 1:7 with the parallel expression "The table of Yahweh has been desecrated and the food that is placed upon it is desecrated" found in Mal 1:12, which is the likely source of the addition.

Zechariah 1:8. The final example of this type of textual alteration creates a parallelism of a different sort from those cited above. In Zech 1:8, the LXX text has the addition *hoi psaroi* "dappled grey (horses)," making the number of colors of the horses of Zechariah's first vision agree with the number of colors

---

[42]See also Mic 3:1a, where the phrase "heads of Jacob" reads in the LXX as "heads of *the house* of Jacob," in harmony with "rulers of *the house* of Israel" of the following stichos.

of the horses accompanying the four chariots of Zech 6:2–3. The LXX addition harmonizes the first of Zechariah's visions with the final vision. This harmonization highlights the other parallel features of these two visions and completes the parallelism by reconciling the number of colors of the horses.[43] The structural parallelism of the first and final visions thus helps to mark clearly the beginning and end of the visionary section of the Book of Zechariah.[44]

Exegetical Harmonizations

The third group of textual alterations share the common feature of attempting to clarify a question or difficulty within the presumed source text. These alterations are therefore explicative in nature. Another significant feature of this group of changes, however, is that they carry out their explication of the text by "borrowing" language from a nearby context. In a sense, such exegetical harmonizations attempt to interpret "Scripture" by "Scripture."

Hosea 12:10. Hos 12:10 (LXX 12:9) is identical to Hos 13:4a in the MT ("I am Yahweh your God from the land of Egypt"). As in LXX Hos 13:4, the LXX of 12:10 adds the phrase *anagagon se* before the words *ek gēs Aigyptou*, creating the reading "I, Yahweh your God, brought you up from the land of Egypt." The retroverted text behind this addition, *haʿălîtîkā*, was present in 4QXII[C] at Hos 13:4 and was therefore most likely also in the Hebrew *Vorlage* of LXX Hos 12:9. The addition transforms the somewhat obscure Hebrew phrase "I am Yahweh your God from (the time of?) the land of Egypt" into an expression that is more

---

[43]For discussion of parallel imagery between the first and final visions of Zechariah, see Meyers and Meyers, *Haggai, Zechariah 1–8*, 332.

[44]A similar harmonization between the beginning and the end of Zechariah takes place in Zech 1:6. In speaking about the divine appointment of "the former prophets," LXX Zech 1:6 adds the phrase *en pneumati mou* "by my spirit" (Heb. *bĕrûḥî*), a harmonization with identical phraseology in Zech 7:12.

common in biblical language.[45] The immediate context of Hos 12.14, "By a prophet Yahweh brought up (*hĕʿelâ*) Israel from Egypt" is the most likely source for the addition.

Amos 1:1. In Amos 1:1, the description in the MT of the visions of Amos as "concerning Israel" reads in the LXX as "concerning Jerusalem." The change was most likely made by a copyist under the influence of the reference to Jerusalem in Amos 1:2, or possibly under the influence of the superscriptions of Isa 1:1, 2:1 and Mic 1:1, each of which refers to Jerusalem as the subject of the divine word. Although not the original reading, LXX Amos 1:1 does reflect the reality that the words of Amos against the Northern Kingdom were later applied to Judah and Jerusalem once the Northern Kingdom had disappeared. In that sense, the LXX reading is similar to the aim of proposed Judean redactions of the Book of Amos.[46]

Amos 1:3. This example of exegetical harmonization has already been discussed above. The text explains the enigmatic offense of Damascus by means of the offense of Gilead in a nearby context. Again, the text of 5QAmos demonstrates that this addition took place within the Hebrew source text of the LXX.

Joel 1:5. In the MT, this verse commands the wine drinkers to lament *ʿal ʿāsîs kî nikrat mippîkem* "over the sweet wine, for it has been cut off from your mouth." The LXX, however, contains two textual changes. First, it has the addition *euphronsynē kai*

---

[45]References in the Hebrew Bible to Yahweh bringing Israel up (Hiphil of *ʿlh*) from the land of Egypt include: Exod 32:1, 7, 23; 33:1; Josh 24:17; Judg 6:8; 1 Sam 12:6; 2 Kgs 17:7; 17:36; Jer 2:6; 16:14; 23:7; and 1 Chr 17:5. This expression occurs in the Minor Prophets in Amos 2:10; 3:1; 9:7; and Mic 6:4.

[46]See the discussions of possible Judean redactions of Amos in Wolff, *Joel and Amos, A Commentary* tr. W. Janzen, S. D. McBride, and C. Muenchow, Hermeneia (Philadelphia: Fortress Press, 1979), 112–13; and W. Schmidt, "Die deuteronomistische Redaktion des Amosbuches," *ZAW* 77 (1965): 168–93.

chara, "joy and rejoicing," at the end of the verse, and second, it translates *ʿal ʿāsîs* by the Greek phrase *eis methēn* "unto drunkenness." The LXX may thus be translated as "Lament, oh drinkers of wine unto drunkenness, for joy and rejoicing have been cut off from your mouths." There is no clear text-critical reason why the the word pair "joy and rejoicing" would have been omitted from the MT. Apparently a tradent of the Hebrew text did not recognize *ʿāsîs* "sweet wine" as the antecedent of the pronominal subject of the Niphal verb *nikrat* "to be cut off." The tradent thus supplied a subject from the nearby context of Joel 1:16, where the word pair *śimḥâ wāgîl* "joy and rejoicing" occurs as the subject of the verb *nikrat.* Although this addition solved the perceived problem of an indefinite subject for the verb *nikrat,* it caused difficulty for the translator. Instead of translating *ʿāsîs* correctly as "sweet wine," the translator rendered it instead as *eis methēn,* "unto drunkenness."[47]

Micah 4:8. The LXX of Mic 4:8 differs from the MT by the addition of the words, *ek Babylonos.* Translated, it reads "To you, tower of the parched[48] flock, daughter Zion, to you will come and to you will enter the former dominion, the kingdom *from Babylon,* to daughter Jerusalem." The addition of "from Babylon" in 4:8 was most likely influenced by Mic 4:10, the only other mention of Babylon in the Book of Micah. In 4:10, daughter Zion is told to prepare to go into exile to Babylon, to be rescued there at a later time. The addition in LXX Mic 4:8 interprets the verse as a promise of the restoration from the exile predicted in

---

[47]Against R. Harrison ("The Unity of the Minor Prophets," 68), who suggests that the addition was added by the translator because of the mistranslation of the subject of the verb. It is more likely that the addition of the words "joy and gladness" in the *Vorlage* of LXX caused the translator difficulty in translating *ʿāsîs,* which he rendered correctly at LXX Joel 3:18 (MT 4:18).

[48]The Greek *auchmōdēs* is a mistaken rendering of the MT *ʿopel* "hill," which occurs only here in the Minor Prophets. The MT reads, "To you, tower of the flock, hill of daughter Zion. . . ."

4:10. It also interprets the promise of 4:10 that states "there (i.e., in Babylon) you will be rescued, there Yahweh will redeem you from the hand of your enemy." This promise does not explicitly state, however, the nature of the anticipated rescue and, specifically, it does not indicate whether the rescue would take place "there" in Babylon or whether it would involve a return to Judah from exile. The addition to 4:8 states clearly that the leadership of Jerusalem would not only be rescued from the enemy while "there" in Babylon (4:10), but that they would also return to Jerusalem "from Babylon."

A significant feature of the addition in Mic 4:8 is that its apparent source, Mic 4:10, is almost universally considered to be a redactional addition as well.[49] The addition preserved in the LXX provides a concrete example of the same kind of editorial activity proposed for Mic 4:10. Despite their similarities, however, Mic 4:10 is labeled as a "redactional" or "editorial" feature of the book, while the addition in LXX 4:8 is generally considered a "textual" phenomenon. The similarity of these two verses as they are preserved in the LXX illustrates the occasional "editorial" role of ancient copyists and thus blurs somewhat the strict distinction between the categories of textual and editorial alterations.

Malachi 1:1. LXX Mal 1:1 contains the following addition at the end of the verse: *thesthe dē epi tas kardias hymōn.* This Hebraism reflects the idiom *śîmû lĕbabkem,* "set your heart (upon something)," which means to consider or to think seriously about a matter.[50] A form of this idiom is found in Mal 2:2: *kî ʾênĕkem śāmîm ʿal lēb* "because you are not laying it to heart." The imperative form of the statement found in LXX Mal 1:1, however, does not occur elsewhere in Malachi. The imperative

[49]For an exception to this interpretation, see L. C. Allen, *The Books of Joel, Obadiah, Jonah and Micah,* NICOT (Grand Rapids, MI: Eerdmans, 1976), 245–46.

[50]Meyers and Meyers, *Haggai, Zechariah 1–8,* 24; Petersen, *Haggai and Zechariah 1–8,* 49.

form of the idiom "set your heart (upon something)" does occur five times, however, in the Book of Haggai (1:5, 7; 2:15, 18 [2x]).

The addition in LXX Mal 1:1 of so prominent a phrase from the Book of Haggai highlights other similarities between these two books. With regard to form, both books employ a question and answer schema to communicate their message. Thematically, both view the restored Second Temple and a reformed cult as central to the economic and political welfare of the province of Judah. Historically, both demonstrate a period in which the functions of prophet and priest had begun to merge together.[51] Linguistically, both employ the phrase *dĕbar yhwh bĕyad* PN "the word of Yahweh by the hand of PN" (Hag 1:1; Mal 1:1) as an introductory formula. Finally, if one interprets the word *malʾākî* with the Targum and the LXX (*aggelou auto= malʾākô*) as an appellative, i.e., my/his messenger, then both Haggai and the anonymous prophet of the Book of Malachi share the identical title of messenger of Yahweh (Hag 1:13).[52]

The expansion in LXX Mal 1:1 not only emphasizes the similarities between Malachi and Haggai but was also possibly motivated by the question, "Who was *malʾākî/ malʾākô* (my/his messenger)?" The Targum answered this question by identifying "Malachi" with Ezra.[53] The Hebrew text behind LXX Mal 1:1, by borrowing a thematic phrase from another "messenger of Yahweh" (Hag 1:13), perhaps offered a subtle suggestion that Haggai was the anonymous messenger of the book. The added phrase that is preserved in the LXX at least suggests that the

---

[51]Cf. Hag 2:10–14 and Mal 2:4–7 and the comments of E. M. Meyers, "Priestly Language in the Book of Malachi," *HAR* 10 (1986): 236.

[52]For other similarities between Haggai and Malachi, see the discussion of these two books in R. Mason, *Preaching the Tradition: Homily and Hermeneutics after the Exile* (Cambridge: Cambridge University Press, 1990); and the observations of Nolgalski, *Redactional Processes in the Book of the Twelve*, 201–205.

[53]See also the Talmudic discussions of Malachi's identity in the *b. Meg.* 15a.

ministry of the anonymous prophet was similar to that of his fellow messenger, Haggai.

Perhaps the greatest significance of LXX Mal 1:1 is that it provides textual verification of the use of catchwords to unify books of the Minor Prophets. By creating a verbal linkage between two prophetic books, LXX Mal 1:1 not only supplements the other numerous literary connections between the books of Haggai, Zechariah, and Malachi,[54] but also demonstrates the reality of the use of the proposed *Stichwörter* technique in the transmission and unification of the biblical text in antiquity. LXX Mal 1:1 demonstrates that verbal cross-references were employed within the textual tradition of the Hebrew *Vorlage* of the LXX as well as that of the MT.

The following two examples, Jon 3:4 and Mic 1:5, differ from the preceding texts in that they are based on variant wordings of the text rather than quantitative differences. The literal translation technique of the LXX Minor Prophets, however, argues for the conclusion that in each case the LXX reading was present within the translator's Hebrew source text. These two texts also share in common a high degree of difficulty in determining which reading is preferable on text-critical grounds. The following treatment of these texts therefore presents the arguments for both possible textual readings.

Jonah 3:4. In the MT, Jonah announces that Nineveh will be destroyed in the span of forty days. The LXX, however, reads "three days." Some have accepted the LXX reading as original because the three day span of the LXX would help to explain the urgency of Nineveh's response to Jonah's message.[55] If so, then the forty day span of the MT would possibly harmonize the reprieve given to Nineveh in the Book of Jonah with the description of Nineveh's doom as stated in the Book of Nahum.

---

[54]Nogalski, *Redactional Processes*, 197–204.

[55]C. A. Keller, *Jonas*, CAT XIa (Paris: Delachaux and Niestle, 1965), 283; A. Jepsen, "Anmerkungen zum Buche Jona," in *Wort-Gebot-Glaube. Festschrift für Walter Eichrodt* (Zürich: Zwingli Verlag, 1970), 297.

The impact of the MT reading would then be that Nineveh's repentance was shortlived; they soon reverted to their former ways and received their just punishment as described in Nahum.[56]

Against the reading of the LXX text as original, Rudolph argues that the forty days of the MT only expresses the outer limit of the timespan for Nineveh's destruction and that the destruction could occur at any time during the forty-day span.[57] This interpretation would explain the urgency of Nineveh's repentance while accepting the reading of the MT. Sasson suggests that the three day time span is possibly an attempt to explain why Jonah is made to wait outside of the city in Jon 4:5. The mention of Nineveh's dimensions in the immediate context of Jon 3:3 as a "three days journey" and also the length of Jonah's stay of "three days and three nights" inside the great fish (2:1) have possibly influenced the LXX reading.[58] In that case, the LXX of Jon 3:4 reflects a harmonizing exegesis of Jonah's actions in Jon 4:5.[59]

Both the MT and the LXX readings of Jonah have supporting arguments for being the original reading. There are also sound explanations why a change may have been made in either the direction of the MT or the LXX. The LXX of Jon 3:4 is possibly an exegetical harmonization influenced by the immediate context of Jon 2:1 and 3:3. The MT of Jon 3:4 is also possibly an exegetical harmonization, although in this case it would

---

[56]For ancient interpretations of Jonah 3:4 as a true prediction of the destruction of Nineveh, see the translation of Jon 4:5 in the Targum to the effect that Jonah sat outside of the city "until he saw what would *ultimately* happen to the city." See also Tobit 14:4 according to the text preserved in Codex Sinaiticus, where the prediction of doom for Nineveh is attributed to Jonah rather than to Nahum as in the primary textual tradition of Tobit.

[57]W. Rudolph, *Joel, Amos, Obadja, Jona*, KAT XIII/2 (Gütersloh: Gerd Mohn, 1971), 355.

[58]Sasson, *Jonah*, 234.

[59]For the difficulties of Jon 4:5 and an explanation on structural grounds, see N. Lohfink, "Jona ging zur Stadt hinaus (Jona 4,5)," *BZ* 5 (1961): 185–203.

harmonize the Book of Jonah with the Book of Nahum found in the larger context of the Book of the Twelve. A conclusive text-critical decision between these two texts is difficult to make since either reading appears to be acceptable. What does not seem acceptable, however, is to describe the alternatives as accepting either the LXX as original while labeling the MT reading as an "editorial" change, or accepting the MT reading as original and labeling the LXX as a "texual" variant. Both the LXX and the MT texts bear the possibility of being editorial changes.

Micah 1:5. Like Jon 3:4, the LXX of Mic 1:5 is an example of a textual variant based on harmonization with its literary context. The MT of Mic 1:5 may be translated:

> All this is for the transgression of Jacob (*peša˓ ya˓āqōb*), and for the sins of the house of Israel (*ḥaṭṭĕ˒ōt bêt yiśrā˒ēl*). What is the transgression of Jacob (*peša˓ ya˓āqōb*)? Is it not Samaria? And what are *the high places of Judah* (*bāmōt yĕhûdâ*)? Is it not Jerusalem?

The difference between the text of the MT and the LXX concerns the phrase *bāmōt yĕhûdâ* "the high places of Judah" and may be illustrated by the following comparison:

MT: *bāmōt yĕhûdâ* "the high places of Judah"
LXX: *hē hamartia oikou Iouda* "the sin of the house of Judah"
(Retroverted Hebrew: *ḥaṭṭĕ˒at bêt yĕhûdâ*)

When retroverted into Hebrew, the LXX represents a reading of *ḥaṭṭĕ˒at* instead of *bāmōt* and the presence of the word *bêt* "house of" before the word Judah.[60] The LXX reading thus repeats the parallel *peša˓ ya˓āqōb // ḥaṭṭĕ˒ōt bêt yiśrā˒ēl* of the first half of the verse.

---

[60] A similar addition is found in Mic 1:15, where the MT phrase "the glory of Israel" is rendered in the LXX as "the glory of *daughter* Israel." The addition of the word *bat* was possibly a harmonization with the phrase "daughter Zion" two verses above in 1:13.

The MT reading "highplaces of Judah" has been problematic for numerous commentators. The parallelism of the preceding lines leads one to expect the word *ḥaṭṭēʾat* "sin of," which is the reading preserved in the LXX. Mays argued, however, that the word *bāmôt* is the original wording of the text. The redactor of Micah 1 connected the theme of the judgment of Samaria with Micah's threat against Jerusalem in Mic 3:12, where *bāmôt* is used in reference to the predicted destruction of Jerusalem.[61] Mays noted that the words *ḥaṭṭēʾat* and *bāmôt* occur in synonymous parallelism in Hos 10:8.

Mays explained the reading of the LXX by suggesting that the Greek translator did not expect the parallel *pešaʿ//bāmôt* and therefore changed the text during the process of translation under the influence of the preceding lines. Such an alteration, however, is inconsistent with the literalism displayed by the translator in the rest of the LXX Minor Prophets and with the general practice of ancient translation. It is more likely that a scribe substituted the Hebrew word *ḥaṭṭēʾat* for *bāmôt* and that this was the reading that the translator had before him. The practice of substituting one member of a synonymous word pair for the other member is an acknowledged scribal technique.[62] The scribe who made such a substitution would have therefore "restored" the parallel *pešaʿ yaʿăqōb // ḥaṭṭēʾôt bêt yiśrāʾēl* of 1.5a.

Although the solution proposed above is a satisfactory explanation for the text of LXX Mic 1:5, the possibility cannot be overlooked that the LXX here preserves a textual reading that is earlier than that of the MT. In this case, the redactor proposed by Mays and Weiser would have interrupted the repeated parallelism of *pešaʿ yaʿăqōb // ḥaṭṭēʾôt bêt yiśrāʾēl* preserved in the LXX by substituting the word *bāmôt* for an original *ḥaṭṭēʾat*. The occurrence of the word *bāmôt* in Mic 1:3 and the important

---

[61]Mays, *Micah: A Commentary*, OTL (Philadelphia: Westminster Press, 1976), 45. See also A. Weiser *Das Buch des XII Kleinen Propheten*, ATD 24 (Göttingen: Vandenhoeck und Ruprecht, 1967), 209.

[62]See the examples provided in Talmon, "The Textual Study of the Hebrew Bible—A New Outlook," 338–43.

connection between *bāmôt* and Jerusalem in 3:12 would have influenced this textual alteration. The resulting comparison between Samaria and the highplace of Jerusalem connects the destruction of Samaria that was predicted by Hosea and Amos with the subsequent prediction of Micah that Jerusalem would become "a heap of ruins, and the temple mount a wooded height (Mic 3:12)." If the LXX of Mic 1:5 is accepted as the original reading, then a comparison of the LXX and MT texts offers a concrete example of the kind of redactional activity that is often proposed to have taken place during the extended transmission history of the Minor Prophets.[63] In such a case, commentators on Mic 1:5 would have a choice between the "original" reading of the LXX and the "final form" of the text represented by the MT.

Lengthy Textual Expansions

The fourth type of textual alteration attested in the text of the LXX Book of the Twelve differs from preceding examples primarily in the length of the addition. These expansions share another common feature, however, other than their relative length. Each of the expansions discussed below is either an imitation or a creative combination of language found elsewhere in biblical literature. As such they are comparable with what has been described by some as the "scribal" character of late biblical prophecy,[64] or by others as a new mode of prophecy designated by the term *Schriftprophetie*.[65] Again the similarity between these "textual" expansions and the literary features of other biblical

---

[63]An extended argument that the comparison between Samaria and Jerusalem in Micah 1 is the result of redactional activity is found in Nolgalski, *Literary Precursors to the Book of the Twelve*, 137–39. Nogalski does not, however, consider the evidence of the LXX text.

[64]For this description see J. Blenkinsopp, *A History of Prophecy in Ancient Israel* (Philadelphia: Westminster Press, 1983), 256–58; D. Petersen, *Late Israelite Prophecy* (Missoula, MT: Scholars Press, 1977), 77.

[65]H. Utzschneider, *Künder oder Schreiber? Eine These zum Problem der "Schriftprophetie" auf Grund von Maleachi 1,6–2,9* (Frankfurt: Peter Lang, 1989).

texts demonstrates the shared roles of scribes and editors in the transmission history of the Hebrew Bible.

Hosea 13:4. The extended addition found in the LXX of Hos 13:4 has been discussed above. It may be translated as follows:

> [I am Yahweh your God] who stretched out the heavens and created the earth, whose hands made all the hosts of heaven, yet I did not reveal them for you to walk after them. And I brought you up [from the land of Egypt].

The addition expands the enigmatic phrase "I am Yahweh your God from the land of Egypt" by introducing material that is similar in form and language and theme to texts from Deutero-Isaiah, Jeremiah, and the hymnic material of Amos 4:13; 5:8–9; and 9:5–6. The phrase "the host of heaven" in LXX Hos 13:4 is also used in Jer 8:2 and 19:3 in the context of a denuncitation of idolatrous astrological practices. The first person form of Hos 13:4 bears similarity to Isa 45:12 and 48:13, which also declare that Yahweh or the hand of Yahweh created the heavens and the earth and commands the heavenly host. The participial form of the verbs ("he who stretched out the heavens and who created the earth"), however, is similar to the forms of the hymnic confessions found in Amos.[66]

The language of LXX Hos 13:4 is more prosaic than the heightened cosmological language of the doxologies of Amos. More importantly, LXX Hos 13:4 lacks the distinctive refrain "Yahweh the God of Hosts is his name" of Amos 4:13; 5:8 ("Yahweh is his name"); and 9:5–6.[67] Perhaps the first person form of Hos 13:4, which preceded the addition of the doxological material preserved in the LXX, prevented the use of

---

[66]F. I. Andersen and D. N. Freedman, *Hosea*, The Anchor Bible, Vol. 24 (New York: Doubleday, 1980), 634.

[67]For the interpretation of this refrain as key to the life setting of the doxologies, see J. L. Crenshaw, *Hymnic Affirmations of Divine Justice: The Doxologies of Amos and Related Texts in the Old Testament*, SBLDS 24 (Missoula, MT: Scholars Press, 1975), 75, 141.

the third person refrain.[68] It is also possible that the addition to Hos 13:4 was made at a time after the refrain had fallen out of use in the corporate life of the worshipping community.

Despite these differences between the doxology preserved in LXX Hos 13:4 and the doxologies in Amos, Hos 13:4 and its immediate context do share at least three of the four central themes that Crenshaw has identified in the doxologies of Amos, namely, creation, judgment, idolatry, and oaths.[69] The addition to Hos 13:4 supplies the theme of Yahweh as creator, which is elsewhere absent in the Book of Hosea. The context of Hos 13:3–16 contains an extended, explicit, and graphic announcement of judgment upon Israel. The denunciation of idolatrous worship of the "hosts of heaven" in LXX 13:4 follows an accusation of idolatry in 13:2 and complements the exclusive Yahwism of 13:4b ("you shall know no god but me, and besides me there is no savior.") Although the theme of false oaths is not explicitly stated, 13:2 does contain an enigmatic reference to speaking to idols in the context of sacrifices. The text of this reference, however, is unclear.[70] Regardless of the meaning of this reference, significant thematic affinities exist between the doxologies of Amos and LXX Hos 13:4.

The doxologies of Amos are generally considered to be late additions to the book that reflect its reception and possible liturgical use in the post-exilic period.[71] The addition to Hos 13:4 preserved in the LXX has in the past been offered as further evidence of the secondary nature of the hymnic material in Amos.[72] This argument, although not conclusive, is strengthened by the confirmation found in 4QXII[C] that the text of the addition to Hos 13:4 was present in the Hebrew *Vorlage* of the LXX.

---

[68]A form of the refrain is found in Hos 12:6. Ibid., 79.

[69]Ibid., 89–90.

[70]Literally, "To them [the idols] they are speaking, those who are sacrificing a human, they kiss calves."

[71]Crenshaw, *Hymnic Affirmations of Divine Justice*, 123, 143.

[72]Ibid., 23–24.

Haggai 2:9. In speaking about the future glory of the reconstructed temple, Hag 2:9 ends with the promise "And in this place I will give peace, oracle of Yahweh of hosts." The LXX includes the following addition to this promise:

kai eirēnēn psychēs eis peripoiēsin panti tō ktizonti tou anastēsai ton naon touton

And [I will give] peace of soul for a possession to everyone who labors to raise this temple.

It is possible to retrovert this statement into Hebrew as follows: *wišĕlōm nepeš lĕsegūlat kōl hakkōnēn lĕhāqîm hahêkal hazzeh.*[73] The most difficult word to retrovert into Hebrew is the dative singular present participle of *ktizein* "to establish, build, create." In the only two other occurrences of this verb in the LXX Minor Prophets, it translates the verb *brʾ* "to create" (Amos 4:13; Mal 2:10). This Hebrew verb is not used elsewhere in the Hebrew Bible to refer to human activity. It therefore seems inappropriate in this context describing human efforts to rebuild the temple. Of the various Hebrew verbs rendered by *ktizein* in the LXX, only the *Polel* of the verb *kwn,* "to establish" is used in the sense required by LXX Hag 2:9. *konen* is used in parallelism with the verb *bnh* "to build" in Hab 2:12: "Woe those who build (*bôneh*) a town with blood and who found (*kōnēn*) a city on iniquity." *ktizein* is used to translate the Polel of *kwn* in Deut 32:6 and Ezek 28:13. The connotations of this root are consistent with the building activity described in the Book of Haggai.

The expansion in LXX Hag 2:9 elaborates upon the promise of peace contained in that verse. The idea, however, that those who rebuild the temple will benefit materially from their efforts is in harmony with the message of both Haggai and Zechariah 1–

---

[73]This reconstruction is based on the following statistics in the LXX Minor Prophets: *eirēnēn = šālôm,* passim; *psychē = nepeš* in all 17 occurrences; *peripoiēsis = segûlâ* at its only occurrence (Mal 3:17); *anistēmi = qwm,* 19 of 20 times; and *naos = hêkal* in all 9 occurrences.

8. Both books emphasize the "peace and prosperity" that is to accompany the restoration of the temple.[74] Even the unique language of the addition, such as the phrase "peace of soul," which is without parallel in the Hebrew Bible, is not entirely incongruous with the language of the final three books of the Minor Prophets. Compare, for example, the innovative combinations of the word *šālôm* in Zech 8:12 ("sowing of peace"), Mal 2:5 ("life and peace"), and especially Zech 8:16 ("judgment of peace") and 8:19 ("love truth and peace").[75] Further, the word *segūlâ* "possession" is attested among the Minor Prophets, outside of this addition, only in Malachi (3:17).[76] I conclude therefore that the expansion is the product of a scribe familiar with both the language and the thought world of Haggai, Zechariah, and Malachi and was inserted into a Hebrew text of Haggai prior to the LXX translation.

Haggai 2:14. The other lengthy expansion in the LXX of Haggai is found in Hag 2:14. The MT of Hag 2:14 may be translated "This people and this nation are unclean before me, oracle of Yahweh, and so are all of the deeds of their hands. That which they bring near, it is also unclean." The LXX contains the following addition:

> *eneken tōn lēmmatōn autōn tōn orthrinōn odynēthesontai apo prosōpou ponōn autōn kai emiseite en pylais elegchontas*

---

[74]C. L. Meyers and E. M. Meyers, *Haggai, Zechariah 1–8*, The Anchor Bible, Vol. 25B (Garden City, NY: Doubleday, 1987), 64–65, 422–23.

[75]S. Amsler sees Zech 8:16–19 as a primary influence upon the gloss in Hag 2:9 (*Aggée, Zacharie 1–8*, CAT XIc [Paris: Neuchatel, 1981], 34).

[76]For other prophetic idioms unique to Haggai, Zechariah, and Malachi, see E. M. Meyers, "The Use of *Tora* in Haggai 2.11 and the Role of the Prophet in the Restoration Community," in *The Word of the Lord Shall Go Forth: Essays in Honor of David Noel Freedman in Celebration of His Sixtieth Birthday*, ed. C. L. Meyers and M. O'Connor (Winona Lake, IN: Eisenbrauns/ASOR, 1983) 69–76; and idem, "Priestly Language in the Book of Malachi," 230–32.

Because of their early gains they will suffer from their labors, and you hate the one who reproves in the gate.

The final phrase of the addition, "and you hate the one who reproves in the gate," is the easiest to retrovert into Hebrew. With the exception of being in the second rather than the third person, it is identical to Amos 5:10 (*śānẹ'û baśśaᶜar môkîaḥ*), which is the likely source of the addition.[77] The second phrase, "they will suffer from their labors," may be reconstructed in Hebrew as *yāhîlû* (or *yāmîrû*) *mĕlipĕnê yĕgîᶜêhem*.[78] The initial phrase "because of their early gains" is the most enigmatic and the most difficult to retrovert into Hebrew. Some commentators have suggested, however, that the translator read *śaḥar* "dawn" instead of *śōḥad* "bribe."[79] Thus the Hebrew *Vorlage* of the translation *eneken tōn lēmmatōn autōn tōn orthrinōn* would have possibly been *kî miqqāḥām śōḥad* "because of their acceptance of a bribe."[80] This reading is compatible with the theme of judicial ethics that is reflected in the quote from Amos.

The addition found in LXX Hag 2:14 attempts to answer the difficult question of the identity of the "unclean" people in this verse.[81] According to the addition, ritual impurity is the result of moral and ethical failure, particularly with regard to judicial fairness. In spite of its secondary status, the expansion is therefore consistent with such moral exhortations as Zech 7:9–10,

[77]For another example of the use of language from the Book of Amos in Haggai, compare Hag 2:17 and Amos 4:6–11.

[78]This reconstruction is based on the following equivalents in the LXX Minor Prophets: (1) *odynēthēsontai*, in its only 2 occurrences translates *hyl* in Zech 9:5 and *mrr* in Zech 12:10; (2) *ponōn autōn* renders *yāgiaᶜ* in Hag 1:11.

[79]P. Haupt, "The Septuagint Addition to Hag 2:14," *JBL* 36 (1917): 149; H. G. Mitchell, *Haggai and Zechariah*, ICC (Edinburgh: T & T Clark, 1912) 73; Rudolph, *Haggai-Sacharja 1–8*, 45.

[80]For the use of the phrase *miqqaḥ śōḥad* "taking a bribe," see 2 Chr 19:7.

[81]See the discussion in H. G. May, "'This People' and 'This Nation' in Haggai," *VT* 18 (1938): 190–97; and K. Koch, "Haggai's unreines Volk," *ZAW* 79 (1967): 52–66.

8:16–17, and Mal 3:5. It also includes language taken from the Book of Haggai itself (cf. *yāgîaʿ* in Hag 1:11), as well as language from the Book of Amos and possibly the Book of Chronicles. The use of the language of "Scripture" to expand upon Scripture is thus similar to the compositional technique of several late prophetic texts in the Hebrew Bible.[82]

Haggai 2:5. The lengthy additions in the LXX of Hag 2:9, 14 call attention to one of the few texts in the Book of the Twelve in which the LXX text is shorter than the MT. The MT of Hag 2:4d–2:5a reads as follows:

> *waʿăśû kî ʾănî ʾitkem nĕʾūm yhwh ʾet haddābār ʾăšer kāratî ʾitkem bĕṣēʾtkem mimmiṣrayim*

> And do, for I am with you, oracle of Yahweh, the word which I cut with you when you came out of Egypt.

The LXX of Hag 2:5a lacks the equivalent of the phrase *ʾet haddābār ʾăšer kāratî ʾitkem bĕṣēʾtkem mimmiṣrayim* "the word which I cut with you when you came out of Egypt." The missing phrase, which supplies a direct object for the imperative of the verb *ʿaśāh* of 2:4d, apparently was not in the *Vorlage* of the LXX translator. The additional phrase in the MT creates an awkward displacement of the direct object from the main verb and also interrupts the parallel between "I am with you, oracle of Yahweh," (2:4) and "my spirit is standing in your midst" (2:5).[83]

---

[82]Thus Petersen, *Haggai and Zechariah 1–8*, OTL (Philadelphia: Westminster Press, 1984), 75; idem, *Late Israelite Prophecy: Studies in Deutero-Prophetic Literature and Chronicles* (Missoula, MT: Scholars Press, 1977); and especially the comments and charts demonstrating the dense intertextuality in Zechariah 9–14 in Meyers and Meyers, *Zechariah 9–14*, The Anchor Bible 25B (New York: Doubleday, 1993), 35–45.

[83]See the comments of Ackroyd, "Some Interpretative Glosses in the Book of Haggai," *JJS* 7 (1956): 163–64. For the meaning of the phrase in the context of the MT text of Haggai, see Meyers and Meyers, *Haggai, Zechariah 1–8*, 52.

The text represented in the LXX of Hag 2:5 may help to explain the source of the enigmatic addition in the MT. Absent the additional phrase, it may be translated "Act, for I am with you, oracle of Yahweh." The use of the verb ʿāśāh with the meaning of "to act" occurs in two other texts that are concerned with temple restoration.[84] In 2 Chr 31:21, the Chronicler attributes the success of Hezekiah's reforms to the fact that "he acted with all his heart" to restore both the temple and the commandments of the covenant. The verb ʿāśāh "to act" is also used in 1 Kgs 8:32, 39, in the context of Solomon's dedication of the First Temple. Interestingly, 1 Kgs 8:9 also contains the closest approximation to the additional phrase "the word which I cut with you when you went forth from Egypt" in MT Hag 2:5.[85] 1 Kgs 8:9 refers to "the two tablets of stone that Moses had placed [within the Ark of the Covenant] at Horeb, which Yahweh cut with the children of Israel when they went forth from Egypt." The addition to Hag 2:5 in the MT shares with 1 Kings 8 and 2 Chronicles 31 the context of temple construction/restoration, reference to the commandments/tablets of the covenant made during the exodus from Egypt, and the use of the verb ʿāśāh in the absolute state.

The coincidences of vocabulary and themes in 1 Kings 8, 2 Chr 31:32, and Hag 2:5 suggest a possible explanation for the additional text of the MT. The use of the verb ʿāśāh "to act" in Hag 2:4 in the context of temple restoration perhaps evoked its use in the similar contexts of Solomon's dedication and Hezekiah's refurbishing of the First Temple. Both of these contexts, however, also included the theme of the preservation and enactment of the covenantal commandments. The addition of the MT text of Hag 2:5 provides this topos and thereby harmonizes the description of the restoration of the Second Temple with events in the history of the First Temple. The displacement of the direct object ʾet haddābār "the word" from

---

[84]For additional uses of the verb ʿāśāh in the absolute state, see Jer 14:7, Ezek 20:9, 14, 22; Ps 22:32; 52:11; Dan 8:12, 24; and 9:19.

[85]Meyers and Meyers, *Haggai, Zechariah 1–8*, 52.

the main verb, however, also preserves the intransitive meaning of ʿāśāh. In the MT, the verb serves a dual function, meaning both "to act" with regard to temple restoration and also "to enact" the covenantal commandments.

The learned allusions to Solomon and Hezekiah's temple activities suggest that the MT text of Hag 2:5 is a sophisticated example of inner-biblical exegesis. Unlike most proposed examples of inner-biblical exegesis, however, Hag 2:5 has the support of corroborating textual evidence in the LXX. The intepretative features of MT Hag 2:5 make this text comparable to the additions in the LXX of Hag 2:9 and 2:14 and suggests that the text of Haggai was expanded independently in the LXX and MT manuscript traditions.

Textual Expansion Attested by a Difference in Sequence

Malachi 3:23–24 (LXX 4:4–6). The final example of an extensive textual expansion in the Hebrew source text of the LXX Book of the Twelve differs from the previous examples given above in that it does not involve a quantitative difference between the text of the MT and the LXX. Rather, the sequence of MT Mal 3:22–24 is altered in the LXX, where verses 23 and 24 precede verse 22. This change in sequence, as well as the textual variants that are found in LXX Mal 4:4–6 (MT 3:22–24), may best be illustrated by a full quotation.

> 4:4 (MT 3:23) And behold I am sending to you Elijah the Tishbite[86] before the the great and terrible Day of the Lord comes.

> 4:5 (MT 3:24) He will restore the heart of a father to a son and the heart of a man to his neighbor,[87] lest I come and utterly smite the earth.

---

[86]The MT reads "Elijah the prophet" (*hannāʾbî*).

[87]The MT here reads "the heart of the parents toward the children and the heart of the children toward the parents."

4:6 (MT 3.22) Remember the law of Moses my servant, which I
commanded to him at Horeb for all Israel, statutes and ordinances.

Rather than ending with the promised return of Elijah, the
LXX ends with the call to remember the Torah of Moses. The
translator of the LXX Minor Prophets has elsewhere strictly
adhered to the word order represented in the MT, and where
deviations occur, they involve individual words rather than
whole verses. Based upon the translation technique of the entire
unit, therefore, the altered sequence would have most likely
been present in the translator's Hebrew *Vorlage*.

As discussed in Chapter Two above, the issue of differences
in sequence has been treated by Tov, who has compared a
number of texts that contain sequence differences between the
LXX and the MT.[88] He observed that many of the texts that have
variant sequences have also been suspected on literary-critical
grounds of being secondary additions within their respective
contexts. He concluded that a sequence difference between the
Vorlage of the LXX and the MT provides further evidence of the
secondary nature of such texts. Tov suggested that the sequence
differences reflected an uncertainty on the part of ancient
copyists about the location of the presumed addition.

The secondary nature of Mal 3:22–24 has long been suspected
within the scholarly literature on the Book of Malachi. The
verses are generally considered to contain two separate
appendices to the Book of Malachi.[89] Mal 3:22[90] concludes either

---

[88]Tov, "Some Sequence Differences Between the MT and LXX and Their
Ramifications for the Literary Criticism of the Bible," *JNSL* XIII (1987): 151–
60.

[89]J. M. P. Smith, *Malachi*, ICC (Edinburgh: T & T Clark, 1912), 81–82, and
most commentators. Summaries are provided in B. Glazier-MacDonald,
Malachi: The Divine Messenger, SBLDS 98 (Atlanta: Scholars Press, 1987), 244–
45; and J. O'Brien, *Priest and Levite in Malachi*, SBLDS 121 (Atlanta: Scholars
Press, 1990), 53–55.

[90]Unless otherwise indicated, the numbering of the text in the MT will be
followed in the discussion below.

the Book of Malachi or the Book of the Twelve as a whole with an exhortation to obey the Mosaic Torah. Mal 3:23–24 is apparently an expansion upon the reference to the messenger of Yahweh in Mal 3:1 that identifies the eschatological messenger with Elijah, whose return will precipitate the Day of Yahweh. The reference to Elijah's reconciliation of parents and children is argued to be a reference to intergenerational conflict in the third century BCE over the issue of Hellenistic customs.[91] The verses have also been suggested to possess canonical implications by extending the perspective of the Book of Malachi and the Book of the Twelve as a whole to include both the Torah and the entire prophetic corpus.[92]

The conclusion that Mal 3:22–24 contains two late additions to the text of Malachi has been challenged, however, in the recent commentary by B. Glazier-MacDonald.[93] Glazier-MacDonald argues that 3:22 possesses sufficient continuity with the Deuteronomic language and general theme of the Book of Malachi to be considered an appropriate conclusion to the message of the book.[94] With regard to the argument that the reference to Elijah's reconciliation of parents and children suggests the events of the Hellenistic period, Glazier-MacDonald rightly criticizes the assumption that the phenomenon of intergenerational conflict was peculiar to a specific time

---

[91]W. Rudolph, *Haggai-Sacharja 1–8–Sacharja 9–14–Maleachi*, KAT XIII/4 (Gütersloh: Gerd Mohn, 1976), 293; R. Mason, *The Books of Haggai, Zechariah, and Malachi*, Cambridge Bible Commentary (Cambridge: Cambridge University Press, 1976), 160.

[92]Rudolph, *Haggai-Sacharja 1–8–Sacharja 9–14–Maleachi*, 291. Rudolph argues that shared language with Josh 1:2, 7, such as the phrase "the Torah of Moses my servant" creates an intentional envelope structure encompassing the entire prophetic canon. See also J. Blenkinsopp, *Prophecy and Canon* (Notre Dame and London: University of Notre Dame Press, 1977), 120–22; and B. Childs, *Introduction to the Old Testament as Scripture* (Philadelphia: Fortress Press, 1979), 495.

[93]*Malachi: The Divine Messenger*, 246–70.

[94]Ibid., 245–51.

period.[95] She argues further that 3:23–24 and 3:1 are references to the same eschatological messenger figure by the same compositional hand, although addressed to different segments of the book's audience.[96]

Tov's analysis of sequence differences suggests that the different placements of Mal 3:22–24 in the LXX and the MT may provide textual evidence that could move the question of the literary history of these verses beyond the impasse between those who interpret them as later additions and those who accept Glazier-MacDonald's defense of their authenticity. Based upon Tov's observations, the differences in sequence suggest that either 3:22 or 3:23–24 is a later insertion. Of the two units, Glazier-MacDonald's arguments for the continuity of 3:22 with the rest of Malachi are stronger than those for 3:23–24. Further, 3:22 seems more appropriate as a conclusion to the Book of Malachi than does 3:23–24. Although Glazier-MacDonald argues that 3:23–24 and 3:1 refer to the same eschatological figure, she fails to explain satisfactorily the placement of 3:23–24 at the end of the book in a context quite removed from 3:1. The recapitulation of the messenger theme in 3:23–24 is anticlimactic to the exhoratory conclusion provided in 3:22.

Beyond the literary objections to the placement of Mal 3:23–24 in the MT, these verses contain two textual variants in the LXX that appear to have been present in the Hebrew *Vorlage*.[97] In 3:23, Elijah is referred to as "Elijah the Tishbite" rather than "Elijah the prophet" of the MT. In 3:24, the second part of Elijah's mission is described as turning "the heart of a man to his neighbor" rather than the MT's chiastic "heart of the children to their parents." The wording of these verses as well as their placement appears to have been uncertain and subject to alteration.

---

[95]Ibid., 254–55.

[96]Ibid., 263–65.

[97]Against Glazier-MacDonald (268), who argues that the LXX variants were the product of the translator.

The textual and literary evidence for Mal 3:22–24 therefore seems to suggest the following explanation of the literary history of these verses. Mal 3:22 was present at the end of the book prior to the insertion of Mal 3:23–24. Whether 3:22 was added to the text by a redactor of Malachi or was instead the original conclusion of the book remains in question, although the arguments of Glazier-MacDonald for its authenticity have merit. The placement of Mal 3:23–24 in the LXX, however, as well as the variant text of the LXX's Hebrew *Vorlage* support the conclusion that these verses were added to the text at a time later than 3:22, and most likely in the position and the textual form attested by the LXX. The placement of 3:23–24 that is reflected in the LXX text would have preserved the previous ending to the Book of Malachi.

If the conclusion about the "originality" of the sequence of LXX Mal 4:4–6 (MT 3:22–24) is correct, then an explanation of the MT sequence and text of these verses is required. Although Tov did not discuss these verses in his essay on sequence differences, he concluded that sequence differences in general were the result of the uncertainty of ancient copyists with regard to the placement of the additional text, which in this case would have been 3:23–24. In this context, however, previous arguments about the "canonical" implications of Mal 3:22–24 are of significance, specifically arguments about the relationship of Mal 3:22–24 to a collection of "Torah and Prophets." If Mal 3:22–24 is to be perceived as a reference to the Torah of Moses and to the prophetic corpus as represented by the typological figure of Elijah, then this perception is the result of the textual/editorial alterations of the tradents of the MT. First, verses 3:23–24 were moved from their position prior to 3:22 in the Hebrew text reflected in the LXX to the end of the book, thus conforming the text to the "canonical" order of the careers of Moses and Elijah. Secondly, the text preserved by the LXX, "Elijah the Tishbite" was changed to read "Elijah the prophet," perhaps to make explicit the connection between Torah and Prophets as represented by Moses and Elijah, respectively.[98]

The final textual difference between the Hebrew text preserved by the LXX and that of the MT is the reference to the conciliatory mission of the eschatological prophet. Although the MT describes the mission of Elijah as turning "the heart of the parents toward the hearts of the children, and the heart of the children toward the parents," the LXX preserves the reading "he will restore the heart of the parents to the children and the heart of a man to his neighbor." The reading of the LXX is possibly supported by Sir 48:10. There Ben Sira describes the future mission of Elijah as "to turn the hearts of parents to their children, and to restore the tribes of Jacob." The reference to the tribes of Jacob in the final line of Sir 48:10 is more likely a paraphrase of the LXX reading "restore the heart of a man to his neighbor" than the reading "heart of the sons to the fathers" of the MT. This conclusion is supported by the use in Sirach 48:10 of the Greek verb *kathistēmi* "to restore," which is also the verb used in the LXX translation of Mal 3:24.

If Sir 48:10 does attest the text of Mal 3:24 preserved in the LXX, then the argument that the MT text refers to the intergenerational conflict of the Hellenistic period may indeed provide an explanation of the variant text of the MT. It is possible that the reading "restore the heart of a man to his neighbor" that is preserved in the LXX was changed in the second century BCE to "return the heart of the children to the parents." The purpose of such a change may indeed have been to address the conflict between those among the younger generation in Palestine who embraced Hellenistic culture and the older generation who adhered to the traditions of the ancestors.

---

[98]Compare the argument by A. G. Auld that the title "prophet" and its verbal forms are more frequent in the later redactional layers of Jeremiah than earlier stages, and are also more frequent in the Chronicler's History than in the earlier parallel accounts of "prophetic" activities within the Book of Kings. See "Prophets and Prophecy in Jeremiah and Kings," *ZAW* 98 (1989): 66–82.

If so, then the MT of 3:24 would have originated subsequent to the time of Ben Sira and possibly in the context of the Maccabean Revolt.

In summary, the preceding analysis of Mal 3:22–24 that is based upon the textual evidence of the LXX agrees with many of the previous literary-critical conclusions about these verses, although the reconstruction of their literary history differs from previous treatments. For example, the textual evidence of the LXX seems to support the conclusion that Mal 3:23–24 is a later addition to the form of the Book of Malachi that ended with 3:22. Verses 23–24, however, were most likely inserted originally into the position that they occupy in the LXX. The previous claim that the perspective of the MT text of Mal 3:22–24 extends beyond the context of the Book of Malachi to include a collection of sacred literature comprised of the Torah and other prophetical books is supported, although I conclude that the "canonical" implications of the MT text of 3:22–24 are the result of a rearranging of the text that is now preserved in the LXX rather than the result of the addition of 3:23–24 at the end of the book. I also agree with the previous claim that the plea for intergenerational reconciliation in the MT of Mal 3:24 may describe the situation of the Hellenistic crisis in the late third and early second centuries BCE. I conclude, however, that the reading of the MT is a result of an alteration to the text that is preserved in the LXX. It therefore does not indicate that Mal 3:23–24 was originally written in the Hellenistic period. There is little reason to conclude that Mal 3:23–24, in the form and sequence preserved in the LXX, could not have been added to the text rather early in the transmission history of the Book of Malachi, even as early as the end of the fifth century BCE. No conclusion is reached regarding the authenticity of Mal 3:22, although the arguments of Glazier-MacDonald regarding the common Deuteronomistic language and shared themes of 3:22 and the rest of the book do support the possibility that 3:22 comes from the same hand as the Book of Malachi.

It is possible to object that the conclusions stated above indulge in the same kind of hypothetical reconstructions that are found in previous literary-critical analyses of Mal 3:22–24. I would argue, however, that the conclusions offered here have the methodological advantage of supporting textual evidence. I do not claim, however, that the conclusions offered above are the only possible explanation of the extant textual evidence. I do wish to argue, however, that debate over the literary history of Mal 3:22–24 and similar texts should begin from a discussion of extant evidence before proceeding to more hypothetical stages of composition.

Conclusion

The quantity of textual differences between the Hebrew source text of the LXX Book of the Twelve and the proto-MT text preserved within the MT is slight in comparison with the great degree of textual agreement attested within these two manuscript traditions. These differences, nevertheless, are significant in three distinct ways. The differences illustrate: (1) the textual relationship between the Hebrew Vorlage of the LXX and the proto-MT text of the Book of the Twelve; (2) the continuity between textual alterations and the techniques of ancient authors and redactors; and (3) the textual and interpretative dynamics of the canonical process.

(1) The limited quantity of differences between the MT and the LXX support the conclusion that the Hebrew *Vorlage* of the LXX and the proto-MT text were based on a single textual archetype that followed two slightly different histories of transmission. The results of the present study offer no evidence that would contradict this conclusion. The textual differences discussed above, however, do illustrate the minor creative role of the tradents of biblical literature prior to the stabilization of the Hebrew text. It should also not be overlooked that the process of transmission influenced not only the Hebrew source text of the LXX, but the proto-MT text as well. In fact, it has been suggested above that the LXX text of Mic 1:5, Jon 3:4, Hag 2:5, and Mal 3:22–24 preserves Hebrew textual readings that have been altered in the transmission history of the MT text.

(2) The alterations preserved with the LXX Minor Prophets also illustrate the point that Talmon had earlier demonstrated regarding the continuity of stylistic techniques between the process of literary composition and the process of textual transmission. The examples given above of parallelism that was created at the stage of textual transmission show that the tradents of the Hebrew source text of the LXX Minor Prophets were attuned to the stylistic techniques of ancient Hebrew composition. The lengthier additions discussed above, such as Hos 13:4 and Hag 2:9, 14 demonstrate that ancient textual tradents were also adept at "biblical" compositions that are comparable to other texts in the Hebrew Bible.[99] Texts such as Mic 4:8, which draws upon Mic 4:10, itself a "redactional" insertion, demonstrate the similarity between the categories of "redactional" alterations and "textual" changes.[100]

The similarities between the textual alterations attested in the LXX Book of the Twelve and texts that are labeled as redactional changes in the MT also have significant methodological implications. Redaction-critical treatments of biblical texts generally suffer from the hypothetical nature of redactional reconstructions and from the often wide variety of proposed redactional hypotheses that result from such an approach. The conclusions of literary and redaction-critical analyses of biblical texts would be strengthened if they were to be based upon textual evidence, or, in light of the limited quantity of such evidence, if such analyses were demonstrated to be clearly analogous to alterations that are supported by textual evidence.

---

[99]Talmon has argued that the literary productions of the Qumran community were also consciously "biblical" compositions. See "The Textual Study of the Bible," 379–81; and also the recent comments of Meyers and Meyers (*Zechariah 9–14*, 35–45) regarding the compositional techniques exhibited in Deutero-Zechariah.

[100]For further discussion of this distinction, see J. W. Watt, "Text and Redaction in Jeremiah's Oracles against the Nations," *CBQ* 54 (1992): 432–47.

(3) Finally, the intepretative character of many of the textual alterations discussed above has implications for the canonical process as it applies to the Book of the Twelve. In Chapter Two above, the primary dynamics of the canonical process were identified as textual transmission and actualizing interpretation. In many of the examples discussed above, these two dynamics occurred concurrently. The act of textual transmission of the Minor Prophets itself assumes that the text is of value for subsequent generations of readers. Interpretation is required, however, in order to ensure that the texts will continue to be meaningful regardless of the vicissitudes of history and culture. Rather than indicating a disregard for the text of the Book of the Twelve, the textual changes discussed above demonstrate a reverence for the text on the part of the ancient tradents that led them to attempt to preserve the meaning and relevance of the text for posterity. Paradoxically, in the act of changing the text, they were yet preserving it, and while preserving the text, they were helping to create it as well.

The growing authoritative status of the Minor Prophets is illustrated not only by the evidence of its textual transmission, but also in the primary mode of interpretation that is attested in the LXX text, namely, harmonization. When exegetical questions arose, such as the nature of the offense of Damascus in Amos 1:3, or possibly the identity of "my/his messenger" in Mal 1:1, the strategy for addressing such questions was to seek an answer from within the other texts of the Minor Prophets corpus. The possibility, for example, that the ministry of "Malachi" was identified with the ministry of Haggai by the addition within LXX Mal 1:1 demonstrates such an approach. This example also suggests that the distinctions between individual texts began to fade as the entire corpus began to take on the sacred status of "Scripture."[101] The same dynamic is at play as well in the

---

[101]The same phenomenon of the blurring of contextual distinctions between the books of Scripture was observed also in the citations of the Minor Prophets in the NT and the Qumran literature discussed in Chapter One. For discussion of the canonical implications of harmonization, see G. Sheppard,

example of inner-biblical exegesis preserved in the MT of Hag 2:5. There the construction of the Second Temple is placed within a "biblical" perspective of similar occasions in the history of the First Temple during the reigns of Solomon and Hezekiah. Further, the imitative style of the extensive additions of such texts as LXX Hos 13:4 and LXX Hag 2:9, 14 also suggest that by the time of these expansions, biblical texts both within and beyond the corpus of the Minor Prophets had become the model and the standard of Hebrew composition, which is yet another indication of the growing canonical status of Israel's ancient national and religious literature.[102]

The preceding examination of the uniqueness of the Hebrew text that has been preserved in the LXX translation has attempted to contribute to the understanding of the development of the received Hebrew text of the Book of the Twelve by calling attention to the pluriform nature of the text of the Book of the Twelve in antiquity. Chapters Four and Five will continue the examination of the textual and literary variety attested for the Book of the Twelve by discussing the significance of the alternative sequences of the Minor Prophets as they are preserved 4QXII[a] and in the manuscript tradition of the LXX.

"Canonization: Hearing the Voice of the Same God through Historically Dissimilar Traditions," *Interpretation* 34 (1982): 21–33.

[102]For an explanation of the origin of canonical literature in general as the result of the need for models of composition within the institutional structure of the school, see J. Guillory, "Canonical and Non-Canonical: A Critique of the Current Debate," *English Literary History* 54 (1987): 483–528.

CHAPTER 4

4QXIIA AND THE POSITION OF JONAH AMONG THE MINOR PROPHETS

The discussion in Chapter Three of variant readings within the MT and the LXX texts of the Book of the Twelve sought to demonstrate the editorial and interpretative nature of some of the alterations that have been made to the Book of the Twelve at the stage of its textual transmission. Beyond the examples of quantitative differences between the textual witnesses to the Book of the Twelve, the example of a difference in sequence of verses between the MT and the LXX of Mal 3:22–24 proved to be useful in evaluating various literary-critical assessments of the redactional history of this particular text. The aim of the next two chapters is to employ the variant arrangements of the Minor Prophets as they are attested in the ancient manuscript witnesses as evidence for the literary growth of the Book of the Twelve. While Chapter Five will address the variant position of the books of Joel and Obadiah in the LXX Book of the Twelve, the placement of the Book of Jonah among the Minor Prophets will be the focus of the present chapter.

Jonah is the only book among the Minor Prophets to occupy three different positions within manuscript witnesses to the Book of the Twelve.[1] Outside of the positions of the book attested in the MT and the LXX manuscript witnesses, a variant placement of Jonah is also found in the text of 4QXII[a]. As discussed in Chapter One, this fragmented scroll of the Twelve Prophets from Qumran Cave IV places the Book of Jonah after the end of the Book of Malachi, presumably as the final book of the scroll. 4QXII[a] not only demonstrates that a variant arrangement of the Book of the Twelve existed in an ancient Hebrew manuscript, but also invites questions about the meaning of its arrangement for the history of the Minor Prophets collection and for the role of the Book of Jonah within this collection. The present chapter will argue that of the three arrangements attested in ancient manuscripts of the Book of the Twelve, 4QXII[a] contains the arrangement that most plausibly reflects the earliest placement of Jonah among the Twelve. Based upon such a conclusion, the positioning of Jonah within the LXX and the MT manuscript traditions may therefore provide evidence of ancient interpretations of Jonah within the context of the Minor Prophets collection. Since I have argued above that the activities of preserving and interpreting texts are the primary dynamics in the process of canonization, the implications of the placement of Jonah among the Minor Prophets for the issue of the canonical process will be examined as well.

The Meaning of the Placement of Jonah in 4QXII[a]

The unique arrangement of books attested in 4QXII[a] raises the legitimate question of whether this particular manuscript is representative of an actual scribal tradition or instead represents an anomalous or erroneous exception in the transmission history of the Book of the Twelve. Ultimately, the latter possibility cannot be entirely excluded. Two factors, however, argue for the conclusion that 4QXII[a] represents a legitimate scribal tradition of arrangement that existed at one time during the transmission history of the Book of the Twelve. These factors

---

[1]See above, Table 2.1.

are: (1) the multiplicity of ancient textual forms attested in the manuscripts from Qumran, and (2) the several correspondences between the placement of Jonah in 4QXII[a] and the results of critical scholarship on the nature and message of the book.

The manuscript discoveries from Qumran have demonstrated that a variety of Hebrew textual traditions was in circulation in the final two centuries before the Common Era. Such a supposition is valid whether one accepts Cross's local texts theory, which postulates three primary textual forms, or the view of Talmon that the three primary textual groups attested at Qumran are representative of an even greater multiplicity of textual witnesses in antiquity.[2] 4QXII[a] fits into the post-Qumran assessment of the history of the biblical text as yet another example of the variety of textual forms in circulation in Judaism during the Hellenistic period.[3]

A second factor that supports the conclusion that 4QXII[a] reflects a wider scribal tradition for the transmission of the Book of the Twelve is the fact that scholarly assessments of the book have also suggested, like 4QXII[a], that Jonah is appropriately placed at the conclusion of the Book of the Twelve. The correspondences between scholarly conclusions about Jonah and its placement in 4QXII[a] include: (1) the uniqueness of Jonah within the prophetic corpus; (2) the probable late date of composition of Jonah; and (3) the primary themes of the book as identified by means of literary assessments of its form, style, structure, and relationships with other biblical texts. Previous

---

[2]F. M. Cross, Jr. "The Evolution of a Theory of Local Texts," in *Qumran and the History of the Biblical Text*, ed. Cross and S. Talmon (Cambridge: Harvard University Press, 1975), 147–72; Talmon, "The Textual Study of the Bible—A New Outlook," *Qumran and the History of the Biblical Text*, 324.

[3]See also the recent discussions of the multiplicity of biblical texts in D. Barthélemy, "Les diverses formes du texte hébreu," in *Critique textuelle de l'Ancient Testament*, OBO 50/3 (Freiburg/Göttingen: University of Fribourg/Vandenhoeck and Ruprecht, 1992) vii–cxvi; and E. Tov, *Textual Criticism of the Hebrew Bible* (Minneapolis/Assen/Maastricht: Fortress Press/Van Gorcum, 1992), 158–63.

scholarly assessments of the Book of Jonah have described it as a didactic, satirical, prophetic story that addresses certain theological issues related to Israelite prophecy. In discussing this description of the Book of Jonah in detail below, I will argue that its placement in 4QXII^a is most plausibly the earliest of the three placements of the book attested in ancient manuscripts.

The Uniqueness of Jonah among the Prophets

The most obvious observation to be made about the position of Jonah in 4QXII^a is that it reflects the critical opinion of scholars ancient and modern that the Book of Jonah is *sui generis* among the books of the Minor Prophets and in the prophetic corpus in general. For example, the Book of Jonah is the only extended prophetic narrative among the books of the Minor Prophets. Although most of the other books are comprised primarily of prophetic speeches, the Book of Jonah contains only one line of prophetic pronouncement, the enigmatic "Yet forty days (LXX: three days) and Nineveh is overturned/turns over" of Jonah 3:4.[4] It has been argued that the distinctive form and content of the Book of Jonah require that it be treated separately from the other prophetic books[5] and that the style, structure, characters, and content of the Book of Jonah combine to make it one of the more "strange books of the Bible."[6]

---

[4]For a discussion of the inherent ambiguity in this oracular statement and its relationship to similar ambiguous oracles in ancient Near Eastern literature, see J. Sasson, *Jonah*, The Anchor Bible Vol. 24B (New York: Doubleday, 1990), 233–34, 346.

[5]See, for example, J. Smart, "Introduction and Exegesis of the Book of Jonah," *The Interpreter's Bible*, Vol. VI (New York: Abingdon, 1956), 871, and most interpreters.

[6]E. Bickerman, *Four Strange Books of the Bible* (New York: Schocken, 1967). The unique stylistic and literary features of the book are treated in detail in J. Magonet, *Form and Meaning: Studies in Literary Techniques in the Book of Jonah* (Sheffield: Almond Press, 1983), a summary of which is provided by Magonet in "Jonah, Book of," *The Anchor Bible Dictionary*, Vol. III (New York:

The uniqueness of the Book of Jonah has indeed provoked arguments about the propriety of its placement among the Minor Prophets at all.[7] K. Budde, in his article on the proposed comprehensive redaction of the Book of the Twelve, argued that Jonah was the last book to be added to the Book of the Twelve; its addition primarily served the numerological interest of creating a book of twelve prophets.[8] Budde had earlier argued that the Book of Jonah had circulated independently from the Book of the Twelve as part of the document identified in 2 Chr 24:27 as "the Midrash of the Book of Kings."[9] As such, the book would have originated as a midrashic expansion on the account of the prophet Jonah given in 2 Kgs 14:25. Budde cited the abrupt beginning of the book and the omission of Jonah's place of origin (included in 2 Kgs 14:25) as evidence that the book was excerpted from this context. As further evidence, he cited a midrashic tradition that counted eleven books within the Minor Prophets, "excluding Jonah, which is a book by itself" (*Bammidbar rabbah* 18:21).

Against Budde's theory it must be argued first of all that there is no positive evidence that the Book of Jonah ever followed the brief mention of the prophet in 2 Kings 14 or that it was part of a compilation known as the Midrash on the Book of

---

Doubleday, 1992), 936–42. See also the comments of P. Trible, "Studies in the Book of 'Jonah'" (Ph.D. dissertation, Columbia University, 1963), 126–27.

[7]E. Dyck has attempted to dispel the questioning of Jonah's placement among the Twelve by employing Childs's canonical approach ("Jonah Among the Prophets: A Study in Canonical Context," *JETS* 33 [1990]: 63–73). He argues that Jonah's consistent placement in manuscripts of the Twelve refutes all questions about its formal dissimilarity with other prophetic texts. Dyck does not address, however, the variant portrayals of the book preserved in the LXX and 4QXII[a].

[8]"Eine folgenschwere Redaktion des Zwölfprophetenbuchs," *ZAW* 39 (1922): 227.

[9]"Vermutungen zum 'Midrasch des Büches der Könige,'" *ZAW* 11 (1892): 40.

Kings.[10] Second, the two occurrences of the term "midrash" in the Book of Chronicles (2 Chr 13:22; 24:27) do not provide contexts sufficient to identify the use of the term there with the kind of material attested in the Book of Jonah. In rabbinic and other post-biblical literature, "midrash" is used to convey a variety of meanings beyond the specific, technical, and relatively late usage of the term to indicate a literary collection.[11] Third, the rabbinic tradition that Budde cites about Jonah being a book in itself is from a late (eighth-ninth century CE) midrashic collection and is motivated primarily by a numerological interest in counting the books of Scripture in such a way as to arrive at the number fifty.[12]

Although Budde's arguments concerning the midrashic genre of Jonah and its circulation independent of the Minor Prophets are ultimately not credible, he nonetheless accurately described the book's tenuous relationship to the other Minor Prophets. Despite the questionable historicity of the midrashic tradition cited by Budde, one does not need further ancient attestation of the book's uniqueness outside of its own contents to conclude with the exegete quoted in *Bammidbar rabbah* 18:21 that, at least in regard to the literary style and content of the book, Jonah remains "a book by itself."[13] The placement of Jonah in 4QXII[a]

---

[10]Trible, "Studies in the Book of 'Jonah,'" 166. Trible rejects the arguments of Budde about the relationship between Jonah and Kings, but retains the category of midrash as the genre of the book.

[11]G. Porton, "Defining Midrash," in *The Study of Ancient Judaism I: Mishnah, Midrash, Siddur*, ed. J. Neusner (New York: KTAV, 1981), 55–92.

[12]Sasson, *Jonah*, 15.

[13]A conclusion similar to that of Budde concerning Jonah's distinctiveness from the other books of the Minor Prophets is found in a recent redaction-critical analysis of the Book of the Twelve by E. Bosshard ("Beobachtungen zum Zwölfprophetenbuch," *BN* [1987]: 36). Bosshard identified parallels between the structure of the Book of Isaiah and the sequence of books in the MT Book of the Twelve. The only books not to fit into the parallel structure identified by Bosshard were the books of Malachi

highlights the uniqueness of the book by setting it apart at the end of the scroll of the Minor Prophets. The question of whether Jonah was appended to the end of an already existing collection of prophetical books may be further illuminated by discussing scholarly conclusions about the date of the book.

The Late Date of the Book of Jonah

The placement of Jonah after Malachi in 4QXII[a] is consistent with the arguments of scholars who conclude that Jonah was among the latest, if not the latest, compositions in the Minor Prophets and possibly the last book to be added to this collection.[14] Attempts at dating the Book of Jonah precisely, however, are frustrated by what A. Berlin succinctly describes as the abstract, theoretical nature of the work.[15] The book contains no historical superscription, the characters are unnamed except for Jonah and Yahweh, and the narration of the book is more concerned with abstract, theological arguments about the nature of prophecy than with addressing a concrete, identifiable historical situation.

The most credible arguments for the dating of Jonah are those that place it generally in the post-exilic or Persian period but do not atttempt to be more specific than the evidence allows. Bickerman, for example, cited the two primary clues for a date of composition in the Persian period.[16] These are: (1) the

---

and Jonah. From this Bosshard suggested that these two books were the last books to enter the collection.

[14] A survey of critical opinion on the date of Jonah prior to 1963 is given in Trible, "Studies in the Book of 'Jonah,'" 104–116. See also the discussion in H. W. Wolff *Obadiah and Jonah: A Commentary*, tr. M. Kohl (Minneapolis: Augsburg Publishing House, 1986), 76–78; and Sasson, *Jonah*, 20–27. Recent scholars who date the book during the early sixth century are D. Schneider ("The Unity of the Book of the Twelve," 111–13) and G. Landes ("Jonah, Book of," *IDBS*, 490).

[15] "A Rejoinder to John A. Miles, Jr., with Some Observations on the Nature of Prophecy," *JQR* 66 (1976): 230.

[16] *Four Strange Books*, 29.

phrase "the God of Heaven" in 1:9, which is a designation for the deity found only in biblical texts from the Persian period;[17] and (2) the royal decree of 3:7 that is issued by "the king and his nobles" according to Persian imperial custom. Trible concluded that certain late words that show Aramaic influence or origins such as *ṭaʿam, ʿāśat, qirîʾâ, ʿāmal,* and *šātaq* provide the most reliable evidence for dating the book and require a date no earlier than the fifth century.[18] Another reasonable argument for a post-exilic date of the book is its degree of literary sophistication. M. Smith, for example, described the book as a sample of the "belletristic" material that emerged under the patronage of the landed gentry of Judah sometime during the late Persian and early Hellenistic periods.[19] Evidence that Jonah either quotes from or directly alludes to biblical texts such as 1 Kings 19 and Jeremiah 18 and 26 indicates a general familiarity with the literary traditions of Israel subsequent to their collection and promulgation during and after the exilic period.[20]

Attempts to locate the date of the book more precisely within the post-exilic or the Persian period, however, have been inconclusive. Feuillet and others, for example, have argued that Jonah 3:9 and 4:2 are quotations of Joel 2:13–14; therefore Jonah is to be dated after Joel, which is often thought to be a fourth century work.[21] Arguments from literary dependence, although

---

[17] For example, Ezra 1:2; 5:12; Neh 1:4; 2:4, 20; Dan 2:18.

[18] "Studies in the Book of 'Jonah,'" 116. See also the similar linguistic arguments in A. Rofé, *The Prophetical Stories*, 1st English ed. (Jerusalem: Magnes Press, 1988), 152–57. Cf., however, G. Landes ("Linguistic Criteria and Date of the Book of Jonah," *Eretz Israel* 16 [1982]: 147–70) and Sasson (*Jonah*, 22–23), who argue that such linguistic evidence is inconclusive.

[19] *Palestinian Parties and Politics That Shaped the Old Testament* (London: SCM Press, 1971), 121–22.

[20] See the discussion of literary dependence in A. Feuillet, "Les Sources du Livre de Jonas," *RB* 54 (1947): 161–86; and in Magonet, *Form and Meaning*, 65–77.

[21] "Les sens du livre de Jonas," *RB* 54 (1947): 355. See also Bickerman, *Four Strange Books*, 48.

superficially appealing, are in reality extremely difficult to prove. Others have argued just the opposite, namely, that Joel is dependent upon Jonah.[22] Since both Jonah 3:9, 4:2 and Joel 2:13–14 are restatements of older material from Exodus 32–34, the possibility that they are independent appropriations of common tradition cannot be excluded.[23]

Several scholars attempt to date the Book of Jonah in the early Hellenistic period because of perceived signs of influence from Hellenistic literature and culture. Wolff, for example, suggests the presence in Jonah 1 of Hellenistic seafaring motifs.[24] A. Faj finds in Jonah similarities with early Stoic philosophy.[25] Others have suggested that the book is an example of the genre of Menippean satire and thus emerged out of a Hellenistic cultural milieu.[26] If similarities with aspects of Hellenistic culture exist in the Book of Jonah, however, they are certainly understated and cannot conclusively be shown to be evidence of influence. Even if Hellenistic influence is present in the Book of Jonah, aspects of Hellenistic culture were introduced into Palestine far earlier than the late fourth or early third century. Therefore a date for Jonah in the early Hellenistic period would not be required.

The arguments for the precise dating of the Book of Jonah alone are too inconclusive, therefore, to make a reliable judgment about the chronological order in which Jonah and

---

[22]Magonet, *Form and Meaning*, 78–79; S. Bergler, *Joel als Schriftinterpret* (Frankfurt an Main: Peter Lang, 1991), 213–14.

[23]This is the conclusion of W. Rudolph, *Joel, Amos, Obadja, Jona*, KAT XII/2 (Gütersloh: Gerd Mohn, 1976), 27.

[24]Wolff, *Obadiah and Jonah*, 78.

[25]"The Stoic Features of the Book of Jonah," *Instituto Orientale di Napoli, Annali* 34 (1974): 345.

[26]J. Ackerman, "Satire and Symbolism in the Song of Jonah," in *Tradition and Transformation*, ed. B. Halpern and J. D. Levenson (Winona Lake, IN: Eisenbrauns, 1981), 227–29; and A. Lacocque and P.-E. Lacocque, *Jonah: A Psycho–religious Approach to the Prophet* (Columbia, SC: University of South Carolina Press, 1990), 37–41.

other books entered the collection of the Minor Prophets. Sasson has argued that it matters little for the interpretation of Jonah whether one dates it in the early fifth or the late third century BCE.[27] The sequence of 4QXII[a], however, when compared with the other arrangements of the LXX and the MT, may provide new evidence for establishing the relative chronology of Jonah in relation to the the Minor Prophets.

As discussed in Chapter Three above, changes in sequence of textual material between manuscript traditions of the Hebrew Bible may be employed as further evidence for the literary history of such texts. It is possible to expand the argument regarding changes in the sequence of individual texts to the evidence of the variant sequences of books among the manuscript traditions of the Minor Prophets. According to such an argument, the Book of Jonah would have been introduced into the scroll of the Minor Prophets after a previous collection of nine or eleven books had already taken shape. The nine books would be those books that are not altered in their sequence in either the MT or LXX arrangements.[28] An eleven-book collection would include the nine books whose sequence is stable in each manuscript tradition and also the books of Joel and Obadiah. Since Joel and Obadiah occupy different places in the MT and LXX manuscripts of the Book of the Twelve, these two books also appear to have been late entries into a previously arranged collection of prophetic books, although not necessarily at the same time as the Book of Jonah.[29] Unlike other scholarly reconstructions of smaller collections of the Minor Prophets prior to the final collection of the Book of the Twelve, the suggestion that the books of Joel, Obadiah, and Jonah were the latest entries into the final collection has the advantage of supporting

---

[27]*Jonah*, 27.

[28]Hosea, Amos, Micah, Nahum, Habakkuk, Zephaniah, Haggai, Zechariah, Malachi. The sequence of Hosea, Amos, and Micah, although interrupted in the MT, is unaltered with respect to the order of the three books themselves.

[29]See the discussion of Joel and Obadiah in Chapter Five below.

manuscript evidence. The variant placements of the three books in ancient manuscripts indicate either an uncertainty about the proper sequence of the later additions or a degree of fluidity and scribal creativity in the placement of the latest books to enter the collection.

Jonah is the only book that occurs in three places among the manuscripts of the Book of the Twelve. Therefore it is most likely that Jonah was the latest book to be added to the collection and the one that possessed either the most uncertainty or the most flexibility in its placement among the Minor Prophets. The position of Jonah as the final book of the Twelve in 4QXII^a is consistent with such a possibility. Although it cannot be said that the sequence of 4QXII^a proves that Jonah was the last book to enter the Book of the Twelve, scholarly arguments about the late date of the book allow for this possibility. The plausibility that Jonah was the final book to enter the Book of the Twelve increases upon consideration of the literary features of the book and the primary themes that it addresses.

The Primary Themes of the Book of Jonah

The placement of Jonah in 4QXII^a is consistent with its uniqueness in relation to the rest of the Minor Prophets and with its probable late date of origin. The sequence of 4QXII^a, however, may also be seen to adumbrate the observations and conclusions of critical research concerning the literary characteristics of the book and the primary messages or themes contained within it. The following treatment of the form and content of Jonah will attempt to demonstrate the validity of this claim.

[*Excursus: Methodological Issues in the Interpretation of Biblical Narratives.* The question of the possible meanings of Jonah, however, raises the methodological issue of how meaning is determined for biblical texts. Scholarship on the meaning of the Book of Jonah generally falls under the headings of either diachronic or synchronic approaches. Diachronic approaches seek to determine meaning for the book by reconstructing the chronological layers of its composition and identifying the intention behind each layer. In such an approach, the meaning of the earliest stage of composition is first identified, followed by an analysis of the new meanings that are given to the text by subsequent redactional layers. By comparison, synchronic approaches determine meaning from the linguistic, stylistic, and structural features of the text in its present form.

Many recent scholars have eschewed diachronic approaches to the narrative of the Book of Jonah. Nevertheless, even among scholars who treat the narrative portions of the book as a literary unity, a diachronic approach is seen in the tendency to dismiss the prayer of Jonah 2:3–10 as either having no meaningful relationship to the narrative, or as altering the meaning of the narrative.[30] Diachronic treatments of the narrative sections of Jonah, however, have also been advanced in recent scholarship on the book.[31] From the perspective of a diachronic approach, the meaning of the present form of the text is contingent upon a reconstruction of the earlier strata, and indeed is often said to contradict or obscure those earlier layers.

As the title of Magonet's monograph on Jonah indicates, in synchronic analyses of biblical texts, "form and meaning" are inseparable.[32] The message of the text is discerned from the presentation of the text. The well known example of the prayer in Jonah 2 is again illustrative of this

---

[30]J. Bewer's comment (*The Book of the Twelve Prophets*, ICC [Edinburgh: T & T Clark, repr. 1961], 21) that the prayer's "inclusion or omission makes no difference to the point of the narrative" is representative of this view, which was even accepted by Trible ("Studies in the Book of 'Jonah,'" 76), who elsewhere shows great sensitivity to the synchronic structures of the narrative sections.

[31]See, for example, the literary-critical treatment of the book in L. Schmidt, *"De Deo." Studien zur literarkritik und Theologie des Buches Jona, des Gesprächs zwischen Abraham und Jahwe in Gen 18:22ff. und von Hi. 1*, BZAW 143 (Berlin: Walter de Gruyter, 1976); and the more recent redaction-critical approach in P. Weimar, "Jon 4,5. Beobachtungen zur Entstehung der Jonaerzählung," *BN* 18 (1982): 86–109. Nogalski (*Redactional Processes in the Book of the Twelve*, 256–62) agrees in general with the redactional analysis of Schmidt, although like Weimar, he dissects the prayer in 2:3–10 into two redactional layers.

[32]Magonet, *Form and Meaning: Studies in Literary Techniques in the Book of Jonah*.

approach. A synchronic approach determines the meaning of the prayer from the perspective of its context in the present form of the book. The subtitle of G. Landes' influential article "The Kerygma of Jonah: The Contextual Interpretation of the Jonah Psalm," is indicative of such an approach.[33] Landes argued that the prayer, whatever its origin or chronological relationship with the narrative, has been well integrated literarily into the structure and meaning of the book as a whole.[34] As Landes's article illustrates, synchronic approaches do not necessarily deny the composite nature of Jonah or even the possibility of redactional accretions. They begin, however, with the manner in which the text "works" as a literary creation as the primary determinant of the text's meaning.[35]

The present work addresses the question of meaning for the Book of Jonah, including the relationship of the prayer to the narrative, from a synchronic perspective, based upon the following presuppositions. (1) Diachronic approaches are often based upon assumptions about ancient Near Eastern perceptions of narrative coherence and meaning that are often neither explicitly stated nor critically examined. These include assumptions such as the inability of a single author to write both prose and poetry, the preference of ancient authors/storytellers for precise consistency in narrative details, and the corresponding assumption of the disposition or insensitivity of ancient redactors toward awkward juxtapositions and interpolations. (2) Even those diachronic treatments of Jonah that attest a high degree of methodological self-awareness and rigor are ultimately based upon hypothetical reconstructions of forms of the texts that exist only in the scholar's reconstruction and can therefore neither be verified nor

---

[33]*Interpretation* 21 (1967): 3–31.

[34]Other arguments to this effect are given in G. H. Cohn, *Das Buch Jona im Lichte der biblischen Erzählkunst*, Studia Semitica Neerlandica 12 (Assen: Van Gorcum, 1969), 93ff.; O. Kaiser, "Wirklichkeit, Möglichkeit und Vorurteil. Ein Beitrag zum Verständnis des Buches Jona," *EvTh* 33 (1973): 91–103; Magonet, *Form and Meaning*, 49–53; Ackerman, "Satire and Symbolism," 217–20; and recently, K. Craig, *A Poetics of Jonah* (Columbia, SC: University of South Carolina Press, 1993), 73–82.

[35]Sasson, *Jonah*, 16–20, 205.

invalidated.[36] (3) The corpus of Hebrew Scriptures does provide a basis of comparison for the identification of synchronic literary features such as the employment of recognizable genres, the use of verbal repetition, parallelism and symmetry of structure, allusions to traditional material, and the creative structuring of dialogue and narration.[37] (4) The identification of such literary features, as I hope to indicate below, has produced cogent and persuasive interpretations of the Book of Jonah as a unified literary text.]

That a variety of messages has been suggested by readers of the Book of Jonah is a tribute to the literary artistry of its author and also to the ambiguity and abundant possibilities of language. Magonet identifies four major themes of the book, although he states that these are only four themes out of other possible selections.[38] Sasson summarizes various views of the meaning of Jonah in a final chapter of his commentary entitled "Interpretations," with an emphasis on the plural form of the title. He concludes that the time-bound assumptions and shifting perspectives of interpreters require that "elucidating Jonah (indeed any biblical text) is a goal that can never be permanently or fully realized."[39] The present exposition of the

---

[36]The Book of Jonah differs in this respect from the Book of Jeremiah, for example, where the redactional history of at least one-seventh of the book may be reliably reconstructed from textual evidence.

[37]Lengthy discussions of biblical stylistics or poetics may be found in R. Alter, *The Art of Biblical Narrative* (New York: Basic Books, 1981); A. Berlin, *Poetics and Interpretation of Biblical Narrative* (Sheffield: Almond Press, 1983); S. Bar Efrat, *Narrative Art in the Bible*, tr. D. Shefer-Vanson (Sheffield: Almond Press, 1989); and J. Licht, *Storytelling in the Bible* (Jersualem: Magnes Press, 1978). See also the discussion of "aesthetic criticism" in J. L. Crenshaw, *Samson: A Secret Betrayed, a Vow Ignored* (Atlanta: John Knox Press, 1978), 21–24.

[38]*Form and Meaning*, 88. These themes take the form of polarities between: (1) knowledge of God/disobedience of God; (2) particularism/universalism; (3) traditional teaching/new experience; and (4) the power of God/the freedom of man. For other themes, see *Form and Meaning*, 145, n. 30.

[39]*Jonah*, 352.

primary messages of the Book of Jonah recognizes that the variety of interpretations of the book indicates not only that multiple meanings are possible, but that multiple meanings are indeed present within the text itself. The following assessment of the text is thus an attempt to weigh the various possible meanings of the text by means of a close reading of its primary literary features.

The hermeneutical clues that enable an interpretation of a text based upon a close reading of its literary features will ideally differ from text to text. Those features that I conclude to be most significant for the Book of Jonah are: (1) the form of the book; (2) the characterization of the prophet Jonah by means of the devices of irony and satire; (3) the structure of the book; and (4) the literary relationships between the book and other biblical literature. The following intepretation attempts to identify the primary messages of the Book of Jonah by incorporating the elements of form, technique, structure, and literary relationships of the book into a single holistic treatment.

The Literary Form of Jonah. The uniqueness of the Book of Jonah has made it difficult for scholars to characterize it satisfactorily by means of a single literary category. Suggestions, therefore, about the genre of the Book of Jonah are as numerous and diverse as the attempts to date the book. Trible listed in her 1963 dissertation no fewer than thirteen literary categories that have been suggested in the previous scholarship, including: historical narrative, didactic fiction, tale, short story, satire, sermon, fable, myth, folk tale, allegory, parable, midrash, and legend.[40] To the list should now be added the categories of

---

[40]"Studies in the Book of 'Jonah,'" 127–30. Subsequent summaries of this issue may be found in M. Burrows, "The Literary Category of the Book of Jonah" in *Translating and Understanding the Old Testament*, ed. T. H. Frank and W. L. Reed (Nashville: Abingdon Press, 1970), 80–107; and T. D. Alexander, "Jonah and Genre," *Tyndale Bulletin* (1985): 35–39.

philosophical book,[41] parody,[42] Menippean satire,[43] and novella.[44]

The difficulty of identifying a single category for the book is further complicated by Sasson's observation that certain categories (e.g., satire, didactic fiction) describe the intentions of an author of a given text, while other categories (parable, fable, midrash, parody) may describe features that an audience may legitimately discover during the process of reading, regardless of authorial intention.[45] The fact that so many readers have located so many generic features within the book appears to validate Sasson's observation. The goal of literary categorizations, however, should not be to squeeze this unique text into a narrow, precast literary mold, but rather to answer the reader's conscious or implied question, "What kind of text am I reading?" The best descriptions of the Book of Jonah are those that describe its general features by means of a combination of the most salient literary elements within the book.

G. von Rad's characterization of the book, for example, is exemplary for both its simplicity and its descriptive power. He classified Jonah as "a story about a prophet," albeit one that exceeds earlier examples of this category in its didactic tone and that "seems to have been the last and strongest flowering of this old and almost extinct form."[46] A similar description is given by A. Berlin, who describes Jonah as "a prophetic story *par excellence*," whose main theme is "the nature of prophecy and its

---

[41]E. Levine, "Jonah as a Philosophical Book," *ZAW* 96 (1984): 235–45.

[42]J. A. Miles, Jr., "Laughing at the Bible: Jonah as Parody," *JQR* 65 (1974–75): 168–81; and A. J. Band, "Swallowing Jonah: The Eclipse of Parody," *Prooftexts* 10 (1990): 177–95.

[43]Ackerman, "Satire and Symbolism," 127; Lacocque, 40.

[44]H. W. Wolff, *Obadiah and Jonah: A Commentary* (Minneapolis: Augsburg Publishing Co., 1986), 84–85.

[45]*Jonah,* 331–34.

[46]*Old Testament Theology,* Vol. II, tr. D. M. G. Stalker (New York: Charles A. Scribners & Sons, 1965), 291; cited in Burrows, "The Literary Category of Jonah," 229.

effect on the prophet."[47] Von Rad and Berlin's description of Jonah as a prophetic story has the advantage of being a category "indigenous to ancient Hebrew literature."[48] This is significant since, as Berlin explains, attempts to classify works by genre began with Aristotle and have dealt primarily with Greek and other Western literature. Biblical works often defy such precise classification.[49]

The classification of Jonah as a prophetic story highlights the affinities of the book with the stories about Elijah and Elisha contained in the Deuteronomistic History. Jonah shares with these narratives the features of an episodic portrayal of the exploits of northern prophets, an interest in the miraculous, and a prophetic mission that extends beyond the boundaries of Israel.[50] T. S. Alexander has observed that the formulation of Jonah 1:1 ("Now the word of Yahweh came to Jonah Ben Amittai saying, 'Arise, go to Nineveh . . .'") is almost identical to the divine address to Elijah in 1 Kgs 17:8–9 ("Now the word of Yahweh came to [Elijah] saying, "Arise, go to Zarephath which is in Sidon . . .'").[51]

As von Rad and Berlin observe in their descriptions of Jonah, the book exceeds the prophetic stories about Elijah and Elisha in its didactic tone. Numerous commentators on the book highlight the didactic aspect of the text. E. Haller, for example, described the book as a "eine Beispielerzählung in der Form einer Prophetenlegende, weisheitlich-didaktisch intendiert."[52] L. Schmidt emphasized the possible sapiential traditions behind the

---

[47]"Rejoinder to John A. Miles, Jr.," 235.

[48]Burrows, "The Literary Category of Jonah," 86.

[49]"A Rejoinder to John A. Miles, Jr.," 229.

[50]See the comments of C. A. Keller, "Jonas. Le Portrait d'un prophéte," *TZ* 21 (1965): 330; Schneider, "The Unity of the Twelve," 111; and Sasson, *Jonah,* 343–45.

[51]"Jonah and Genre," 56. See also 1 Kgs 17:2 and 21:17.

[52]"*Die Erzählung von dem Propheten Jona* (Munich: Chr. Kaiser, 1958), 50.

book by labeling it a "erzählte Dogmatik."[53] Scholars who label
the book as "parable" generally use the term to emphasize the
didactic aim of the narrative as its primary characteristic.[54] Such
an emphasis, for example, motivates A. Rofé's designation of the
book as a prophetic parable.[55] Because the term "parable,"
however, more precisely describes a simple story or comparison
with a clearly expressed meaning, others argue that the term
"didactic narrative" or "didactic fiction" is a better description
of the complex composition and rather open-ended meaning of
the Book of Jonah.[56] The category "didactic prophetic story"
describes the general form of Jonah and also marks its differences
with the Elijah and Elisha cycles.

Beyond its didacticism, Jonah differs in yet another way
from the Elijah and Elisha tales. Unlike those stories, the central
character of the Book of Jonah is portrayed in a definitely
negative light. E. Sellin suggested that Jonah was an expression of
a type of folk literature that chronicled the foibles of prophetic
figures as a counter-argument against stern prophetic
denunciations.[57] Certain stories within the Elijah and Elisha tales,
such as Elijah's flight and the story of Elisha's servant Gehazi,
may fall into this category. Evidence of popular opposition to
prophetic figures in ancient Israel makes Sellin's suggestion
plausible.[58] The questions of how such a category of folk
literature may have influenced the composition of the Book of

---

[53]"*De Deo*," 113. Wolff (Obadiah and Jonah, 83) thinks that this
designation emphasizes too much the theological tenor of the book.

[54]As observed by E. M. Good, *Irony in the Old Testament* (London: SPCK,
1965), 40.

[55]*The Prophetical Stories* (Jerusalem: Magnes Press, 1988), 159–66.

[56]See the discussions to this effect in B. Childs, *Introduction to the Old
Testament as Scripture*, 421–22; Alexander, "Jonah and Genre," 40; and Sasson,
Jonah, 335–36.

[57]*Das Zwölfprophetenbuch*, 2nd ed., KAT 12 (Leipzig: Deichert, 1929), 285–6.

[58]See, for example, the reconstruction of popular opposition to prophetic
utterance in J. L. Crenshaw, *Prophetic Conflict: Its Effect upon Israelite Religion*,
BZAW 124 (Berlin: Walter de Gruyter, 1971), 24–36.

Jonah and why a derisive story about an eighth century prophet was used to address a post-exilic audience may be illuminated by discussing further the characterization of the prophet Jonah that is contained in the book.

Characterization of the Prophet Jonah. Numerous commentators have identified the techniques of irony and satire as the primary means by which the author of Jonah has chosen to portray the book's central character. E. M. Good labeled the book a thoroughly ironic work of satire "that portrays the prophet in order to ridicule him."[59] Burrows, after an exhaustive summary of previous categorizations of Jonah, chose satire as the proper literary category of the book.[60] Burrows describes satire as a form of verbal caricature that employs "the humor of deliberate hyperbole, which makes the object of attack ridiculous by incongruity and grotesque exaggeration." Against the conclusions of Burrows and Good, it should be pointed out that irony and satire more appropriately describe literary devices that are used by the author of Jonah, rather than the generic category of the book.[61] For this reason, Wolff classifies the book as a novella that begins with satire, described by Wolff as a derisive use of humor, and ends with irony, which is a less severe form of educational humor.[62]

The satirical nature of the Book of Jonah may be seen in its depiction of the central prophetic character. Whereas the narratives about Elijah and Elisha portray the prophets as the heroes of these stories, Jonah is depicted negatively as a caricature of the prophetic hero. He is a prophetic anti-hero who openly rebels against his prophetic mission and submits only

---

[59] *Irony in the Old Testament*, 41.

[60] "The Literary Category of the Book of Jonah," 95–96.

[61] This point is made by J. C. Holbert, "'Deliverance Belongs to Yahweh!': Satire in the Book of Jonah," *JSOT* 21 (1981): 60.

[62] *Obadiah and Jonah*, 84–85. See also the references to Jonah's satirical and ironic qualities in Feuillet, "Le Sens du livre de Jonas," 346–52; and T. E. Fretheim, *The Message of Jonah* (Minneapolis: Augsburg, 1977), 51–60.

after the ordeal and indignity of being swallowed and then vomited by a "great fish." Although the prophet's resistance to the divine call is not an uncommon biblical motif (Exodus 3–4; Isaiah 6; Jeremiah 1), Jonah's flight as described in chapter one exaggerates this theme to comic proportions.[63] The extremity of Jonah's resistance to his prophetic mission is shown by such items as his chartering an entire ship to go to Tarshish (1:3),[64] by his deep sleep in the midst of the storm, in contrast to the panicked sailors (1:5), and by his request to be thrown overboard (1:12). The two latter actions are indicative of Jonah's resignation to face death rather than to fulfill his prophetic calling.[65]

Another example of the hyperbolic element of satire in the Book of Jonah is the fourteen uses of the word *gādôl* "large, or great," which is the most frequently used word in the brief book.[66] The items designated in the Book of Jonah as being of great dimensions include: Nineveh (four times); the storm; the fish; the fear of the sailors (two times); and the anger of Jonah. Other exaggerated features in the book include: the size of Nineveh (a three days journey in diameter); the extremity and totality of Nineveh's repentance, including its livestock; the rapid growth of the *qîqāyôn* plant; and the dramatic swings of Jonah's temperament from great delight to extreme depression over the sudden appearance and sudden loss of a plant. Hyperbole in the Book of Jonah takes on the features of the grotesque or fantastic in such narrative elements as the storm in chapter one and the supernatural features of the divinely appointed fish (2:1), plant (4:6), worm (4:7) and wind (4:8). Although Sasson cautions that the number of humorous elements

---

[63]See the comments of Miles, "Laughing at the Bible," 72–73; and Holbert, "'Deliverance Belongs to Yahweh!'" 64–65.

[64]For the the interpretation of the Hebrew phrase *wayyittēn śĕkārâ*, "and he paid its hire" as indicating that Jonah hired the entire ship and its crew to take him to Tarshish, see Sasson, *Jonah*, 83–84.

[65]Magonet, *Form and Meaning*, 17, 68.

[66]A. Jepsen, "Anmerkungen zum Buche Jona," in *Wort-Gebot-Glaube: Festschrift für Walter Eichrodt* (Zürich: Zwingli Verlag, 1970), 298.

in Jonah have often been overstated,[67] few commentators have failed to note the grotesque humor of Jonah's unceremonious deposition onto dry land by means of the intestinal distress of the great fish.

By comparison with satire, irony is a literary device that exposes and exploits incongruity without the ridiculing tone of satire.[68] The incongruity may consist of differences between pretense and reality, between expectations and outcomes, between words and actions, or between the level of knowledge possessed by the characters and by the reader. An example of irony is Jonah's flight to Tarshish, which symbolizes the farthest destination in the opposite direction from Nineveh. One does not expect such an incongruous response to a divine appointment. There is also irony in the total repentance of Nineveh and in Jonah's angry response to that repentance, since both outcomes are far from what a reader would expect.

The majority of ironic features in the Book of Jonah, however, occur in the speeches of its characters. For example, Jonah attempts to flee the presence of Yahweh (1:3), yet he confesses that Yahweh is "the God of heaven, who made the sea and the dry land" (1:9). In 1:6, the captain of the ship urges Jonah to pray to his god that he might save them, not knowing that Jonah's god has caused the storm that threatens them. The most bitterly ironic statement in the book occurs in 4:2, when Jonah turns the ancient confession of Yahweh's attributes of mercy and compassion into an angry accusation of divine injustice.

Magonet has argued that a demonstrable narrative technique of the Book of Jonah is to make the speeches of the pagan characters into ironic evocations of traditional Israelite confessions.[69] For example, in 1:14 when the sailors pray to Yahweh (!) "For you, Yahweh, have done as you desired," their words are identical to Israelite confessions contained in Ps 115:3 and 135:6. In 3:9, the king's statement, "Perhaps God will turn

---

[67]*Jonah,* 331.

[68]Holbert, "'Deliverance Belongs to Yahweh!'" 60.

[69]*Form and Meaning,* 70–71.

and repent and turn away from his fierce wrath," uses language identical to the intercessory prayer of Moses in Exod 32:12. The pagans in Jonah ironically speak like pious Israelites while Jonah utters traditional confessions that are either completely incongruous with his actions (1:9) or with the narrative context of the confession (4:2).

It is possible, following Magonet's observation about the ironic content of the speeches in Jonah, to interpret the prayer in Jonah 2:3–10 as the most prominent example of ironic speech in the book. Literary critics have consistently concluded that the prayer is an interpolation that disrupts the narrative of the book. Some of the inconsistencies between the prayer and the narrative include the following:[70] (1) The psalm is a prayer of praise and thanksgiving when a lament or a supplication might be expected. (2) Jonah's request to be thrown overboard is an indication of his resignation to his own death, which is incongruous with the joyous emotions of the prayer's conclusion. (3) Details in the prayer, such as the descriptions of Jonah's plight, the wish to return to the holy temple, and the mention of idolatry, have no correspondence with the rest of the narrative. (4) The prayer and the narrative contain distinctive vocabularies that do not correspond with one another. (5) The prayer interrupts the symmetry between the first part of the narrative and the second part, which are marked by the parallels between 1:1 and 3:1. Finally, (6) it is argued that the narrative holds together with or without the prayer.

Although the distinctions between 2:3–10 and the rest of the Book of Jonah are serious ones, a tendency within the scholarly literature of the last three decades has been to affirm the unity of the psalm and the narrative, or at least the appropriateness of the psalm in its present context. Bickerman noted that ancient readers easily recognized the appropriateness of a prayer of

---

[70]See the detailed discussion in Trible, "Studies in the Book of 'Jonah,'" 77–80; and also the summaries in G. M. Landes, "The Kerygma of the Book of Jonah," *Interpretation* 21 (1967): 3–5; and J. Ackerman, "Satire and Symbolism," 214–16.

thanksgiving for rescue from drowning, and they saw the fish as the vehicle of that rescue.[71] Sasson, although he does not dismiss the distinctions listed above between the prayer and the narrative, concludes that these distinctions are themselves "organic to the distinct dictions" of prose and poetry and therefore do not speak to the issue of the psalm's appropriateness within its present context.[72] Landes argued that the psalm fit into the symmetrical structure of the book as a parallel to the dialogue between Jonah and God in chapter four, particularly Jonah's address to God in 4:2–3.[73]

Magonet has observed that the psalm fits well with certain literary features of the book, particularly the narrative progression of the psalm and the practice of inserting incongruous or ironic speeches into the mouths of the characters in the book.[74] The psalm, like Jonah's confessions in 1:9 and 4:2, does not correspond to Jonah's previous actions or with the expected consequences of the previously narrated events. Even the dramatic shift in mood from resignation in 1:12 to exultation in 2:9–10 is paralleled in the narrative of chapter four, in which Jonah's disposition changes suddenly from one of extreme joy over the plant to utter depression over its loss.[75] It is legitimate, therefore, to interpret Jonah's prayer in 2:3–10 to be the surpassing irony in a book that is marked through and through by ironic and incongruous features.[76] The significance that the speeches in the Book of Jonah and their ironic content have for the meaning of the book may be further illustrated by a discussion of the book's literary structure.

The Structure of the Book of Jonah. If the purpose of irony is to instruct by means of exposing the incongruity of certain

---

[71]*Four Strange Books of the Bible,* 11.

[72]*Jonah,* 202.

[73]"Kerygma of the Book of Jonah," 16–17.

[74]*Form and Meaning,* 51–53.

[75]Landes, "Kerygma of the Book of Jonah," 19.

[76]Ackerman, "Symbolism and Satire," 227–29.

attitudes or behaviors, then the ironic quotations in the Book of Jonah provide insight into the didactic aim of the book. The significance of these quotations increases after a consideration of their placement within the structure of Jonah. Each of the ironic speeches in the Book of Jonah is prominently marked by structural parallels with the rest of the book.

An example of the structural significance of the quoted speeches in the Book of Jonah is Jonah's confession in 1:9. Jonah's statement ("I am a Hebrew and I fear Yahweh the God of heaven who made the sea and the dry land") is ironic because it exposes the futility of his flight from Yahweh's presence. Yahweh's status as Creator not only enables Yahweh to chasten a rebellious Jonah, but also provides the rationale for Yahweh's act of sparing Nineveh (4:10). As Bickerman observes, "The story of Jonah teaches us that God is merciful, but He is merciful because He is the Creator."[77] The ironic speech quoted in chapter one scores the theological point that, as Creator, Yahweh acts with complete freedom.

The significance of Jonah's ironic statement in 1:9 for the message of the book is emphasized by its place in the structure of chapters one and two. N. Lohfink observed that Jonah 1:4–16 has a concentric structure that places 1:9 at the center of the literary unit.[78] Nogalski has extended Lohfink's observations to include 1:1–3 as a narrative introduction to the unit and 2:1–2,11 as the narrative conclusion.[79] This analysis of the organization of 1:1–2.11 highlights, both structurally and literarily, the significance of Jonah's ironic confession.

Nogalski's primary reason for extending the concentric structure of Jonah 1–2 to include 2:1–2, 11 is to argue that the prayer in 2:3–10 does not fit into the symmetry of the chapter and therefore does not belong to the original composition.

---

[77]Bickerman, *Four Strange Books*, 48.

[78]"'Jona ging zur Stadt hinaus' (Jona 4,5)," *BZ* NF 5 (1961):185–203. See also R. Pesch, "Zur konzentrischen Struktur von Jona 1," *Biblica* 47 (1966): 577–81.

[79]"Redactional Intentions and Layers," 458–59.

Another structural feature of the Book of Jonah, however, makes it possible to understand 2:3–10 as structurally appropriate and functional within its present context. The text of Jonah 1–2 exhibits an interlocking structure that unites it with the episode of Jonah in Nineveh as portrayed in Jonah 3 and with the dialogue between Jonah and Yahweh in Jonah 4.

The interlocking structure between Jonah 1 and 3 is seen first of all in the relationship between 1:1–3 and 3:1–3. The first verses of Jonah 3 are a nearly verbatim repetition of 1:1–3. Jonah 3:1–3 divides the book into two parts and also furthers the narrative by means of its distinctions from chapter one.[80] The relationship between Jonah 1 and 3 is further strengthened by the parallels between 1:6 and 3:9. The verses begin with the synonymous interrogatives *'ûlay* "perhaps" and *mî yôdēa'* "who knows."[81] Both verses also end with the identical phrase *wĕlō' nō'bēd* "that we may not perish." Both verses are spoken by non-Israelites and both convey the same emphasis upon the efficacy of praying to *hā'ĕlōhîm* "the supreme god." As was the case with Jonah 1:9, these two ironic quotations in which pagans model the appropriate awareness of the sovereignty of the supreme deity are emphasized by the structural organization of the book, in this case, the parallelism between chapters one and three.

The parallelism between chapters one and three is complimented by similar parallelism between chapters two and four.[82] Whereas Jonah 1 and 3 feature Jonah in the midst of non-

---

[80]See the discussion of the distinctions between 1.1–3 and 3.1–3 in Sasson, *Jonah*, 225–34.

[81]For the synonymous meaning of these interrogatives, see J. L. Crenshaw, "The Expression *mî yôdēa'* in the Hebrew Bible," *VT* 36 (1986): 274–88.

[82]As observed by Landes, "The Kerygma of the Book of Jonah," 16–17. Sasson (*Jonah*, 203) rightly criticizes Landes's overwrought attempt to identify parallels within the internal structure of 2:3–10 and 4:2–3. They are parallel nonetheless because both are direct addresses of Jonah to Yahweh and because both are incongruous with Jonah's situation. See also the list of catchwords between Jonah 2:3–10 and 4:2–3 that are listed in L. Allen, *The*

Israelites, Jonah 2 and 4 feature Jonah alone in dialogue with Yahweh. The parallelism between Jonah 2 and 4 is established through the prayer in 2:3–10 and Jonah's complaint/prayer in 4:2–3. Again, the structural features of the book highlight quoted speech that is ironic in character. In Jonah 2:3–10, one finds a thanksgiving psalm where one would expect to find a lament. In Jonah 4:2–3, after Nineveh has repented of its evil ways because of the preaching of Jonah, one finds a lament where one might expect to find thanksgiving. A further incongruity is established by comparing Jonah's exclamation following his personal rescue that "Salvation belongs to Yahweh!," and Jonah's complaint and wish to die following the reprieve that is given to Nineveh.

The tendency within the Book of Jonah to place ironic speeches upon the lips of its characters and to emphasize those speeches in the structure of the book reaches its climax in Jonah 4:2–3. These verses not only reveal the reason for Jonah's flight, a "gap" that is left unfilled until this point in the narrative, but they also contain the climactic issue toward which the previously quoted speeches pointed. According to Jonah's complaint in 4:2–3, the reason for his flight and the primary issue of the book is the question of the justice of God. The classic confession of Yahweh's compassionate and merciful attributes becomes for Jonah a bitter accusation of injustice in light of the great wickedness of Nineveh. Jonah's complaint is not that Yahweh's mercy extends to a non-Israelite nation; any anti-foreign sentiment in the book is certainly understated.[83] Jonah's problem has more to do with Nineveh's wickedness than its foreignness. The central question addressed by Jonah's complaint in 4:2 is, as Fretheim has argued, the question of theodicy.[84]

Books of Joel, Obadiah, Jonah and Micah, NICOT (Grand Rapids, MI: Eerdmans, 1976), 198–99, n. 108.

[83]Fretheim, *The Message of Jonah*, 22.

[84]"Jonah and Theodicy," *ZAW* 90 (1978): 227–37; see also the comments of Ackerman in "Jonah," in *The Literary Guide to the Bible*, ed. R. Alter and F. Kermode (Cambridge: Belknap Press, 1987), 240. For a discussion of parallels

Jonah objects to divine mercy when it is extended to those who deserve judgment. The response that the book gives to the question of justice delayed is found in the speeches of Jonah, the sailors, and the king of Nineveh, namely, that the god of heaven who made the sea and the dry land does whatever the god pleases, including turning away from divine wrath.[85]

The preceding assessment of the primary message of the Book of Jonah may therefore be summarized as follows: Jonah is a didactic narrative that explores theological issues related to prophecy. The use of satire in describing the character Jonah is suggestive of a type of folk tale that emphasized negative characteristics of prophetic figures. The primary vehicle, however, for communicating the message of the book is the use of ironic speech. Two different uses of ironic speech are employed. In one use, pagan characters are made to utter traditional Israelite confessions; they are models of proper responses to divine action and judgment. A second type of ironic quotation is found in the speeches of Jonah, who utters traditional confessions that do not agree with his own actions and circumstances. Jonah's complaint in 4:2–3 answers the question of the reason for Jonah's flight, which was previously left unanswered, and also reveals the central theological problem of the book, which is the issue of theodicy, particularly the question of the delay of divine justice for the wicked. This reading of the primary themes of Jonah and its implications for the historical context of the book may be further supported by a discussion of the literary relationships between Jonah and other biblical texts, particularly the Book of Malachi.

---

and contrasts between Jonah and Job, see B. Vawter, *Job and Jonah: Questioning the Hidden God* (Ramsey, NJ: Paulist Press, 1983).

[85]See the discussion of the issue of delayed justice in R. P. Carroll, "Eschatological Delay in the Prophetic Tradition," *ZAW* 94 (1982): 47–58.

Literary Relationships between Jonah and Malachi

The primary problem addressed in the Book of Jonah is described above as the issue of theodicy, specifically the delay of divine justice against the wicked. Of the numerous possible historical contexts in which this issue could have arisen, Fretheim has suggested that the narrative strategy of Jonah best fits the situation that is described in the Book of Malachi.[86]

Theodicy in the Post-Exilic Prophets. In Mal 2:17, the people are accused of complaints such as "Everyone who does evil is good in the eyes of Yahweh and he is pleased with them," or "'Where is the God of justice?" Again in 3:13–15 the complaint is registered that those who serve God do so without profit while "evildoers not only prosper, but when they put God to the test they escape (NRSV)." According to Fretheim, Jonah's protest against the extension of divine mercy to the wicked is an ironic reflection of the popular questioning of divine justice described in Malachi.[87] The narrative strategy of the Book of Jonah was to lead the presumed post-exilic audience to identify with the character of Jonah and his complaint of divine injustice, and thus also to experience with Jonah the didactic effect of the book's final rhetorical question.

Although the issue of theodicy is stated most strongly in Malachi among post-exilic prophetic writings, the issue of the delay of justice against the nations is also present in other late prophetic texts. Hag 1:1–11 and Zech 1:11–12 provide further evidence of eschatological expectations of divine judgment against the nations within the post-exilic Judean community. In Hag 1:1–11, the prophet blames the delay of eschatological

---

[86]"Jonah and Theodicy," 30. See the similar comments of Wolff (*Obadiah and Jonah*, 168), although he dates Jonah a century and a half later than Malachi and suggests that the problems in Malachi persisted into the early Hellenistic period (78).

[87]"Jonah and Theodicy," 31.

promises upon the returnees' neglect of the Jerusalem Temple.[88] Despite this past neglect, however, Haggai promises in 2:6 that Yahweh will judge the nations in "yet a little while," presuming that construction of the Temple is completed. In Zech 1:11–12, a part of Zechariah's first vision, the interpreting angel responds to the report that the nations of the earth are dwelling at rest with the lamenting cry, "How long!," followed by a prayer of intercession on Judah's behalf. Such a response apparently reflected popular disappointment with the delay of judgment that had been promised against the nations.[89]

Israel and the Nations in Jonah and Malachi. Fretheim's suggestion that Jonah was written to address a situation similar to that described in the Book of Malachi is strengthened by other similarities between the two books. Nogalski, for example, cites Mal 1:11–14 as the closest parallel to Jonah in the entire Book of the Twelve.[90] Mal 1:11–14 contrasts the honor given to Yahweh among the nations with the defilement of Yahweh's name by the Judean priesthood. This situation is analogous to the contrast in the Book of Jonah between the piety of the sailors and the Ninevites and the negative description of the character of Jonah. The identification of Jonah with a disobedient Judean community, however, does not require an allegorical reading of the book. Jonah is identified with the post-exilic community by his traditional confession in 1:9, and by his complaint of divine injustice in 4:2–3 that identifies him with the Judean audience that made similar complaints.

The comparison made in Mal 1:11–14 between appropriate reverence for Yahweh among the nations and disobedience of

---

[88]R. P. Carroll, "Eschatological Delay in the Prophetic Tradition?" *ZAW* 94 (1982): 56–58.

[89]C. L. Meyers and E. M. Meyers, *Haggai, Zechariah 1–8*, Anchor Bible Vol. 25B (Garden City, NY: Doubleday, 1987), 131; D. L. Petersen, *Haggai and Zechariah 1–8*, OT Library (Philadelphia: Westminster Press, 1987), 146–47.

[90]*Redactional Processes*, 272. Nogalski also finds similarity between the view of the nations in Jonah and in Zech 8:20–23.

Yahweh among the descendants of Israel is also made in an understated way in the Book of Jonah through allusions to another prophetic text, Jeremiah 36.[91] The confrontation between Jonah's words and the king of Nineveh in Jonah 3 stands in sharp contrast with the confrontation between Jeremiah's prophecy and King Jehoiakim reported in Jeremiah 36. Whereas the people and the king of Nineveh "believed in god," "proclaimed a fast" (3:5), and "turned from their evil ways" (3:10), King Jehoiakim and the people of Jerusalem and Judah "would not listen" (Jer 36:31) to the words of Jeremiah.

Jonah and the "Mosaic" Prophets. The allusion to Jeremiah 36 within Jonah 3 calls attention to another feature of the Book of Jonah that it shares with the Book of Malachi. Although the Book of Jonah includes numerous evocations and reminiscences of events and themes from Israel's prophetic literature, the strongest of these allusions are to the prophetic careers of Elijah and Moses. The prominence of these two prophetic figures in the conclusion to the Book of Malachi provides another connection between this text and the Book of Jonah.[92]

The Elijah traditions are echoed in Jonah in a number of ways. Mention has already been made of the similarity between the form of Jonah and the Elijah/Elisha narratives, as well as the similar wording of Jonah 1:1–2 and the divine address to Elijah in 1 Kgs 17:8. The story of Elijah's flight in 1 Kings 19 is particularly prominent in the Jonah narrative since it forms the narrative

---

[91]Feuillet, "Les Sources du livre de Jonas," 171; see also the discussion of Magonet, *Form and Meaning*, 76–77.

[92]As mentioned above, the other figure whose biography and literary legacy are prominent in Jonah is the prophet Jeremiah. See Feuillet, "Les Sources du livre de Jonas," 169–71; and Magonet, *Form and Meaning*, 71, 76. The significance of the ties between Jonah and Jeremiah will be discussed below in the context of the MT sequence of the XII. For an argument that Elijah and Jeremiah are depicted in Scripture as "Mosaic" prophets, see R. Wilson, *Prophecy and Society in Ancient Israel* (Philadelphia: Fortress Press, 1980), 197–99; 237.

frame for the entire Book of Jonah.[93] Jonah's flight toward
Tarshish and his deep sleep aboard the ship in chapter one are
echoes of Elijah's flight from Jezebel and his slumber in the
wilderness. The entirety of Jonah 4 appears to be modeled after
the dialogue between God and Elijah in 1 Kings 19. Elijah sits
under a broom tree; Jonah sits under a *qîqāyôn* plant. The deity's
twice repeated question, "What are you doing here, Elijah?" is
paralleled by the twice repeated question, "Do you do well to
be angry?" in Jonah 4:4 and 4:9. Jonah's two requests to die, in 4:3
and 4:8 are in fact a divided quotation of Elijah's similar request
in 1 Kgs 19:4:

> *And he asked for his life to end* and he said, "Enough *now, Yahweh, take
> my life*" (1 Kgs 19:4).

> *And he asked for his life to end* (Jonah 4:8).

> *And now, Yahweh,* please *take my life* from me (Jonah 4:3).[94]

Sasson has compared Jonah's request to die with similar
requests elsewhere in the Hebrew Bible and finds its closest
parallels in Elijah's flight to Horeb, which Jonah quotes directly,
and in the petitions of Moses that Yahweh end his life.[95] The first
such petition of Moses occurs in Exod 32:32, in the context of the
Golden Calf episode. The broader context of Exodus 32–34 has
already provided source material for the king of Nineveh's
statement in Jonah 3:9, for the divine response in 3:10, and for
the confession of the divine attributes in 4:3. The second of
Moses' two recorded requests to die is found in Num 11:10–15.
There Moses complains about the unfair and unbearable burden

---

[93]Magonet, *Form and Meaning,* 67–69.

[94]The similarity was not lost on the Syriac translator(s), who harmonized
Jonah 4:8 with 1 Kgs 19.4 by adding the phrase "for I am no better than my
ancestors." See A. Gelston, *The Peshitta of the Twelve Prophets* (Oxford:
Clarendon Press, 1987), 198. For a discussion of the technique of divided
quotations in Jonah, see Magonet, *Form and Meaning,* 73–75.

[95]Sasson, *Jonah,* 284–86.

of his leadership responsibilities and asks strongly that God kill him (*horgēnî nāʾ hārōg*) as an act of mercy. Sasson finds in Jonah's evocation of Elijah's and Moses's despair a message of protest against divine abuse of prophets.[96]

Jonah and the "End" of Prophecy. The echoes of the Elijah and Moses traditions in the Book of Jonah, along with the other similarities between Jonah and Malachi, may help to explain why an editor or compiler might have appended the book to the end of the scroll of the Minor Prophets following the conclusion to the Book of Malachi, in which Elijah and Moses are the representative heroes of Israel's religious heritage. Malachi, however, is not the only post-exilic prophetic text to contain a retrospective view of the phenomenon of prophecy. A primary example of a retrospective orientation toward Israelite prophecy is the threefold reference to "the earlier prophets" in Zechariah (1:4; 7:7, 12). Although the Book of Zechariah recognizes the presence of contemporary prophets (7:3; 8:9), Zechariah's words are consciously identified with the authority of the prophets who spoke "when Jersalem was inhabited and in prosperity."[97] Another example of a view of prophecy as primarily a phenomenon of the past is found in Joel 3:1-5. This text projects prophecy into the near but indefinite future as a universal phenomenon that will appear prior to the Day of Yahweh. Even within this future context, prophecy is conceived of according to an ancient (Mosaic) tradition, in this case the story recorded in Numbers 11 of the pouring out of the spirit of prophecy within the Israelite camp.[98] Texts such as these indicate a trend in the post-exilic community toward locating prophecy within a past "prophetic age" and thus conceiving of

---

[96]Ibid., 286.

[97]Meyers and Meyers, *Haggai, Zechariah 1–8*, 94; Petersen, *Haggai and Zechariah 1–8*, 132.

[98]D. L. Petersen, *Late Israelite Prophecy*, SBLMS 23 (Missoula: Scholars Press, 1977), 77.

contemporary prophetic speech as a secondary level of revelation.[99]

A final point of similarity that the Book of Malachi shares with Jonah may help to explain further both the choice of Jonah as the central character of the book and also the satirical portrayal of his character. From the perspective of the respective audiences of both works, Malachi and Jonah both contain somewhat unflattering portraits of the prophet as an embattled and self-serving figure. In Malachi, this portrayal comes through in the form of prophetic disputation employed within the book.[100] The manner of speech employed in Malachi has been described by Crenshaw as "a weapon of warfare" whose "pedagogic value . . . is minimal, owing to the great gulf between prophet and people, a chasm enlarged by abusive language."[101] In the face of popular skepticism and opposition, prophets in the post-exilic period ultimately became embattled figures concerned primarily with their own reputation. This concern, whether legitimate or not, could easily be caricatured as an extreme preoccupation with self.

Such a caricature of the self-absorbed prophet may be detected in the Book of Jonah. The interpetation that Jonah's flight from his prophetic mission was primarily an attempt to protect his own reputation is an ancient and often-repeated

---

[99]The further development of this transformation in the Second Temple period from "primary" revelation to "secondary" revelation is discussed in M. Fishbane, "From Scribalism to Rabbinicism," in *The Garments of Torah* (Bloomington, IN: University of Indiana Press, 1989), 64–78.

[100]E. Pfeiffer, "Die Disputationsworte im Buche Maleachi," *EvTh* 19 (1959): 546–68. Although J. O'Brien has challenged the description of Malachi as a disputation speech in favor of the form of covenant lawsuit, the same antagonism and accusatorial tone are present within both forms. See *Priest and Levite in Malachi*, SBLDS 121 (Atlanta: Scholars Press, 1990), 60–63.

[101]J. L. Crenshaw, "Popular Questioning of the Justice of God in Ancient Israel," *ZAW* 82 (1970): 393. Crenshaw describes the ultimate aim of the prophetic disputation speech as the defense of God and thereby also as an exercise in self-vindication for God's prophetic spokesperson.

observation.[102] Although Sasson has argued that this interpretation is exaggerated,[103] Jonah's overriding concern for his own comfort and well-being is certainly emphasized in both the narrative and in the prayer of chapter two. Jonah's slumber aboard the ship, the prominence of the pronoun "I" in the psalm, his construction of the *sūkkâ*, and his delight in the plant indicate Jonah's preoccupation with his own comfort and security.[104] A post-exilic audience might have identified such behavior as an exaggerated yet not unfamiliar portrait of prophetic figures.

The negative perception of prophecy in the post-exilic period may help to answer the question of why the author of Jonah chose the form of a satirical prophetic narrative to communicate a message of divine justice. A reading of late prophetic literature exhibits evidence of an increasing degree of difficulty and effort required of prophets who would attempt to address an audience directly.[105] The Haggai-Zechariah-Malachi corpus offers evidence of such a development. The form of the Book of Haggai has been described as a brief prophetic biography that was intended to present an apologetic portrait of the prophet's words and deeds.[106] Apparently such an apologetic tone was necessary in a context of resistance to prophetic figures. Haggai also bears the title "messenger of Yahweh" (Hag 1:13), which may also indicate a further assertion of "prophetic" status.[107] The dense use of the messenger formula

---

[102]See, for example, *Pirqe R. El.* 10.

[103]*Jonah*, 332.

[104]Magonet, *Form and Meaning*, 49–51, 95.

[105]For a treatment of resistence to prophetic speech in the post-exilic community from the perspective of the social sciences, see T. Overholt, "The End of Prophecy: No Players without a Program," *JSOT* 42 (1988): 103–115.

[106]Petersen, *Haggai and Zechariah*, 35–36.

[107]The term *maPāk* in post-exilic texts describes a mediator figure who possesses both human and supernatural characteristics. See Meyers and Meyers, *Haggai, Zechariah 1–8*, 114; and N. Cohen, "From *Nabi* to *Mal'ak* to Ancient Figure," *JJS* 37 (1987): 12–24.

"Thus says Yahweh of hosts" and the oracular formula "oracle of Yahweh" in Haggai and Zechariah 1–8, which occur there with a frequency unparalleled in prophetic literature, is perhaps another indication of an exerted effort to gain prophetic authentication in the post-exilic setting.[108]

Another indication of popular resistance to prophecy in the post-exilic period is found in the innovation of the interpreting angel within the vision reports of Zechariah. This device shifts the authority of the vision intepretations from the human to the supernatural realm.[109] There is also in Zechariah the threefold appeal to the authority of "the earlier prophets" as a means of establishing Zechariah's own authenticity. The developing picture of resistance to contemporary prophets continues in Zechariah 9–14 and Malachi, in which prophetic speech employs the strategy of pseudonymity or anonymity in order to gain a receptive hearing.

Hostility toward contemporary prophets in the post-exilic period reaches its climax in Zech 13:2–6, where prophets are equated with idolatry and unclean spirits, and a day is envisioned when one will prophesy under the threat of death and Amos's famous statement of prophetic compulsion (Amos 7:14) will become an defense of prophetic reticence (Zech 13:5). The language of Zech 13:2–6 suggests that these verses were intended as a critique of the phenomenon of false prophecy.[110] If one accepts, however, that ancient Israel was unable to formulate an effective means of distinguishing between true and false prophets, then by the post-exilic era skepticism toward prophetic figures would have grown to include all forms of self-consciously prophetic activity.[111] Therefore, although something of the phenomenon of prophecy may have been preserved in

---

[108]Meyers and Meyers, *Haggai, Zechariah 1–8*, 101–102. See also the self-vindicating claim, "Then you will know that Yahweh has sent me" in Zech 2:14, 16.

[109]Fishbane, *Biblical Interpretation in Ancient Israel*, 507.

[110]Meyers and Meyers, *Zechariah 9–14*, 370–71.

[111]For this conclusion, see Crenshaw, *Prophetic Conflict.*

the institutions of the cult and in the transmission and interpretation of prophetic traditions, Zech 13:2–6 portrays little tolerance for the continuing activity of publicly prophetic figures.[112]

Summary. Interpreting Jonah against a background similar to that of the Book of Malachi and other post-exilic prophetic texts places it in a context in which traditional forms of prophetic speech are accepted with increasing difficulty. In this context, the Book of Jonah would represent the fruition of a broader tendency toward literary innovation in the crafting of prophetic speech.[113] The innovative rhetorical strategy of the Book of Jonah may be summarized as follows. The author has chosen a historical prophet from the remote past as the vehicle for his didactic narrative.[114] The unflattering caricature of Jonah's rebelliousness, self-centeredness, and mercurial temperament would have most likely appealed to a post-exilic audience with a hostile view towards contemporary prophets, whose unrealized predictions and increased concern for self-vindication had made them increasingly unpopular figures. Such a negative portrayal of the prophet may even have been imitative of similar anti-prophetic stories in the folk literature of the post-exilic community.

The humorous and satirical elements of the Jonah story, however, constitute only one part of the author's narrative

---

[112]Meyers and Meyers, *Zechariah 9–14*, 402–403.

[113]For a discussion of the transformation of the prophetic role in post-exilic times from an oral to a literary activity, see E. Davis, *Swallowing the Scroll: Textuality and the Dynamics of Discourse in Ezekiel's Prophecy* (Sheffield: Almond Press, 1990).

[114]Fretheim, ("Jonah and Theodicy," 230) argues that the prophet Jonah ben Amitai was an appropriate choice to illustrate the author's point about the sovereignty of divine mercy. The reference to Jonah in 2 Kgs 14:25–27 is a unique and somewhat surprising tradition about an act of mercy that Yahweh extended to the Northern Kingdom, which is otherwise disparaged in the Deuteronomistic History.

strategy. Wolff has rightly observed the subtle shift in the story from the ridiculing satire of the first two chapters to the more instructive device of irony in chapters three and four.[115] If the Book of Jonah was written in a context similar to that described in Malachi 2:17 and 3:15, then Jonah's complaint in 4:2–3 about the indefinite delay of divine justice also reflects the complaint of Jonah's audience. Therefore, although the satire of the initial chapters of the book invites the audience to view Jonah negatively as a ridiculous prophetic figure, the irony of the latter chapters leads the audience to identify with Jonah's complaint against the deity. The satirical portrait of the prophet is the bait of the narrative; the irony of Jonah's words, particularly 4:2–3, is the didactic hook. The delay in reporting Jonah's motives for his flight, which is the most noticeable feature of the story's plot, facilitates the ironic turn in the narrative. Jonah's reason for fleeing from Yahweh, which is also the audience's own complaint against Yahweh, is revealed in chapter four only after the audience's defenses have been lowered by the humorous caricature of the prophet's adventures, and their interest has been piqued by the surprising events of chapter three.

The rhetorical effect of Jonah's theological complaint in 4:2–3 is that Jonah's problem has become the audience's problem and thus the solution in 4:11, in the form of a rhetorical question, becomes the answer to the audience's complaint as well. The fact that the use of irony in the narrative leads the audience to identify with Jonah, however, highlights a secondary theme of the book, namely, the nature of Israelite prophecy. By leading the audience to identify with the pathos of a prophetic figure from the past, the narrative invites a more sympathetic view of the plight of Israel's prophets.[116] The evocations in the Book of

---

[115] *Obadiah and Jonah,* 84–85. "The writer of our novella has made a caricature of Jonah, so that he can more easily free the reader, who is in a similar state of mind, from his fatal dilemma [i.e., his anger unto death]."

[116] A similar argument for the vindication of Israel's prophets in an exilic or post-exilic text is made in J. Blenkinsopp, "Abraham and the Righteous of Sodom," *JJS* 33 (1982): 119–132. Blenkinsopp argues that Gen 18:22–33 is a

Jonah of Elijah's despair at Horeb, Moses' frustration in the wilderness, and Jeremiah's peril as described in Jeremiah 26 and 36 emphasize the difficulties of the prophetic task and the not infrequent prophetic claims of divine abuse.[117] The use of irony in the Book of Jonah was a more subtle and more effective means of expressing the sufferings of Israel's prophets than the self-justifying disputations of Malachi.

Jonah's subtle apologetic for prophecy therefore exposes the weakness of J. A. Miles's claim that the book is a parody of prophetic literature.[118] Miles argues that the frequency in Jonah of themes and characters typical of prophetic literature indicates that it was primarily intended as a comic treatment of Israel's literary traditions. The interpretation described above, however, suggests that the caricature of the prophet presented in the Book of Jonah is a reflection of popular contempt for prophetic figures during the post-exilic period; the author exploited such contempt by means of satire in order to lure the audience into an identification with the complaint and the plight of the prophet. The density of literary allusions in Jonah does not require an intepretation of the book as parody. Instead, it demonstrates both the literacy and the creativity of the author of Jonah.

---

proto-midrashic interpolation intended to refute the charge that the fall of Jerusalem is the result of the prophets' failure to intercede for the people.

[117]On the conscious comparisons between Jonah and Elijah, Moses, and Jeremiah in the Book of Jonah, see Magonet, *Form and Meaning*, 99–106. For a discussion of Jonah's exposure of the unfair treatment of Israel's prophets, see Sasson, *Jonah*, 286. Magonet argues that comparisons between Jonah and the three "Mosaic" prophets diminish the character of Jonah. Sasson, however, reads the portrayal of Jonah as a portrait that is sympathetic to his suffering as a prophet. The turn in the narrative from satire to irony supports Sasson's interpretation.

[118]"Laughing at the Bible," 169. Miles's conclusion is rejected by Berlin ("A Rejoinder to John A. Miles, Jr.," 227–28), but supported in A. Band, "Swallowing Jonah: The Eclipse of Parody," *Prooftexts* 10 (1990): 177–95.

To the extent that the author of Jonah exploited existing prophetic texts to create his didactic tale, scholarly claims about the midrashic, or more correctly, proto-midrashic character of the book are justified.[119] The Book of Jonah is the product of a learned, literate mind who created a melange of literary styles, themes, and allusions in order to communicate to an audience that had ceased to recognize the legitimacy of contemporary prophecy. To the extent that the Book of Jonah communicated a new message about the nature of Yahweh and the nature of prophecy through the creative use of traditional materials, it partook of the reinterpretative methods and self-critical spirit of Israelite prophecy and thus secured its place within the prophetic corpus.[120]

Conclusion

The interpretation of the Book of Jonah given above may be seen as entirely consistent with the placement of the book in 4QXII[a]. Jonah is a reflection on issues of divine justice and fairness that were inherent within Israelite prophecy. The book uses texts and traditions from Israel's prophetic heritage to create an *apologia* for both the phenomenon of prophecy and for the deity proclaimed therein. It may accurately be described as a postscript or an epilogue to Israel's prophetic literature. As such, its placement in 4QXII[a] is appropriate to the literary character and message of the book. The appropriateness of Jonah's position at the end of the Book of the Twelve may even be expressed by a kabbalistic interpretation of the population of Nineveh given in the final verse of the book. One might argue that the distress or injustice that Yahweh's sovereign mercy may

---

[119]O. Loretz, "Herkunft und Sinn der Jona-Erzählung," *BZ* 5 (1960): 28; Feuillet, "Le Livre de Jonas," *La Sainte Bible* (Paris: Les Editions du Cerf, 1957), 18. See also Trible ("Studies in the Book of 'Jonah,'" 177), who designated Jonah as a "midrashic legend."

[120]Von Rad, *Old Testament Theology*, Vol. II, 292; Magonet, *Form and Meaning*, 106.

have caused for the remnants of the twelve tribes of Israel or for Yahweh's twelve representative prophets is outweighed in the divine economy by the Creator's compassion for the "more than twelve myriads" (Jonah 4:11) of his creatures, both human and animals.

Given the appropriateness of its context in 4QXII^a, the question arises, therefore, of how the Book of Jonah moved from what I argue to be its earliest position among the Twelve to the positions that it occupies in the LXX and MT manuscript witnesses. The meaning of the placement of Jonah within the MT Book of the Twelve will be addressed in the conclusion to the dissertation in Chapter Six below and the sequence of the books of the Minor Prophets in the LXX textual tradition, including the placement of Jonah within the LXX, is the topic of Chapter Five. Some of the conclusions to be reached in these two chapters, however, may be anticipated here.

First, the scribal factors at play in Jonah's varying positions among manuscripts of the Twelve appear to have been primarily the result of the late date at which Jonah entered the collection of Minor Prophets. Tradents of the Minor Prophets would have already possessed a collection of books with a previously defined order of arrangement. Since the addition of the Book of Jonah to the end of the corpus did not possess the authority of established scribal tradition, it afforded an opportunity for tradents of the Book of the Twelve to interpret the contents of Jonah in relation to the other writings of the prophetic corpus. A possible solution to the question of the different positions of Jonah in manuscripts of the Twelve may therefore be seen in the different interpretations of the book that are implied in the respective manuscript traditions of the MT and the LXX, which may themselves reveal something of the scribal and interpretative dynamics of the canonical process as these dynamics apply to the Book of Jonah.

To anticipate the conclusions of Chapters Five and Six, the placement of Jonah in the LXX arrangement appears to be based primarily upon verbal affinities with the Book of Joel and upon the theme of Nineveh that is shared with the Book of Nahum. In this sequence, Jonah is seen no longer as simply a story about a prophet, and by extension about prophecy in general, but rather as a prophetic book in its own right on a scale with the other Minor Prophets. In the MT arrangement of the Twelve, however, the Book of Jonah is placed among the corpus of the eighth century prophets and is associated particularly with the Book of Micah. In this arrangement, the historical figure of the eighth century prophet Jonah takes precedence over the literary content of the book. The focus of the Book of Jonah thus evolves from Israelite prophecy in general (4QXII[a]) to the contents of the book as prophetic literature (the LXX), and finally to the person and career of the eighth century prophet (the MT). The evidence and justifications for these conclusions about the interpretative history of the Book of Jonah and the chronological relationships between the LXX and MT arrangements of the Book of the Twelve constitute Chapters Five and Six, respectively, to which the discussion now turns.

CHAPTER 5

THE FORMATION OF THE BOOK OF THE TWELVE ACCORDING TO THE EVIDENCE OF THE SEPTUAGINT

The present chapter continues the investigation of the textual evidence for the formation of the Book of the Twelve by exploring the internal coherence and literary unity of the arrangement of books preserved in the LXX manuscript tradition. As I have argued above in the case of Mal 3:22–24 and also regarding the placement of Jonah in 4QXII[a], differences in sequence between biblical manuscripts may in certain cases provide supporting evidence for the literary history of biblical texts. The present chapter will examine the alternative sequence of the Minor Prophets that is preserved in the LXX manuscript witnesses, and particularly their arrangement of the books of Joel and Obadiah. To anticipate the results of this examination, it will be argued that (1) the LXX sequence of the Minor Prophets represents an integrated literary corpus, the unity and coherence of which is similar to that proposed for the MT sequence; (2) the placement of the books of Joel and Obadiah within the LXX Book of the Twelve is chronologically prior to their placement within the MT sequence and possibly reflects the position that they were given when these two books entered a pre-existing collection of prophetic texts; and (3) the placement of Jonah within the LXX Book of the Twelve is an alteration of the arrangement preserved in 4QXII^a, although it is also chronologically prior to the placement of Jonah within the MT textual tradition.

The LXX Arrangement of the Twelve in Previous Research

In Chapter Three above, I argued that some of the textual alterations attested by the LXX Minor Prophets were quite similar to changes that are often identified as being redactional in nature. In an article on redactional stages in the Book of Jeremiah that are attested by textual evidence, J. W. Watts has observed that different value judgments often accompany the labeling of a particular variant reading as either a textual or a redactional alteration.[1] The labeling of a variant as a textual change bears the somewhat negative evaluation of being a secondary, corrupt, or inferior reading. A redactional reading, however, may be evaluated positively as an integral part of the final form of the text.[2] Watts explained the tendency to evaluate one textual edition as superior and others as inferior as a result of the (legitimate) need of modern commentators, scholars, faith communities, and publishers for a single biblical text. In this manner, modern scholars and publishers perform a function analogous to that of ancient scribes: they each are responsible for transmitting the biblical text. The practical dimension of this task requires the selection of a single, superior text from among the multiplicity of possible variant texts presented by the ancient Hebrew and versional manuscripts.[3]

---

[1]Watts, "Text and Redaction in Jeremiah's Oracles against the Nations," *CBQ* 54 (1992): 437–38.

[2]Ibid., 438. Watts qualified his broad generalization to include scholars who value textual changes for their own sake and also those who dismiss all redactional changes as secondary.

[3]Ibid., 441. See also the discussion in E. Ulrich, "Double Literary Editions of Biblical Narratives and Reflections on Determining the Form to Translate," in *Perspectives on the Hebrew Bible: Essays in Honor of Walter J.*

The evaluations implicit in the distinctions between textual and redactional changes may be illustrated by the treatment of the LXX Book of the Twelve in previous studies. Schneider, for example, sought to minimize the differences in sequence between the MT and the LXX.[4] He explained the differences in sequence as a result of two different ways of incorporating the books of Joel, Obadiah, and Jonah into the Minor Prophets collection. The MT order was the more "original" sequence, according to Schneider, because he concluded that Joel and Obadiah were intentionally composed to fit precisely into the places that they occupy in the MT sequence. The LXX collection was more conservative in nature and therefore preserved the older collection of Hosea-Amos-Micah intact. The fact that the subgrouping of Joel-Obadiah-Jonah follows Hosea-Amos-Micah in the LXX sequence and that they have the same order as the MT within their sub-grouping led Schneider to conclude that the LXX sequence was directly dependent upon the MT sequence.

Schneider's conclusion about the "original" order of the MT Book of the Twelve includes the value judgment that the LXX order is a secondary and inferior corruption of the original and superior structure of the book. The LXX order is therefore comparable to a corrupt textual variant. It belongs to the textual history of the Book of the Twelve but plays no role in its literary history. Schneider, therefore, did not attempt to find the kind of literary unity within the LXX sequence of the Twelve that he carefully sought out in the MT text.

Nogalski's treatment of the LXX Book of the Twelve is similar to that of Schneider, only more emphatic in its identification of the MT as the only coherent, unified arrangement of the Book of the Twelve. Nogalski dimisses the LXX arrangement of the

---

Harrelson, ed. J. L. Crenshaw (Macon, GA: Mercer University Press, 1988), 101–16.

[4]Schneider, "The Unity of the Book of the Twelve," (Ph.D. dissertation, Yale University, 1979), 224–25.

Twelve with a footnote to Schneider's conclusion.[5] He then argues that the catchwords shared by the beginning and ending sections of contiguous books in the MT Book of the Twelve are the results of conscious redactional changes that were intended to unify the Book of the Twelve as a single volume in its MT arrangement. The clear implication of Nogalski's argument about the redactional formation of the Book of the Twelve is that an interruption of the "original" MT sequence is a corruption of the book's literary unity. The LXX Book of the Twelve therefore belongs to the textual history of the book and is comparable to an inferior textual variant.

Schneider and Nogalski's treatment of the LXX Minor Prophets is a logical result of their use of the MT sequence as the starting point for their investigation of the formation of the Book of the Twelve. Although the historical endurance and authoritative transmission of the MT text may indeed qualify it to be the privileged textual tradition in the continuing scholarly process of the preservation of the Hebrew Bible,[6] an exclusive focus upon the MT nevertheless obscures the evidence for alternative textual and literary editions of books of the Hebrew Bible that may be preserved in the ancient manuscript witnesses. The present study attempts to bracket out questions of priority and superiority of texts by examining the LXX arrangement of the Book of the Twelve as a literary collection in its own right. The results of such a study will show that the LXX text not only manifests a degree of literary unity and coherence that is equal to the MT Book of the Twelve, but the LXX also contains evidence that indicates that its internal arrangement is also possibly chronologically prior to the MT as well.

The point to be made in arguing that the LXX arrangement of the Book of the Twelve is chronologically prior to that of the

---

[5] *Literary Precursors to the Book of the Twelve,* BZAW 217 (Berlin: Walter de Gruyter, 1993), 2, n. 8.

[6] See the comments of Tov (*Textual Criticism of the Hebrew Bible* [Minneapolis: Fortress Press, 1992], 21) concerning the legitimacy of the privileged position of the MT in the textual criticism of the Hebrew Bible.

MT is not, however, that the MT should be relegated to the status of secondary corruption now occupied by the LXX. The significance of such a conclusion instead lies in the possible existence in antiquity of multiple arrangements or editions of the Book of the Twelve, of which the MT arrangement was but one. The fact that the MT has been preserved as the primary textual witness to the Book of the Twelve is not challenged by the existence of other or even prior arrangements of the Twelve. Rather, as will be argued for the LXX text of the Book of the Twelve, variant editions of biblical texts that existed in antiquity may be used to shed light on the final stages in the otherwise obscure literary history of the received Hebrew text of this ancient collection of prophetical writings.

In order to demonstrate the evidence for the unity of the LXX arrangement of the Twelve and its chronological priority with respect to the MT, the remainder of the chapter will proceeds as follows. First, I will examine textual evidence that indicates that the LXX arrangement of the Minor Prophets was not dependent upon the MT sequence. This evidence comes in the form of a redactional catchword in the MT text of the Book of the Twelve that is not present in the text of the LXX and, as I shall argue, was most likely not present in the Hebrew *Vorlage* of the LXX translator. Secondly, I will argue that the arrangement of the books of Joel and Obadiah in the LXX Book of the Twelve is not only well integrated into its surrounding context, but that their placement in the LXX reflects the position that they most likely occupied when these two books were first added to the Minor Prophets collection. Thirdly, I will address the issue of the relationship between the sequence of Joel and Obadiah in the LXX and their placement in the MT arrangement of the Twelve. Fourth, I will discuss the placement of the Book of Jonah in the LXX and its relationship to other placements of Jonah in the ancient manuscript traditions. Finally, I will address the issue of the chronological relationship between the LXX and MT arrangements of the Twelve and attempt to elaborate on the contribution of the LXX evidence to the literary history of the Book of the Twelve.

A Missing Catchword: LXX Amos 9:12

According to the methodology described in Chapter Three for using the LXX as evidence for the textual criticism of its Hebrew source text, it is acceptable to presume that the sequence of books followed in the LXX manuscripts of the Minor Prophets reflects the sequence of its Hebrew *Vorlage*. Since the LXX Minor Prophets exhibits a fairly high degree of literalness in its translation, particularly with respect to word order, one may reasonably conclude that it would also follow the source text's sequence of books as well. Beyond this methodological assumption, however, other textual evidence supports the conclusion that the sequence of the LXX translation was also that of its source text.

The textual evidence that the arrangement of the LXX Book of the Twelve reflects the sequence of its Hebrew source text is found primarily in LXX Amos 9:12. The Greek translation of this verse differs in no small way from the reading of the MT. The MT preserves the following text:

lĕmaʿan yîrĕšû ʾet šĕʾērît ʾĕdôm wĕkol haggôyim ʾăšer niqrāʾ šĕmî ʿalêhem nĕʾūm yhwh ʿōśeh zōʾt

That they might possess the remnant of Edom, and all the nations over whom my name has been called, oracle of Yahweh who does this.

The LXX, however, rendered its source text as follows:

hopōs ekzētēsōsin oi kataloipoi tōn anthrōpōn kai panta ta ethnē ephʾ hous epikeklētai ton onoma mou epʾ autous legei kyrios o poiōn tauta

That the remnant of *humanity might seek* [me], and all the nations over whom my name is called, declares Yahweh who does this.

Commentators have been in agreement that Amos 9:12 is an important text for the literary unity of the (MT) Book of the

Twelve.[7] The reference to the "remnant of Edom" in this verse provides a connection and a transition to the oracle against Edom contained in the Book of Obadiah. Furthermore, the use of the verb *yrš* "to possess" in Amos 9:12 echoes the fivefold repetition of this verbal root in Obad 17–21. In the LXX text, however, both of these verbal connections between Amos 9:12 and the Book of Obadiah, namely the reference to Edom and the verb *yrš*, have either disappeared in the process of translation or were not present in the translator's source text.

Previous Explanations of LXX Amos 9:12

Although scholars have long noted the different reading of the LXX, they have rarely treated it as a true variant reading in the LXX translator's Hebrew *Vorlage*. It is usually explained as either an erroneous translation, or more benignly, as an example of the translator's exegetical skill and universalistic interests. There are good reasons to question these two explanations, however, and to conclude that LXX Amos 9:12 attests a reading of a Hebrew text that is distinct from the MT and that this textual distinction is appropriate in its context within the variant sequence of the LXX Book of the Twelve.

If LXX Amos 9:12 is the result of an erroneous translation, then the translator's error was threefold. First, for *yîrĕšû* "they will possess," the translator read *yidrĕšû* "they will seek." Wolff explains this change as a result of the LXX's having presupposed a reading of *yidrĕšû* for *yîrĕšû*.[8] Such a mistaken reading or a

---

[7]F. Delitzsch, "Wenn weisagte Obadja?" *ZfdgLThK* 12 (1851): 92; U. Cassuto, "The Sequence and Arrangement of the Biblical Sections," *Biblical and Oriental Studies, Vol. I: The Bible*, tr. I Abrahams (Jerusalem: Magnes Press, 1973), 5; Schneider, "The Book of the Twelve," 96–97. Nogalski, *Literary Precursors*, 113–16.

[8]Wolff, *Joel and Amos*, Hermeneia Commentary tr. W. Janzen, S. D. McBride, and C. Muenchow (Philadelphia: Fortress Press, 1977), 350–51. Wolff does not clarify whether he means that the LXX translator had a variant reading before him or whether the translator made a mistaken translation.

textual change is explainable given the similarity between the two words, the only difference being the second consonant, which is either a quiescent *yodh* or a *daleth*. A survey of scripts represented at Qumran shows that these two letters could at times appear quite similar.[9] It is unclear, however, whether the change from *yîrĕšû* to *yidrĕšû* was made by the translator or whether the variant was already present in the source text.

The second difference between the MT and the LXX is that the LXX reading corresponds to the word *ʾādām* "humanity" whereas the MT reads *ʾĕdôm* "Edom." This difference is also based on an orthographic similarity. Most commentators conclude that the translator erroneously translated the Hebrew word *ʾĕdôm*.[10] The third difference between the MT and the LXX of this verse is that the translator understood the noun *šĕʾērît* to be the subject of the main verb, and therefore either ignored, misread, or lacked in his source text the sign of the definite direct object that precedes the word *šĕʾērît* in the MT. Commentators generally see this rendering as the third in a series of three translational mistakes in this single verse.[11]

Another explanation of LXX Amos 9:12 views the Greek reading as less of a series of mistakes than a freely interpretative

---

[9] See for example the scripts described by Cross in "The Oldest Manuscripts from Qumran," *JBL* 74 (1955): 147–72, Figure 2, particularly 4QSam[b]. In fact, such a transformation between *yîrĕšû* and *yidrĕšû* occurred not only in antiquity but in Wolff's own commentary on the Book of Amos. The verb that Wolff discussed in the text of his German commentary in the *Biblischer Kommentar* series, *yîrĕšû*, appears mistakenly in the English translation of Wolff's text as *yidrĕšû*, the reading "presupposed" by the LXX. Cf. Wolff, *Dodekapropheton 2, Joel und Amos*, BKAT 14/2 (Neukirchen-Vluyn: Neukirchener Verlag, 1969), 404; and idem, *Joel and Amos*, 350.

[10] Wolff, *Joel and Amos*, 351. See also the comments to this effect by K. Budde "Zu Text und Auslegung des Buches Amos," *JBL* 44 (1925): 118; E. Hammerschaimb, *The Book of Amos: A Commentary*, tr. J. Sturdy (New York: Schocken Books, 1970), 142; and S. Paul *Amos*, Hermeneia (Philadelphia: Fortress Press, 1991), 347.

[11] For example, see the comments of Hammerschaimb, *Amos*, 142.

treatment of the source text. This view is represented by F. F. Bruce.[12] Bruce claims that the LXX translation is an example of "a general tendency" of the Septuagint translators "to conform the wording [of the text] to their own religious outlook." The rendering of Amos 9:12 thus reflected "the hope of many Jews of the dispersion that Gentiles would seek and find the true God."[13]

The conclusion that the variant in LXX Amos 9:12 arose at the stage of the Greek translation is based upon a combination of at least two of three possible assumptions about the translator's source text and the manner in which the task was performed. These are: (1) the assumption that the translator was rendering a consonantal text identical to the MT; (2) the assumption that the translator was unable to render the source text accurately; and (3) the assumption that the translator intentionally departed from the sense of the *Vorlage* in order to make a certain theological point or to reflect an interpretative tradition. The textual variants described in Chapter Three as belonging to the Hebrew *Vorlage* of the LXX Minor Prophets call into question the first assumption. The existence of a Hebrew source text that was different from the MT is a possibility not to be dismissed. The other two possible assumptions relate to the way that the Greek translator went about the task of translation and must therefore be addressed by means of the translation tendencies of the LXX Minor Prophets in general and the Book of Amos in particular. Two questions are therefore required concerning the translation tendencies of the LXX Minor Prophets. They are: (1) was the LXX translator prone to making multiple mistakes such as those suggested for LXX Amos 9:12? and (2) did the translator of the LXX freely adapt the source text for theological purposes?

---

[12]"Prophetic Interpretation in the Septuagint," *BIOSCS* 12 (1979): 17–18.

[13]Ibid. See also W. Rudolph, *Joel, Amos, Obadja, Jona,* KAT XIII/2 (Gütersloh: Gerd Mohn, 1971), 279.

LXX Amos 9:12 and the Translation Technique of the LXX Minor Prophets

In general, the answer to the question of whether the translator was capable of mistakes such as those proposed for Amos 9:12 is in the affirmative. If taken individually, each of the three differences between the MT of Amos 9:12 and its LXX translation is a credible example of erroneous translation of a kind that is not infrequent in the LXX. Taken as a whole, however, the presence of three such translational errors within such close proximity is unparalleled within the remainder of the LXX Minor Prophets. Instead, the translation of the rest of the LXX Minor Prophets shows that the Greek translator was certainly capable of translating the text of the MT had it been present in the source text. The LXX translated the verb of MT 9:12, *yrš*, successfully in Amos 2:10 and in its other eight occurrences in the Minor Prophets,[14] each time employing the same Greek root *klēronomai*. The translator also accurately rendered the verb *drš* of the retroverted LXX reading in each of its four occurrences in Amos[15] and in its three other occurrences in the Minor Prophets,[16] each time using the Greek verb *ekzētein*. Also, four times in Amos[17] and four other times in the Minor Prophets[18] the LXX translator accurately translated the proper name Edom. The word *'ādām* is correctly rendered in Amos 4:13 and its other twenty-two occurrences in the Book of the Twelve.

Statistics such as those cited above do not require that the translator would have necessarily translated the words *yîrěšû* and *'ĕdôm* correctly had they been present in the Hebrew *Vorlage* of Amos 9:12. A mistaken reading on the part of the translator in this one instance remains a possibility. The statistics, however, do testify to the ability of the translator to render accurately the

---

[14]Hos 9:6; Mic 1:15; Obad 17–21 (5x); and Hab 1:6.

[15]5:4; 5:5; 5:6; and 5:14.

[16]Hos 10:12; Mic 6:8; and Zeph 1:6.

[17]1:6, 9, 11, and 2:1.

[18]Joel 4:19; Obad 1, 8; Mal 1:4.

Hebrew of the MT of 9:12, as well as the presumed Hebrew of the LXX.

The question of whether the translator mistakenly omitted the particle *ʾet* is a more difficult issue to address. Tov cautions that such grammatical particles are methodologically impossible to reconstruct from a translation.[19] He does note, however, that the more literal the translation, the more likely it is that even such particles as these may be reconstructed. It is significant, therefore, that the Old Greek translation of the Minor Prophets is quite literal with regard to the representation of individual Hebrew elements by corresponding Greek elements, even at the risk of awkwardness in the target language. The Hebrew relative clause with *ʾăšer* is a good example. In Amos 9:12, for example, each element of the phrase *ʾăšer niqrāʾ šĕmî ʿălêhem* "over whom my name is called" is rendered in Greek as *eph' hous epikeklētai to onoma mou ep' autous* "over whom my name is called over them."[20] This tendency to represent each Hebrew element by a corresponding Greek element of course does not mean that the translator was required to translate accurately the *nota accusativi* in MT Amos 9:12. Nevertheless, it is worthy of mention that the LXX rendered every other definite direct object preceded by *ʾet* in the MT of Amos by an accusative noun. Therefore, while it is possible that in the case of Amos 9:12 the translator made three consecutive mistakes in the same context, such a conclusion contradicts the evidence of the translation of the rest of the LXX Minor Prophets.

These examples bring us to our second translation technique question: Did the translator freely adapt the source text? Amos 1:3, for example, would appear to be such an exegetical alteration on the part of the translator. The reference there to Damascus's mistreatment of Gilead is supplemented in the LXX by the phrase *tas en gastri echousas* "those who were pregnant in Gilead," an obvious harmonization with the identical phrase in

---

[19]Tov, *The Text-Critical Use of the Septuagint* (Jerusalem: Simor, 1981), 100.

[20]See also LXX 4:7 and the remarks of G. Howard, "Some Notes on LXX Amos," *VT* 20 (1970): 111.

Amos 1:13. As discussed in Chapter Three, however, the LXX reading for Amos 1:3 is attested in a Hebrew manuscript from Qumran Cave V. Such external evidence suggests that the harmonization was present in the Hebrew text which the LXX faithfully translated. Evidence such as this has caused some textual scholars recently to question the assumption that the LXX translators freely altered or supplemented their source text.[21] Nevertheless, variations between the LXX and the MT must still be evaluated on a case by case basis.

Bruce argued that LXX Amos 7:1 is an example of an exegetical translation that is illustrative of Amos 9:12.[22] Following the introductory formula of Amos's vision report, the MT preserves the following text:

wĕhinnēh yôṣēr gōbay bithillat ʿălôt hallāqeš wĕhinnēh leqeš ʾaḥar gizzê hammelek

And behold he was forming locusts at the beginning of the spring growth, and behold this was the growth after the king's mowings.

The LXX text, however, preserves the following reading:

kai idou epigonē akridōn erchomenē heōthinē kai idou brouchos heis Gōg ho basileus

And behold the offspring of locusts were coming at dawn, and behold one grasshopper was Gog, the king.

The verse obviously caused considerable difficulty for either the translator or perhaps for the tradents of the translator's Hebrew *Vorlage*. The translator or copyists had to reckon twice in this text with the *hapax legomenon*, *leqeš*, the first occurrence of which was rendered as "at dawn" and the second which was

---

[21]Aejmelaeus, "What Can we Know about the *Vorlage* of the LXX?" *ZAW* 99 (1987): 87; and E. Ulrich, "The Canonical Process, Textual Criticism and latter Stages in the Composition of the Bible," 286.

[22]Bruce, "Prophetic Interpretation in the Septuagint," 18–19.

apparently read as *yeleq,* "grasshopper." The word *ʾaḥar* "after" is represented in the LXX as if it were *ʾeḥad* "one," the result of a *daleth / resh* confusion. The other difficult word was the term *gizzê* "mowings," which occurs only four times in the Hebrew Bible and only here in the Book of the Twelve.[23] It is represented in the LXX by the name Gog.

Bruce viewed these differences to be the result of an elaborate interpretative tradition which identified Amos's locusts with Gog's army as described in Ezekiel. This identification was mediated by the comparison in Joel 1–2 between a plague of locusts and an invading army from the north (Joel 2:20). By way of Joel, Amos's locusts are identified with Gog's army as depicted in Ezekiel. Although the interpretative tradition that Bruce identifies is plausible, it is not clear why the changes described above must be assumed to have taken place at the translational stage and not at the stage of the transmission of the Hebrew *Vorlage* of the LXX. Because of the rare and technical vocabulary, the meaning of Amos 7.1 would have presented challenges for Hebrew scribes as it does for modern commentators. F. Andersen and D. N. Freedman conclude that the LXX text "points to a [Hebrew] *Vorlage* already corrupt or else to great freedom in interpreting an obscure text allegorically and apocalyptically."[24] Such freedom, however, is elsewhere absent in the LXX translation of the Minor Prophets.

Ironically, Bruce himself provided evidence that counters his assumption that the changes in LXX Amos 7:1 were made by the translator. In order to strengthen his argument, Bruce cites a similar occurrence of the word "Gog" in the LXX version of Balaam's oracle in Num 24:7. There the MT reading *ʾāgag* "Agag," the king of Amalek, is represented in the LXX as *Gōg.* In order to prove that the Greek reading is not merely a Greek transcription

---

[23]The verb *gzz,* "to shear," occurs 15 times in the Hebrew Bible and at Mic 1:16 and Nah 1:12 in the Book of the Twelve. At those two places the LXX translates the verb correctly.

[24]F. Andersen and D. N. Freedman, *Amos,* The Anchor Bible Vol. 24A (New York: Doubleday, 1989), 741–42.

of the Hebrew name ʿ*ōg* (Og, king of Bashan), Bruce cites the reading of Num 24:7 in the Samaritan Pentateuch, which like the LXX has the name "Gog," the eschatological enemy mentioned in Ezekiel. The significance of the Samaritan version's reading is not, as Bruce concluded, that it confirms the presence of the figure of Gog in the LXX of Num 24:7, but rather that it shows that the transformation attested in the LXX was also present in a *Hebrew* manuscript. The reading of Num 24:7 in the Samaritan Pentateuch, therefore, supports the possibility that a similar change took place in the Hebrew *Vorlage* of LXX Amos 7:1.

Contrary to Bruce's argument, therefore, there is no conclusive evidence that the LXX translator of the Minor Prophets freely altered the text of his Hebrew *Vorlage* according to exegetical traditions current in his intellectual milieu. Another argument weighing against the free rendering of Amos 9:12 is the difficulty of the LXX reading. Specifically, the verb "to seek" has no object. As will be demonstrated below, the absence of a pronominal object is more acceptable in the syntax of Classical Hebrew than in Greek. It does not seem likely that a translator would change the subject, the object, and the verb of the *Vorlage* but would not supply as much as a pronoun as a direct object for the new reading. Such would represent a strangely limited kind of translational freedom.

The results of the study of the translation tendencies of the LXX Minor Prophets suggest that the reading of LXX Amos 9:12 was not due to either a mistaken or tendentious translation. This conclusion leads to the possibility that the variant reading reflects the translator's Hebrew *Vorlage*. In order to assess this possibility, it is necessary to reconstruct a Hebrew text underlying LXX Amos 9:12.

The Hebrew Vorlage of LXX Amos 9:12

According to the methodology described by Tov for retroverting Greek texts into Hebrew, reliable retroversions should: (1) be based on sound Greek-Hebrew equivalences; (2) be textually probable; and (3) be linguistically plausible.[25] The LXX of Amos 9:12 poses no problems with regard to the first criteria of sound Greek-Hebrew equivalences. The Greek clause *opōs ekzētēsousin oi kataloipoi tōn anthrōpōn* retroverts easily into the Hebrew *lĕmaʿan yidrĕšû šĕʾērît ʾādām*. The Greek-Hebrew equivalent *ekzētein=daraš* is used for all seven occurrences of the word in the Book of the Twelve, including four times in Amos. The Greek word *anthrōpos* renders *ʾādām* at the only other occurrence of that word in Amos (4:13), and also in its twenty-two other occurrences in the Minor Prophets. Likewise, the Greek word *kataloipos* is used throughout the LXX Minor Prophets to translate the Hebrew word *šĕʾērît*.

Tov's second criterion of textual probability means that the existence of the retroverted variant should be explainable by normal processes of textual change. In Amos 9:12 three textual changes occurred. The first is the change from either an original *yyršw* to *ydršw* or vice versa. Tov has stated that reconstructions based on differences due to similar letters and involving words remote in meaning should be considered as highly reliable retroversions.[26]

The second textual difference attested in LXX Amos 9:12 involves the presence or absence of a *matres lectiones* in the Hebrew root *ʾdm*. Andersen and Freedman note that Edom is never spelled defectively in the Hebrew Bible. They suggest, however, that it could have possibly been spelled defectively at the time of the LXX translation.[27] Tov has argued that the development of Hebrew orthography makes it likely that the Hebrew *Vorlage* of the LXX was in general more defectively written than the MT, and that for this reason *matres lectiones* may often be disregarded for purposes of textual reconstruction.[28]

The third textual difference in the LXX of Amos 9:12 concerns the presence or absence of the particle *ʾet* in the LXX

---

[25] *The Text-Critical Use of the Septuagint*, 101–25.

[26] Ibid., 132.

[27] Andersen and Freedman, *Amos*, 890.

[28] Tov, *The Text-Critical Use of the Septuagint*, 206.

Vorlage. The presence of this particle should not have allowed the translator to render the text as he did. Since this particle seems to be faithfully translated elsewhere in the LXX Minor Prophets, I conclude that it was not present in the source text of LXX 9:12.[29]

Tov's third criterion for retroverted variants is that of linguistic plausibility. The most serious question is whether the LXX phrase "that the remnant of humanity may seek" is a grammatically acceptable reading since it lacks a direct object for the verb "to seek."[30] The context of Amos 9:11–12 is a series of statements by Yahweh in the first person, which indicates that the pronominal object "me" is to be expected as the object of the verb (i.e., "that the remnant of humanity might seek [me]"). In Biblical Hebrew, pronominal objects are frequently omitted elliptically when such objects can be supplied from the immediate context.[31] The Greek versions of Amos had no difficulty supplying the object of the verb from the context, either by adding as an object the word "me" in the case of the Lucianic manuscripts or "the Lord" as supplied in Codex Alexandrinus and related manuscripts. Based on the evidence of the translation technique of LXX Amos and upon the methodological guidelines of Tov, I conclude that it is methodologically sound to reconstruct the Hebrew *Vorlage* of LXX Amos 9:12 as a consonantal Hebrew text that read *lmʿn ydršw šʾryt ʾdm.*

---

[29]For a suggested example of the secondary insertion of the accusative marker *ʾet* into a biblical text, see the comments of I. Willi-Plein on the text of Amos 4:11 in *Vorformen der Schriftexegese innerhalb des Alten Testaments*, BZAW 123 (Berlin: Walter de Gruyter, 1971), 29.

[30]The question of whether the phrase *šʾryt ʾdm* could be the subject of the plural verb *yidrēšû* is answered by Amos 1:8, where a similar phrase *šĕʾērît pĕlištîm* also takes a plural verb. The similar phrases "remnant of my people" in Zeph 2:9 and "remnant of Israel" in Zeph 3:13 also take plural verbs.

[31]*Gesenius' Hebrew Grammar*, ed. E. Kautzsch and A. E. Cowley (Oxford: Clarendon Press, 2nd ed. 1910), para. 117f.

Evaluation of the Hebrew Vorlage of LXX Amos 9:12

The previous discussion has sought to reconstruct the Hebrew text lying behind the LXX translation of Amos 9:12. The next question to be addressed concerns how to evaluate this variant reading and its relationship to the text of the MT. The question of the evaluation of these variants is more difficult to answer than has often been assumed. The difference between the MT and the LXX concerning the phrase *š'ryt 'dm* is one of vocalization rather than textual variation. The phrase may be vocalized to read either the accusative [*'et*] *šĕ'ērît 'ĕdôm* "remnant of Edom" of the MT or the nominative *šĕ'ērît 'ādām* "remnant of humanity" of the LXX. Both of these possible vocalizations are dependent upon the text of the main verb. This verb was either *yyršw* or *ydršw*. The difference between the two verbs is the whether the second letter was a quiescent *yod* or a *daleth*, letters which are graphically similar in some ancient Hebrew hands.

Both textual readings of the main verb of Amos 9:12, *yidrĕšû* and *yîrĕšû*, pose difficulties for their respective contexts. The difficulty with the LXX reading *yidrĕšû* is, as mentioned above, the omission of a direct object, although such an omission is not infrequent in Biblical Hebrew when the object can be identified from the context. The MT reading *yîrĕšû*, however, has just the opposite problem of having no clearly identified subject. Some scholars conclude that the antecedent of "they will possess" is the restored "booth of David" of 9:11, i.e., the renewed Davidic dynasty.[32] Another possibility is that the phrase "all the nations over whom my name is called" is the subject of the verb, with the *waw* being translated as a resumptive conjunction ("they shall dispossess the remnant of Edom, *even* all the nations . . .").[33]

---

[32]Among those who identify the subject of "they will possess" as the renewed Davidic dynasty are Hammershaimb, *Amos*, 141; Paul, *Amos*, 291; M. Polley, *Amos and the Davidic Empire* (New York: Oxford University Press, 1989), 70–74; Rudolph, *Joel, Amos, Obadja, Jona*, 281; and Wolff, *Joel and Amos*, 353.

[33]Andersen and Freedman, *Amos*, 890.

Wolff contended that neither alternative was sufficient to hide the secondary nature of MT 9:12 in its present context.[34] Another scholar to question the authenticity of 9:12 in its context is R. Coote.[35] Coote argues that the oracle of Amos 9:11–15 takes its inspiration from the festival of *Sukkoth,* particularly the reference to the booth of David in 9:11 and the agricultural imagery of abundant grain and wine in 9:13–15. Coote particularly objects to the reference to the dispossession of Edom and the nations because it "comes close to betraying the original intent" of the oracle, which is to proclaim Yahweh's imponderable mercy.[36]

The work of Nogalski provides the most recent treatment of the redactional status of Amos 9:12. On the basis of a thorough analysis of Amos 9:11–15, Nogalski concludes that Amos 9:12a has little connection either grammatically or thematically to its immediate context.[37] Nogalski argues that the literary horizon of Amos 9:12a lies beyond the boundaries of the Book of Amos and anticipates the denunciation of Edom in Obadiah, particularly Obad 17–21. Amos 9:12a is therefore concluded to be a secondary addition from the redactional hand that united the Minor Prophets into a single "Book" of the Twelve.[38]

Before evaluating Nogalski's conclusions, it is important to note that neither Wolff, Coote, nor Nogalski considers the relationship between the LXX reading of Amos 9:12, the context of Amos 9, and the Book of Amos as a whole. There are four reasons why the LXX reading may be considered to be appropriate to this context. First, the reference to the "remnant of humanity" that will seek Yahweh fits with the image in Amos 9:8–10 of a remnant who will survive Yahweh's "sifting" of Israel "as with a sieve" (Amos 9:9). Second, LXX Amos 9:12 universalizes the worship ("seeking") of Yahweh to include the

---

[34]*Joel and Amos,* 352–53.

[35]*Amos Among the Prophets* (Philadelphia: Fortress Press, 1981), 122.

[36]Ibid., 123.

[37]*Literary Precursors,* 108–109.

[38]Ibid., 113–16.

remnant of humanity "and all the nations over whom [Yahweh's] name is called."[39] The universal perspective of LXX 9:12 is similar to the perspective of 9:7, which compares Yahweh's intervention on the behalf of Israel with similar actions toward the Ethiopians, the Philistines, and the Arameans.

The third reason for concluding that LXX Amos 9:12 is appropriate to its literary context within the Book of Amos is the use of vocabulary that is familiar to the book as a whole. The verb *drš*, "to seek" is found four times in Amos, all in chapter five (5:4, 5, 6, and 14). The term *šĕʾērît* "remnant" is found at two other places in the book, at Amos 1:8 ("remnant of the Philistines") and 5:15 ("remnant of Joseph").[40] The occurrence of both *drš* and *šĕʾērît* in the same context of Amos 5:14–15 calls attention to an observation of Wolff about the relationship between these verses and Amos 9. Wolff noted that the suggestion in 5:14–15 of a possible remnant of those who "seek" the good is reiterated in the implied remnant of the sieve metaphor Amos 9:9–10.[41] The vocabulary of Amos 9:12 extends the theme of a pious remnant to include "the nations over whom Yahweh's name is called."[42]

---

[39]Mal 1:11 uses the similar language of "name theology" to portray universal worship of Yahweh. "For from the rising of the sun to its setting, great is my name among the nations; and in every place incense is offered to my name and a pure offering; for great is my name among the nations."

[40]The word *ʾādām* of LXX 9:12 also occurs in Amos at 4:13. This verse is widely suspected, however, of being a post-exilic addition. It is therefore difficult to determine the chronological relationship between 4:13 and 9:12. For another example of the use of the verb *drš* and the noun *ʾādām* in an eighth century prophetic collection, see Mic 6:8 ("He has declared to you, o mortal [*ʾādām*], what is good and what Yahweh seeks [*drš*] from you.").

[41]*Joel and Amos*, 347.

[42]If the phrase "nations over whom my name is called" refers to the nations of Amos 1–2, then another connection between 9:12 and the rest of Amos is established. See Polly, *Amos and the Davidic Empire*, 73. See also Wolff's comments about the similar perspective toward the relationship

Finally, LXX Amos 9:12 appears to be appropriate to its context because it adds another element of the *Sukkoth* tradition to the imagery in verses 11–15, namely, the theme of the pilgrimage of the nations to celebrate the festival and to worship Yahweh in Jerusalem. Such a pilgrimage is described in Zech 14:16: "Then all who survive from all the nations who came against Jerusalem shall go up year after year to worship the King, Yahweh of hosts, and to keep the festival of *Sukkoth*." The references in Amos 9:11–12 to the restored "booth" of David and to the remnant of humanity seeking Yahweh create a montage of festal, royal, and universalistic themes similar to Zech 14:16.[43] These four arguments do not disprove the conclusion that Amos 9:12 is a secondary redactional addition to the Book of Amos. They do, however, support the conclusion that, unlike the MT text of Amos 9:12, the LXX reading is literarily well integrated into its immediate context.

Although the MT reading of 9:12 appears to be intrusive to the context of Amos 9:11–15, it does have significant ties, as Nogalski and others have noted, to the larger context of the Book of the Twelve, particularly the succeeding book of Obadiah. The MT's reading "that they may possess the remnant of Edom" not only links the end of Amos with the address to Edom in Obad 1, but also with the fivefold repetition of the verb *yrš* in Obad 17–21. The presence of a verbal linkage between Amos and Obadiah in the MT causes no problem for the LXX reading of 9:12, however. In the LXX sequence, Micah, not Obadiah, follows the Book of Amos. The catchword principle of association is preserved, however, in the LXX sequence of Joel and Obadiah by the reference to Edom in Joel 4:19. In other words, the catchword that is absent in the LXX of Amos 9:12 is present in

---

between the nations and Yahweh in Amos 9:7 and Amos 1–2 (*Joel and Amos*, 346).

[43]For an intepretation of the booth of David in Amos 9:11 as representing Jerusalem, see Andersen and Freedman, *Amos*, 889. A similar portrayal of the nations flowing to Jerusalem occurs in the Book of Micah (4:1–4), which follows Amos in the LXX sequence of the Book of the Twelve.

Joel 4:19, which is contiguous with the Book of Obadiah in the LXX Book of the Twelve.

Summary

The preceding treatment of the text of Amos 9:12 agrees with Nogalski and others that the primary context of the MT text of Amos 9:12 is the larger literary horizon of the MT Book of the Twelve rather than the surrounding literary unit of Amos 9:11–15. I would disagree, however, with Nogalski's conclusion that the MT text of Amos 9:12 is a redactional insertion designed to unify the books of Amos and Obadiah. Rather, based upon the evidence cited above, I would argue that the MT of Amos 9:12 is a redactional alteration of the Hebrew text that is preserved in the LXX. The alteration required only the changing of a single letter, from *ydršw* to *yyršw*, and the revocalization of *ʾdm* from *ʾādām* to *ʾĕdôm*.[44] Rather than being a textual corruption, however, this change instead represents an ingenious scribal/redactional linkage of Amos and Obadiah that is based upon a recognition of an exegetical connection between the text of Amos and the Book of Obadiah.[45] As with other examples cited in Chapter Three above, the textual evidence of the LXX appears to preserve a concrete example of the phenomenon of inner-biblical exegesis within the textual transmission of the Book of the Twelve.[46]

---

[44]The accusative marker *ʾet* and the plene spelling of Edom are already present in the Hebrew scroll from Wadi Murabba'at (ca. 100–150 CE). P. Benoit, J. T. Milik, and R. de Vaux, *Les Grottes de Murabba'at*, DJD II (Oxford: Clarendon Press, 1961), 183.

[45]For analogous examples of textual variants that are based upon a combination of an interchange of graphically similar letters and different vocalizations of the consonantal text, see S. Talmon, "DSIa as a Witness to Ancient Exegesis of the Book of Isaiah," *ASTI* 1 (1962): 62–72.

[46]The creation of a new textual reading by means of substitution of letters and paranomasia (i.e., *ʾĕdôm/ʾādām*) is similar to exegetical techniques employed in the Qumran *pesharim*. See for example the comparison between the exegetical methods of the Habakkuk Pesher and dream intepretation in

The absence of a catchword linkage between Amos 9:12 and Obadiah in the Hebrew text of Amos that is now preserved only in the LXX is best explained by the conclusion that the books of Amos and Obadiah were not contiguous in that Hebrew text of the Book of the Twelve. The books of Joel and Obadiah are contiguous in the LXX Book of the Twelve, however, and these books are connected in the LXX sequence by the same catchword linkage as the MT of Amos 9:12, i.e., the proper noun Edom (Joel 4:19). The catchword linkage uniting the arrangement of Joel and Obadiah in the LXX calls attention to other literary and thematic ties between the books of Joel and Obadiah in the LXX Book of the Twelve. The literary unity and coherence of the sequence of the books of Joel and Obadiah further suggest that the textual alteration that is proposed for the MT of Amos 9:12 may indeed be directly dependent upon the catchword relationship between Joel 4:19 and Obad 1. This possibility will now be explored by means of a further demonstration of the unity and distinctiveness of the edition of the Book of the Twelve that is preserved in the LXX.

The Literary Unity of the LXX Book of the Twelve

The textual distinctions between the LXX and the MT of Amos 9:12 suggest that the two arrangements of the Book of the Twelve attested by these manuscript traditions were based upon different conceptions of how the Minor Prophets were to be ordered. Previous scholars have carefully and thoroughly identified the chronological, verbal, and thematic ties that bind the MT Book of the Twelve into an intelligible literary unity. An examination of the literary coherence of the LXX Book of the Twelve will demonstrate a similar unity behind this manuscript tradition. Since, however, the final six books of the Minor Prophets, Nahum, Habakkuk, Zephaniah, Haggai, Zechariah, and Malachi follow the same sequence in both the MT and the LXX

L. Silberman, "Unriddling the Riddle: A Study in the Structure and Language of the Habakkuk Pesher (1QpHab)," *RQ* 3 (1961–62): 323–64.

manuscript traditions, attention here will be given primarily to the order of the first six books in the LXX arrangement of the Minor Prophets. Further, because the text of Amos 9:12 has called attention to the possible connections between Joel and Obadiah, special attention will be given to the position of these two books in the LXX arrangement of the Twelve.

Hosea-Amos-Micah

Schneider has argued that the sequence of the first three books of the Minor Prophets as they are preserved in the LXX represents the original collection of prophetic books at the heart of the Book of the Twelve.[47] Beyond the common chronological background of the events of the eighth century, the sequence Hosea-Amos-Micah may be explained on the basis of: (1) length of books, with the longest book first and the shortest third; (2) content, with Hosea 1–3 serving as a frontispiece to the larger collection and Micah 7 forming an appropriate conclusion; and (3) geographical orientation, beginning with a northern prophet in the north, followed by a southern prophet in the north, and thirdly a southern prophet in the south.[48]

D. N. Freedman has supplied additional arguments for an original collection of Hosea-Amos-Micah based on the chronological information contained in their respective superscriptions.[49] The superscription of Hosea provides a chronological framework for all three books. The Israelite and Judean kings named in Hos 1:1 (Uzziah, Jotham, Ahaz, and Hezekiah of Judah, and Jeroboam of Israel) are also named in the combined superscriptions of Amos (Uzziah and Jeroboam, Amos 1:1) and Micah (Jotham, Ahaz, and Hezekiah, Mic 1:1). The information contained within the superscriptions unites and organizes the three books under the rubric of chronology and also explains the position of Hosea at the head of the collection.

---

[47]"The Unity of the Book of the Twelve," 36–38.

[48]Ibid., 42–43.

[49]Freedman, "Headings in the Books of the Eighth Century Prophets," *AUSS* 25 (1987): 9–26.

The prophecy of Micah concludes the collection and unifies it by applying the historical lessons of the fate of Samaria (Mic 1:1, 5–7) to Judah and Jerusalem (Mic 1:5; 3:9–12). Freedman suggests a date for a common editing of an early form of these three books, plus Isaiah 1–39, in the time of Hezekiah.[50] The literary, thematic, and chronological ties that Schneider and Freedman have identified explain well the arrangement of these books in the LXX.

The conclusions of Schneider and Freedman that the LXX preserves the original sequence of Hosea, Amos, and Micah when these three books were first collected in a compendious work are both supported and extended in the work of Nogalski. Nogalski argues for the redactional integration of the books of Hosea, Amos, and Micah within the context of a Deuteronomistic collection of prophetical writings that included these three books plus the Book of Zephaniah.[51] Nogalski notes how the superscription of Zephaniah overlaps the chronological information of Mic 1:1 by the mention of the name Hezekiah, while also extending the chronological framework of the collection to include the reign of Josiah (Zeph 1:1). Whether the books of Hosea, Amos, and Micah were not collected together until the formation of the Deuteronomistic corpus as proposed by Nogalski,[52] or whether an earlier collection of the three eighth century prophets was supplemented by the later addition of the Book of Zephaniah, as Schneider and Freedman would argue, the arguments for the coherence, cohesiveness, and originality of

---

[50]Ibid., 26. Schneider (41–42) agrees with a Hezekian date for this collection.

[51]For arguments similar to those of Schneider and Freedman concerning the unity of the Hosea-Amos-Micah sequence, see Nogalski, *Literary Precursors*, 137–44.

[52]For other proposals of a sixth century, Deuteronomistic origin for the superscriptions of these books plus Jeremiah, see Wolff, *Dodekapropheton 1. Hosea*, BKAT 14/1 (Neukirchen-Vluyn: Neukirchener Verlag, 1965), 3–6; and T. Lescow, "Redaktionsgeschichtliche Analyse von Micha 1–5," *ZAW* 84 (1972): 61–64.

the Hosea-Amos-Micah sequence preserved in the LXX remain quite convincing.

Joel-Obadiah

Although the LXX sequence of Joel and Obadiah has received far less attention from scholars than that of the eighth century prophets Hosea, Amos, and Micah, careful study shows that these two books possess a high degree of literary and thematic affinity. Although scholars have long recognized certain literary relationships between these books, their arrangement in the LXX manuscript traditions has not been thought to reflect a unified collection. If, however, one is willing to suspend the assumption of the priority, if not the privilege, of the MT, a different picture of the position of these two books in the LXX emerges. Careful review of the books of Joel and Obadiah will show that the books bear literary ties not only to one another, but also to those books that precede and follow them in the LXX Minor Prophets.

The connection between Joel 4:19 and Obadiah 1 has already been noted above. Other parallels are present within the texts of Joel and Obadiah, however, that also serve to give a sense of unity to these two distinct books. The literary relationships between Joel and Obadiah have been thoroughly reviewed in the recent work of S. Bergler[53] and have also been frequently cited in the history of scholarship on these two books. It is surprising, therefore, that scholars have not been receptive to the idea they were transmitted together in a contiguous arrangement in ancient Hebrew manuscripts. The evidence for just such a practice, however, is quite strong.

Bergler, for example, has listed no less than fourteen examples of verbal ties between the books of Joel and Obadiah, each of which he attributes to the literary dependence of Joel upon Obadiah.[54] Since several of Bergler's arguments for literary relationships between Joel and Obadiah depend more upon the

---

[53]*Joel als Schriftinterpret* (Frankfurt am Main/Bern/New York: Peter Lang, 1988), 295–327.

[54]Ibid., 321–22.

weight of the cumulative evidence of literary ties between the two books than upon direct linguistic evidence, many of his fourteen examples bear only the slightest hint of evidence of any literary dependence. Some of the arguments are in fact based upon the common usage of a single word.[55] I will therefore discuss here only those parallels that may be considered to be the strongest examples of literary connections between the books of Joel and Obadiah.

The most convincing example of a literary parallel between Joel and Obadiah is to be found in Joel 3:5b and Obad 17a, 18b.

Joel 3:5b	Obad 17a, 18b
kî běhar ṣiyyôn	(17) *ûběhar ṣiyyôn*
ûbîrûšālayim	
tihěyeh pělêtâ	*tihěyeh pělêtâ*
kaʾăšer ʾāmar yhwh	
ûbaśśěrîdîm	(18) *wělōʾ yihěyeh śārîd*
ʾăšer yhwh qōrēʾ	*lěbêt ʿeśāw*

The phrase *kaʾăšer ʾāmar yhwh* "just as Yahweh has said" appears to be a citation formula.[56] The wording of Obad 17–18 makes it the likely source for such a citation.[57] Bergler concludes that Joel 3:5 has adopted the wording of Obad 17 and has added the words "and in Jerusalem" in parallel to "on Mount Zion," followed by the citation formula.[58] The promise of survivors (*śěrîdîm*) in Joel 3:5 creates a contrast with the plight of Edom in Obadiah 18, for whom there will be no survivor (*śārîd*).

---

[55]See the critique by Nogalski, *Redactional Processes in the Book of the Twelve*, BZAW 218 (Berlin: Walter de Gruyter, 1993), 46, n. 118.

[56]Wolff, *Joel and Amos*, 5, 68.

[57]Cf., however M. Fishbane (*Biblical Interpretation in Ancient Israel*, 289 n. 53), who identifies "just as Yahweh has spoken" as a citation formula, but interprets it as a citation of an anonymous source rather that the Book of Obadiah.

[58]Bergler, *Joel als Schriftinterpret*, 301.

According to Bergler, Joel 4:17 also contains verbal ties with the Book of Obadiah.[59] The words "mountain of my holiness" in Joel 4:17 also describe Zion in Obad 16. The phrase "and Jerusalem will be holy" supplies the only two words (*wĕhāyâ qōdeš*) in Obad 17a that were not cited in Joel 3:5a. Finally, Joel's promise that "strangers (*zērîm*) will not pass through [Jerusalem] again" provides the only use of the noun *zērîm* in Joel and echoes the description of the looting of Jerusalem by *zērîm* in Obad 11. According to Bergler, Joel 4:17 echoes Obadiah's promise of refuge in Zion as a contrast to the description of the plundering of Jerusalem given in Obad 11.

A third example of literary parallels between Joel and Obadiah has to do with Joel's description of the offenses committed by the cities of the Phoenician and Philistine coastlands against Judah.[60] These offenses and the punishment awaiting those regions are again described in language that echoes Obadiah's denunciation of Edom. Joel 4:3 employs the phrase "they cast lots (*yaddû gôrāl*) for my people," echoing Obad 11, "they casts lots (*yaddû gôrāl*) for Jerusalem."[61] Joel 4:4 and 4:7 repeat Yahweh's promise that Phoenicia and Philistia's punishment will resemble their own deeds ("I will return your deeds upon your heads"). Identical language (*gĕmulkā yāšûb bĕrō'šekā* "he will return your deed upon your head") is addressed to Edom in Obad 15. Bergler concludes that Joel interprets Obadiah's denunciation of Edom typologically and applies it to the coastal regions' offenses against Judah during his own time. Just as Obadiah singles out Edom from among the nations to be judged on the Day of Yahweh, so Joel singles out the Phoenician and Philistines coastlands for judgment.[62]

---

[59]Ibid., 305.

[60]Bergler, *Joel als Schriftinterpret*, 325–26.

[61]The phrase *yaddû gôrāl* occurs elsewhere only at Nah 3:10.

[62]Bergler, *Joel als Schriftinterpret*, 315. For the argument that in the post-exilic period Edom came to represent the quintessential enemy of Israel, see B. Cresson, "The Condemnation of Edom in Post-Exilic Judaism," in *The Use of the Old Testament in the New and Other Essays: Studies in Honor of William*

A fourth common feature of the books of Joel and Obadiah is the use of the Day of Yahweh tradition.[63] Both books describe the Day of Yahweh as imminent and as a day of judgment against all nations (Joel 4:14; Obad 15). Both also single out particular nations (Edom, Phoenicia/Philistia) for judgment. Both books contain the element of the call of the nations to battle (Joel 4:9, 11; Obad 1). The use of the Day of Yahweh tradition shows that Joel and Obadiah share thematic as well as linguistic parallels.

Bergler mounts an extensive argument for Joel's dependence upon and conscious employment of Obadiah. Literary dependence, however, is a difficult claim to prove conclusively. Alternative explanations often present themselves, such as the common use of shared traditions[64] or the harmonizing tendencies of a common redactor or tradent.[65] Even if dependence can be demonstrated, the direction of the borrowing may be ambiguous.[66] A thorough demonstration of literary dependence, however, is not essential to the conclusion that an ancient redactor would have recognized the linguistic and thematic relationships between the books of Joel and Obadiah and thus collected them as a contiguous unit within a collection of prophetic books. The presence of shared language that could serve as *Stichwörter* for an ancient editor, regardless of the presence or direction of literary dependence, is sufficient to explain the juxtaposition of Joel and Obadiah in the LXX Book

---

Franklin Stinespring, ed. J. M. Efird (Durham, NC: Duke University Press, 1972), 125–48.

[63]Bergler, *Joel als Schriftinterpret*, 315.

[64]Wolff (*Joel and Amos*, 81), for example, explains the parallels between Joel 4:17 and Obad 16 as a part of "the cultic language of the time."

[65]For this explanation of the parallels between Joel and Obadiah, see P. Weimar, "Obadja: Eine redaktionskritische Analyse," *BN* 27 (1985): 94–99; and Nogalski, 156.

[66]Rudolph (*Joel, Amos, Obadja, Jona*, 73) contended that the literary dependency between Joel 3:5 and Obad 17 was the opposite of that argued by Bergler.

of the Twelve. Schneider and others, for example, have explained the consecutive arrangement of Amos and Obadiah in the MT on the basis of the single reference to Edom in Amos 9:12.[67] Following Schneider's argumentation, therefore, the reference to Edom in Joel 4:19 ("Edom will become a desolate wilderness on account of the violence against the children of Judah") is sufficient to explain its connection with the oracle against Edom that comprises the whole of Obadiah.[68] Bergler's demonstration of the numerous other connections between Joel and Obadiah strengthens the argument for the coherence and cohesiveness of their contiguous arrangement within the manuscript tradition of the Hebrew *Vorlage* of the LXX.

At this point it is helpful to make a comparison between the argument of Nogalski concerning the literary parallels between Joel and Obadiah and the conclusions of the present study. Although Nogalski is critical of some of Bergler's arguments for the literary dependence of Joel upon Obadiah, he accepts Bergler's demonstration of the many literary and thematic parallels between the two books. Nogalski, however, attributes these parallels to the hand of the common redactors or tradents who incorporated both Joel and Obadiah into the Book of the Twelve.[69] Nogalski argues that the books of Joel and Obadiah were composed specifically for their positions within the MT Book of the Twelve and therefore had no prior transmission history outside of the group who incorporated the books into the Book of the Twelve.[70]

The present study agrees with Nogalski on two points, namely, that the books of Joel and Obadiah circulated together within a common transmission circle and that they entered the

---

[67]Schneider, "The Unity of the Book of the Twelve," 96–97. Cf. Ruth 1:1 ("in the days when the judges judged . . .") for a similar verbal linkage between Ruth and the Book of Judges.

[68]See especially Obad 10, "on account of the violence against your brother Jacob."

[69]*Redactional Processes*, 46–47.

[70]Ibid., 276–77.

collection of the Minor Prophets at the same time. I disagree with
Nogalski, however, that Joel and Obadiah necessarily entered the
Book of the Twelve in the positions which they occupy in the
MT arrangement. I have already discussed the internal
relationships between Joel and Obadiah that would support the
authenticity of their sequence in the LXX arrangement of the
Twelve. Two other sets of literary relationships support the
argument that Joel and Obadiah entered the Minor Prophets
collection in the sequence in which they occur in the LXX
textual tradition. These are: (1) the literary relationships
between Joel, Obadiah, and the books of Jonah, Nahum, and
Habakkuk which follow them in the LXX; and (2) the
relationship between Joel and Obadiah and the books of Hosea,
Amos, and Micah which precede them in the LXX sequence.

Joel-Obadiah and Nahum-Habakkuk

The argument for the literary unity of the LXX Book of the
Twelve is strengthened by the literary affinities that the books of
Joel and Obadiah share with one another and with the books that
follow them in the LXX arrangement of the Twelve. Based on
the arguments in Chapter Four above, however, the Book of
Jonah, which directly follows Joel and Obadiah in the LXX,
should be treated separately from the other sequential books in
the LXX Minor Prophets. In Chapter Four, I argued that the
textual evidence of 4QXII[a] supports other literary evidence that
the Book of Jonah was the final book to enter the Book of the
Twelve and that it originally was appended to the end of the
collection following the Book of Malachi.

The conclusion that the position of Jonah in 4QXII[a] is earlier
than its position in the LXX is strengthened by two features of
the LXX arrangement of the Book of the Twelve. First, a
negative argument from the LXX arrangement of the Twelve is
that the books of Jonah and Obadiah, although contiguous in
both the LXX and the MT, share no verbal ties with one another
and only the broad thematic connection of Israel's relationship

to the nations.[71] Second, and more positively, the books of Joel and Obadiah do possess significant literary parallels with the books of Nahum and Habakkuk. These parallels indicate that the books of Joel and Obadiah may have been adjoined to the books of Nahum and Habakkuk prior to the inclusion of the Book of Jonah within the Minor Prophets collection. For these reasons, the relationship between the Book of Jonah and the books of Joel and Obadiah will be examined following a treatment of the ties between Joel and Obadiah and the books of Nahum and Habakkuk.

When one removes the Book of Jonah from consideration, a relatively high degree of literary affinity exists between the books of Joel and Obadiah and the Book of Nahum. These affinities range in nature from verbal parallels to thematic ties, and include a possible unifying redactional gloss as well. Three examples of verbal parallels exist between the books of Joel, Obadiah, and Nahum. These verbal parallels are: (1) the only three occurrences of the phrase *yaddû gôrāl* "they cast lots" in the Hebrew Bible, which are found in Nah 3:10, Joel 4:3, and Obad 11; (2) the elsewhere unattested phrase *kōl pānîm qibběṣû pāʾrûr* "all their faces grow pale(?)," found in Nah 2:11 and Joel 2:6; and (3) the use of the metaphor of stubble (*qaš*) consumed (*ʾkl*) by fire to describe the destruction of an advancing army, which is found in Nah 1:10, Joel 2:5, and Obad 18.

Beyond these linguistic affinities, the books of Joel, Obadiah, and Nahum share some common themes as well. K. Cathcart has concluded, for example, that the divine warrior language of the Day of Yahweh tradition provides the common background for

---

[71]Schneider ("Unity of the Twelve," 98–99) is correct in rejecting the rabbinic argument that Jonah represents the "messenger among the nations" of Obad 1. The messenger of Obad 1 is sent to rouse the nations to war against an enemy of Israel. Jonah, who is not referred to as a messenger, is sent with a message of divine judgment against the city Nineveh. Nogalski (*Redactional Processes*, 270) mentions the presence of the word "lots" in Jonah 1:7 and Obad 11 as a possible catchword, although he justifiably does not give it much weight as a unifying feature.

the linguistic parallels within Joel, Obadiah, and Nahum.[72] Beyond the common theme of the divine warrior motif, the books of Joel, Obadiah, Nahum, and also Habakkuk are united in their emphasis upon the theme of Yahweh's judgment against the nations.

Nogalski has noted further evidence of similar language and themes in the books of Joel, Obadiah, and Nahum and attributes them to the redactional work of a common tradition circle. He connects the use of the locust metaphor to describe Assyria in Nah 3:15–17, for example, with the portrayal of an invading army as a locust plague in Joel 1.[73] On literary critical grounds, Nogalski argues that the locust imagery in Nah 3:15–17 is the result of a redactional gloss that interprets the Assyrian invasion of Israel and Judah in the context of the succession of invasions depicted metaphorically in Joel 1:4. The gloss therefore helped to integrate the books of Joel and Obadiah into the larger context of the Book of the Twelve.

Nogalski indeed argues that the books of Joel, Obadiah, Nahum, and Habakkuk bear sufficient signs of common redaction to conclude that these books most likely entered the Minor Prophets collection at the same time and at the hands of the same tradition circle.[74] Although Nogalski does demonstrate well the unity of the books of Nahum and Habakkuk, the argument that Nahum and Habakkuk were unified by the same redactor(s) who added the books of Joel and Obadiah to the Book of the Twelve appears to exceed the available evidence.[75] Regardless of the

---

[72]"The Divine Warrior and the War of Yahweh in Nahum," in *Biblical Studies in Contemporary Thought*, ed. M. Ward (Somerville, MA: Trinity College Biblical Institute, 1975), 72–76.

[73]*Redactional Processes*, 123–27.

[74]Ibid., 180–81.

[75]For example, Nogalski argues that the primary unifying features between Habakkuk and Joel is the use of agricultural motifs in Hab 3:17 (Ibid., 176–78). Hab 3:17, however, employs vocabulary that is generally distinct from that of the agricultural imagery in Joel 1–2. Further, agricultural imagery is extremely common in the Hebrew Bible, as one

validity of Nogalski's thesis concerning the creation of the books of Joel, Obadiah, Nahum, and Habakkuk by the same redactional hand, the affinities that he observes between these four books nevertheless strengthen the arguments for the unity of the LXX sequence of the Book of the Twelve more so than the arrangement of the MT. For example, if one removes the Book of Jonah, which Nogalski himself considers to be the latest addition to the collection, then the LXX sequence is the closest approximation of the redactional complex of Joel, Obadiah, Nahum, and Habakkuk that is posited by Nogalski. Therefore, although Nogalski's arguments for the redactional unity of Joel, Obadiah, Nahum, and Habakkuk fail to convince the present writer, his observations still call attention to the sequence of these books in the LXX and strengthen the impression of the literary coherence of that sequence.

A final example of the unity and coherence of the LXX sequence of Joel, Obadiah, Nahum, and Habakkuk is found in the evidence of the superscriptions to these books. The superscription to the Book of Joel ("the word of Yahweh which came to Joel, the son of Pethuel") is most similar to the superscriptions of the books of Hosea, Amos, and Micah that directly precede Joel in the LXX order. The superscription to the Book of Obadiah ("the vision of Obadiah") is most similar to the superscription of the Book of Nahum ("An Oracle of Nineveh. The Book of the Vision of Nahum the Elkoshite"), which follows Obadiah in the LXX sequence. The superscriptions to both the Book of Joel and the Book of Obadiah provide the least amount of information among the books of the Minor Prophets and have the greatest appearance of artificiality. It is possible to conclude that each superscription was created to

---

would expect of literature that originated in the social and cultural milieu of the central highlands of Palestine. Such imagery alone, therefore, is insufficient evidence of common redaction.

fit into the position that the books of Joel and Obadiah occupy in the LXX Book of the Twelve.[76]

To summarize, the arguments for the cohesiveness of the LXX placement of the books of Joel and Obadiah are as follows. First, the two books demonstrate a high degree of literary unity with one another. These include catchwords such as Joel 4:19 and Obad 1, 10, the apparent citation of Obad 17–18 in Joel 3:5, and thematic similarities such as the denunciation of specific nations (Edom, Phoenica, Philistia) in the context of universal judgment upon all nations. Second, the books of Joel and Obadiah possess linguistic, thematic, and possibly even redactional ties to the books of Nahum and Habakkuk that follow them in the LXX Book of the Twelve.

Hosea-Amos-Micah and Joel-Obadiah. The appropriateness of the superscriptions of Joel and Obadiah to their context in the LXX arrangement of the Twelve raises the question of the relationship of Joel and Obadiah to the Hosea-Amos-Micah collection that precedes them. Previous studies of the unity of the Book of the Twelve have dealt with these relationships, but only with reference to the sequence of the MT manuscript tradition. On the basis of the MT arrangement, both Schneider and Nogalski have concluded that the books of Joel and Obadiah were deliberately composed to fit into the seams of the Hosea-Amos-Micah collection.[77]

In support of the conclusion of Schneider and Nogalski concerning the originality of the MT placement of the books of Joel and Obadiah, it must be said that the MT arrangement of the Twelve is unified by several literary connections between the

---

[76]Nogalski gives a treatment of each of the superscriptions in Joel, Obadiah, Nahum, and Habakkuk, but only in the context of the MT sequence. Ibid., 277–78. See also G. Tucker, "Prophetic Superscriptions and the Growth of a Canon," *Canon and Authority*, ed. G. W. Coats and B. O. Long (Philadelphia: Fortress Press, 1977), 56–70.

[77]Schneider, "The Book of the Twelve," 84, 97; Nogalski, *Redactional Processes*, 276.

books of Joel and Obadiah and their literary contexts within the seams of the Hosea-Amos-Micah collection. The presence of these literary relationships, however, does not provide conclusive evidence that the position of Joel and Obadiah in the MT is either their original position or the only literarily coherent position of these books among the Minor Prophets. Four distinct arguments may be made against the conclusion that the MT arrangement of Joel and Obadiah is the original arrangement of these books within the Minor Prophets collection. The evidence for the first two of these arguments has already been discussed above. First, the evidence of Amos 9:12 suggests that the MT sequence of Amos and Obadiah was based upon a textual alteration that was itself influenced by the use of the word Edom as a catchword in Joel 4:19 and Obad 1. Second, the ties between the books of Joel and Obadiah and their surrounding contexts in the LXX arrangement of the Twelve demonstrate that the LXX arrangement is a literarily coherent alternative to the MT arrangement of these two books.

Two other arguments call into question the conclusion that the MT sequence of Joel and Obadiah necessarily reflects the original placement of these books in the Minor Prophets collection. First, the argument that verbal correspondences or even shared redactional material between two separate books of the Minor Prophets demand that these books be arranged contiguously must be questioned. There are numerous examples of literary parallels and even evidence of common redaction of books that are not contiguous in any extant textual tradition of the Book of the Twelve. Second, there are numerous literary relationships between the books of Joel and Obadiah and texts within the books of Hosea, Amos, and Micah that are not located in the seams of this collection. These parallels suggest that the books of Joel and Obadiah were composed or edited with a view toward a wider literary horizon than has been previously proposed by those who have focused exclusively upon the MT arrangement of the Book of the Twelve. The arguments against positing the MT arrangement of the Twelve as the original sequence of the collection may be further illustrated by a discussion of the specific literary relationships between Joel, Obadiah, and their surrounding contexts within the MT Book of the Twelve.

Joel and Hosea. The relationship between the books of Joel and Hosea helps to illustrate the arguments against the conclusion that the MT placement of Joel and Obadiah is necessarily the original placement of these books. Schneider argued, for example, that the contrast between the promise of Israel's fertility at the conclusion of Hosea and the description of the despoliation of the land at the beginning of Joel was an intentional design of the author of the Book of Joel.[78] He also noted that the language of Yahweh's promised restoration in Joel 2:19 was similar to that of Hos 2:23–24. Cassuto suggested that the recurrence of the root *šwb* in Hosea 14 and the importance of this root in Joel 2:12 was also a reason for the arrangement of the two books in the MT.[79] These similarities, however, are either quite general, as in the contrast between fertility and desolation, or based on very commonly used language such as the word *šwb*. With regard to the relationship between Joel 2:19 and Hosea 2:23–24, however, it is significant that this example does not occur within the seams of the two books in their arrangement within the MT Book of the Twelve.

Nogalski sought to strengthen the argument that Joel was consciously written for its placement within the MT Book of the Twelve by examining catchwords that reoccur in the both the beginning of Joel and the end of Hosea. The most significant catchwords are found in Hos 14:8, "they will grow *grain* (Joel 1:10); they will flourish like the *vine* (Joel 1:7, 12); his name will be like the *wine* (Joel 1:5) of Lebanon." Nogalski argues on literary-critical grounds that Hos 14:8 is secondary to its context.[80] He concludes on the basis of the catchwords with Joel

---

[78]Schneider, "The Book of the Twelve," 84.

[79]Cassuto, "The Sequence and Arrangement of the Biblical Sections," 5.

[80]*Literary Precursors to the Book of the Twelve*, 65–68.

1 that the verse is a redactional gloss on the part of the author of Joel that was intended to link Hosea 14 with Joel 1.[81]

Although Nogalski's conclusion regarding Hos 14:8 and Joel 1 is a plausible one, it has two primary weaknesses. First, despite Nogalski's careful analysis, the evidence is not conclusive that Hos 14:8 is a later addition to the context of Hos 14:2–10. The three catchwords, grain, vine, and wine, are not so infrequent in the Hebrew Bible that dependency upon the Book of Joel is the only satisfactory explanation of their appearance in Hos 14:8.[82] Further, the reference to these food stuffs is compatible with the fertility imagery of Hos 14:2–10.[83]

If one does accept Nogalski's argument, however, that Hos 14:8 is a redactional gloss intended to harmonize the agricultural imagery of Hosea 14 with the imagery of Joel 1, such a conclusion still does not require that the two texts were contiguous at the time at which the gloss was made. The evidence that a unifying gloss between two texts does not demand that the texts be contiguous is provided by Nogalski himself. Nogalski identifies several texts within the Book of the Twelve as redactional glosses that are intended to create literary unity across the boundaries of the Minor Prophets collection. These texts include: Nah 3:15; Hab 3:17; Hag 2:19; Zech 8:12; and Mal 3:10–11.[84] These texts are similar in language and imagery to the proposed gloss in Hos 14:8 and to the dominant imagery of Joel 1–2, and yet, these proposed glosses are not located in texts that adjoin the Book of Joel. It follows, therefore, that the presence of a similar gloss in Hos 14:8 does not require that Hosea 14 and Joel 1 be contiguous within the arrangement of the

---

[81]Ibid., 72–73.

[82]According to BDB, the word *yāyin* "wine" occurs 141 times in the Hebrew Bible; *gepen* "vine," 56 times, and *dāgān* "grain," 40 times.

[83]Andersen and Freedman (*Hosea*, 643) explain the change from third person plural pronouns to third person singular pronouns in Hos 14:8b, which Nogalski argues is a sign of a later hand, on the basis of a patterned occurrence of such changes elsewhere in the Book of Hosea.

[84]"Redactional Layers and Intentions," 124–27; 176–78.

Book of the Twelve. They are contiguous in the MT; in the LXX, however, they are not.

Joel and Amos. The most noticeable literary relationships between the books of Joel and Amos consist of the parallel language shared by Joel 4:16, 18, and Amos 1:2, 9:13.

Joel 4:16	Amos 1:2
yhwh missiyôn yiš²āg	*yhwh missiyôn yiš²āg*
ûmîrûšāla(y)im yittēn	*ûmîrûšāla(y)im yittēn*
qôlô	*qôlô*
wĕrā'ăšû	*wĕ²ābĕlû*
šāmayim wā²āreṣ	*nĕ²ôt hārô'îm*
	wĕyābēš rô²š hakkarmel
Yahweh roars from Zion	*Yahweh roars from Zion*
and from Jerusalem	*and from Jerusalem*
utters his voice	*utters his voice*
the heavens and	the pastures of the
the earth shake.	shepherds mourn and the
	head of Carmel withers.
Joel 4:18	Amos 9:13
wĕhāyāh bayyôm hahû²	*hinnēh yāmîm bā²îm*
	nĕ²ūm yhwh [. . .]
yittĕpû hehārîm ʿāsîs	*wĕhittîpû hehārîm ʿāsîs*
wĕhaggĕbāʿôt	*wĕkol haggĕbāʿôt*
tēlaknâ ḥālāb	*titmôgagnâ*
And it will happen	Behold, *days* are coming,
on that *day* that	oracle of Yahweh,
the mountains will	*when the mountains will*
drip sweet wine	*drip sweet wine*
and the hills	*and* all *the hills*
will flow with milk.	will flow with it.

Schneider argued that the author of Joel borrowed from Amos for the express purpose of combining his book with that of

Amos.[85] Bergler, however, thinks that the verses in Amos are the work of a later hand and are borrowed from Joel.[86] Nogalski offers a more nuanced conclusion to the relationship between Joel 4:16, 18 and Amos 1:2; 9:13. He argues that Joel 4:16 borrowed from Amos 1:2 and that Amos 9:13 is a gloss that is dependent upon Joel 4:18.[87]

The differences between Schneider, Bergler, and Nogalski illustrate the difficulty of deciding cases of possible literary dependence. There is, however, also a fourth possibility as suggested by Rudolph, namely, that both Joel and Amos independently employ common traditions.[88] For the case of Joel 4:18 and Amos 9:13, the explanation of independent appropriation of a common tradition seems to be the most likely conclusion. The language of the two texts, although similar, differs in too great a degree to merit the conclusion of intentional citation or allusion. With regard to Joel 4:16 and

---

[85]Schneider, "The Book of the Twelve," 79–80. See also Wolff, *Joel and Amos*, 81.

[86]Bergler, *Joel als Schriftinterpret*, 144–45. Bergler argues that features of Joel 4:16, 18 such as Yahweh's judgment from Zion and the restored fertility of the land are integral to the structure and context of Joel, while Amos 1:2 and 9:13 are isolated statements uncharacteristic of that book as a whole. Bergler suggests that the tradent responsible for the collection of the Book of the Twelve added the Joel material into Amos.

[87]*Redactional Processes*, 42–46. Nogalski argues that Amos 1:2, although secondary, is well integrated into its context, while the location of Yahweh at Zion/Jerusalem in Joel 4:16 is in conflict with 4:2, 14 in which Yahweh judges the nations in the valley of Jehoshaphat (See also Wolff, *Joel and Amos*, 81). Joel 4:18, on the other hand, is well integrated into its context, while Amos 9:13 appears to be secondary on literary-critical grounds.

[88]*Joel, Amos, Obadja, Jona*, 86. For the case of Joel 4:16//Amos 1:2, for example, compare Jer 25:30 ("Yahweh roars from on high, and from his holy habitation utters his voice") and the comments of A. Kapelrud, *Joel Studies* (Uppsala: A. B. Lundequist, 1948), 164. For the view that Joel 4:18 and Amos 9:13 are independent appropriations of common traditions, see Andersen and Freedman, *Amos*, 922–23.

Amos 1:2, however, I would tend to agree with Nogalski that Joel is dependent here upon Amos 1:2, which even if secondary, would have entered the text of Amos fairly early in its transmission history. Given the general tendency for dating Joel in the late fifth to early fourth century BCE, it should be no surprise that this text would be influenced by the Book of Amos. Similar cases of influence may be seen in other texts such as Hag 2:17 and Amos 4:9, or Zech 13:6 and Amos 7:14, for example.[89] Such examples of literary parallels or literary dependence may therefore explain, but do not demand, the contiguity of the books of Joel and Amos.

Joel and Micah. Given Schneider and Nogalski's argument that an early collection of Hosea-Amos-Micah formed the germ of the Book of the Twelve and that the Book of Joel was composed under the influence of the books of Amos and Hosea, one would also expect to find connections between Joel and the third book in this authoritative collection, the Book of Micah. Neither Schneider nor Nogalski, however, address these connections, even though their respective theses make the existence of such connections likely. Apparently an exclusive focus upon the sequence of the MT Book of the Twelve caused them to overlook the relationships between the Book of Joel and the Book of Micah.

An obvious connection between Joel and Micah is the Zion traditions contained within each book. Jerusalem is the center of both divine and human activity in the Book of Joel. It is the place of Joel's proclaimed assembly and fast (2:1, 15), the place of refuge on the day of Yahweh (3:5), the place of Yahweh's judgment against the nations (4:16), and the place of Yahweh's eternal dwelling (4:17, 21). Of the three eighth century prophets in the Book of the Twelve, the Book of Micah gives the most

---

[89]Bergler cites another connection between Amos and Joel that is not discussed by either Schneider or Nogalski. He interprets Joel's call to repentance in 2:12 as an allusion to the fivefold call to repentance in Amos 4:6–11. See *Joel als Schriftinterpret*, 73.

prominence to Jerusalem. This is most noticeable of course in the eschatological portrait of Zion in Mic 4:1–4 (// Isa 2:2–4). This text shares with Joel the themes of the gathering of the nations to Zion/Jerusalem (4:1; Joel 4:2), the emanation of the word of Yahweh from Zion (4:2; Joel 4:16), and Yahweh's judging of the nations in Jerusalem. As Bergler has argued, however, Joel has turned the positive effects of these themes in Micah 4 into negative consequences for the nations.[90] In Joel the nations gather for judgment rather than salvation. Yahweh will judge against the nations rather than between them. These reversals culminate in the even more dramatic reversal in Joel 4:9–10 of Micah's call for the cessation of warfare and the conversion of martial weapons to peaceable implements.[91] The very different portraits of the eschatological fate of the nations within the books of Micah and Joel may possibly indicate the motivation for the inclusion of Joel, and also the similar Book of Obadiah, within the Minor Prophets collection.

Obadiah and the Hosea-Amos-Micah Collection. In comparison to the Book of Joel, the Book of Obadiah contains fewer parallels with the Hosea-Amos-Micah collection. Most of the parallels that do exist, however, have been discussed by Nogalski, who uses them as evidence for the redactional origin of the position of Obadiah in the MT sequence of the Book of the Twelve. As was the case with the Book of Joel, I argue that the literary parallels cited by Nogalski and others do not necessarily require the originality of the MT arrangement of the Twelve; they may indeed legitimately support the originality and unity of the LXX arrangement.

---

[90] *Joel als Schriftinterpret*, 27–28.

[91] H. W. Wolff, "'Schwerter zu Pflugscharen—Missbrauch eines Prophetenwortes?' Praktische Fragen und exegetische Klärungen zu Joël 4,9–12, Jes 2,2–5 und Mi 4,1–5," *EvTh* 44 (1984): 280–92.

Nogalski argues first of all that Obad 1–5 and 15–21 have been shaped redactionally in light of Amos 9.[92] The strongest example of redactional shaping is seen in Obad 4 and Amos 9:2b.

If they go up into the heavens, from there I will bring them down (Amos 9:2b).

If you ascend like the eagle, and if you set your nest between the stars, from there I will bring you down, oracle of Yahweh (Obad 4).

Nolgalski argues that the introductory particle *kî* of the parallel text in Jer 49:16 has been altered in Obad 4 to *'im* in order to repeat the *'im/ miššām* structure that is so prominent in Amos 9:1–4. Both Amos 9:2b and Obad 4 also include the rare verb form of the 1 c. s. Hiph. of *yrd* + suffix, "I will bring them/you down," which Nogalski offers as further evidence of the redactional shaping of Obad 1–9 in light of Amos 9. The identical verb form, however, is also present in the parallel text of Jer 49:16. Nogalski does not sufficiently explain why the presence of the verb *'ôrîdekā* in Obad 4 cannot be the direct result of its presence in the parallel text of Jer 49:16 rather than a result of the shaping of Obadiah in light of Amos 9.[93] Even if Nogalski's conclusion is correct, however, that Obadiah has been shaped redactionally under the influence of Amos 9, again this may explain but does not *require* the arrangement of Amos and Obadiah in the MT Book of the Twelve. One should not be surprised that a

---

[92] *Redactional Processes*, 61–69. The analysis of Obad 1–5 demonstrates Nogalski's concerns and contributions to methodological issues in the literary-analysis of biblical texts. Nogalski bases his conclusions upon a comparison of Obad 1–5 and Jer 49:9, 14–6. He compares the changes introduced into the Jeremiah text by Obad 1–5 with the language and structure of Amos 9.

[93] Ibid., 64–65.

relatively late book such as Obadiah has been influenced by the Book of Amos.[94]

Nolgalski does discuss the one example of a literary connection between Obadiah and the larger context of the corpus of Hosea, Amos, and Micah. Obad 19 contains a reference to the Judeans possessing "the field of Ephraim and the field of Samaria." Nogalski notes that the references to Ephraim and Samaria in the Book of the Twelve occur almost exclusively in the books of Hosea, Amos, and Micah.[95] Further, Nogalski argues that the references to the "field" of Ephraim and the "field" of Samaria hearken back to descriptions of those localities in the books of Hosea and Micah. When seen in light of the description of Ephraim in Hosea, the term "field of Ephraim" appears to be more of a literary allusion than a geographic one.[96] Nogalski reads the elsewhere unattested phrase "field of Samaria" in light of the statement in Mic 1:6 that Yahweh will make Samaria "a heap in the field." Obad 19 therefore appears to be another example of a text within Joel and Obadiah that alludes to the wider literary context of the Hosea-Amos-Micah collection rather than the more narrow context of the seams of this collection.

The preceding examples of ties between Joel and Obadiah and the entire corpus of the Hosea-Amos-Micah collection are cited in support of the argument that the placement of Joel and Obadiah in the LXX arrangement of the Book of the Twelve is literarily connected to the broad context of the three books which precede them in that sequence. Previous treatments cite only those textual parallels between Joel-Obadiah and Hosea-Amos-Micah that explain the MT sequence of these five books. I

---

[94]Bergler and Nogalski's arguments concerning the close relationship between Joel and Obadiah suggest that these two books, at least as they appear in their present form, are to be dated in roughly the same time period, ca. the late fifth to early fourth centuries BCE. See Bergler, *Joel als Schriftinterpret*, 315–20; and Nogalski, *Redactional Processes*, 48–59, 92.

[95]Ibid., 82–83. The only exceptions occur in Zechariah 9, which is either an archaic or archaizing poem.

[96]Ibid., n. 58.

have tried to demonstrate that the books of Joel and Obadiah have a broader literary horizon in view than simply those passages that occur in the seams of the Hosea-Amos-Micah collection. Such a broader literary perspective would be appropriate to the placement of Joel and Obadiah in the LXX Book of the Twelve and in fact helps to unify that arrangement of the Minor Prophets collection.

Jonah in the LXX Book of the Twelve

Having addressed the issue of the placement of Joel and Obadiah in the LXX arrangement of the Twelve, I now turn to the question of the placement of the Book of Jonah in the LXX manuscript tradition. As suggested in Chapter Four above, the position of Jonah within the LXX arrangement of the Twelve is likely a secondary alteration of the position of Jonah that is attested in 4QXII^a. The change in the placement of Jonah reflected in the LXX Book of the Twelve is analogous to the examples of changes in the sequence of textual units that were discussed in Chapter Three. There it was argued that a change in sequence is most likely the result of both scribal uncertainty about the proper sequence of the textual unit being copied and also of the limited freedom of ancient scribes to interpret their textual traditions by means of their organization of the material. The placement of the Book of Jonah in the LXX, therefore, may contain clues to how this book was interpreted at a very early point in its reception and transmission history.

Jonah and Nahum

The most obvious connection between Jonah and its context in the LXX Book of the Twelve is with the Book of Nahum. The juxtaposition of these two prophetic books reflects two different attitudes about the justice of God toward the nations as they are represented by the city of Nineveh. Jonah teaches that the sovereignty of divine mercy may permit a reprieve to be extended even unto a people as wicked as the legendary city of Nineveh. Nahum, on the other hand, reflects the belief that

God's universal justice will not be stayed, but rather will be fully executed against the enemies of God and God's elect.

Nogalski argued that the Book of Jonah was added to the Book of the Twelve specifically to counter the perspective of Nahum.[97] When viewed in the light of the argument for the priority of the placement of Jonah in 4QXII[a], however, I conclude that the direct relationship between Jonah and Nahum is a part of Jonah's reception history subsequent to its inclusion within the Book of the Twelve. The tension between divine mercy as portrayed in Jonah and divine justice as proclaimed in Nahum has a mutual influence on the reading of each book. The message of Jonah provides something of an apologetic for prophets of doom, such as Nahum, when their threats against the nations do not come to fruition. Divine freedom and not prophetic deceit may be responsible for justice's delay.[98] Conversely, when read from the perspective of Nahum's vivid portrayal of divine judgment upon Nineveh, Jonah's depiction of Nineveh's repentance may be understood as exaggerated and shortlived. Such an interpretation had already worked its way into the Targum of Jonah 4:5, which described Jonah as waiting outside of Nineveh after its repentance to see "what would happen *ultimately* (*bswp* > MT) in the city."[99] This interpretation of Jonah is also found in the alternative Greek tradition to Tobit 14:3–4, 15, where Jonah is credited with a truthful prophecy of doom against Nineveh.

Joel and Jonah

As stated above, the books of Jonah and Obadiah share few if any literary or thematic similarities. The Book of Jonah does, however, possess significant literary relationships with the Book

---

[97]Ibid., 270–71. See also the comments of T. F. Glasson, "Nahum and Jonah," *Expository Times* 81 (1969/70): 54–55.

[98]E. Bickerman, *Four Strange Books of the Bible* (New York: Schocken, 1967), 42.

[99]J. Sasson, *Jonah*, The Anchor Bible Vol. 24B (New York: Doubleday, 1990), 289.

of Joel. It is possible that the literary relationships between Joel and Jonah would be sufficient to bind these two books together across the boundaries, as it were, of the intervening Book of Obadiah. A similar cross-reference across the boundaries of individual books was demonstrated in Chapter Three above between the Book of Haggai and the Book of Malachi, particularly in the cases of the LXX text of Mal 1:1.[100]

Joel and Jonah do indeed possess strong literary ties, as has been observed often in the history of biblical scholarship.[101] The primary linguistic ties occur in Joel 2:13–14 and Jonah 3:9, 4:2.

Joel 2:13	Jonah 4:2
kî hannûn wĕrahum hûʾ	*kî ʾatâ ʾēl hannûn wĕrahûm*
ʾerek ʾappayim	*ʾerek ʾappayim*
wĕrab hesed wĕnihām	*wĕrab hesed wĕnihām*
ʿal hārāʿâ	*ʿal hārāʿâ*

Joel 2:14	Jonah 3:9
mî yôdēaʿ yāšûb wĕniham	*mî yôdēaʿ yāšûb wĕniham*
wĕhišʾîr ʾahărāyw	*hāʾĕlōhîm wĕšāb mēhărôn*
bĕrākâ	*ʾapô*

The verbal ties between these texts allow a number of possible explanations. Jonah may have borrowed language from Joel, as several scholars have concluded.[102] A second possibility is that both texts may have independently appropriated the enumeration of the divine attributes in Exod 34:6 and similar texts and also may have independently employed a common phrase "who knows whether he may turn and repent?"[103] More

---

[100]See above, pp. 104–105.

[101]See the recent treatment of this issue, with bibliography and review of research in T. Dozeman, "Inner-Biblical Interpretation of Yahweh's Gracious and Compassionate Character," *JBL* (1989): 207–23; and Bergler, *Joel als Schriftinterpret*, 213–14.

[102]Rudolph, *Joel, Amos, Obadja, Jonah*, 360; Wolff, *Joel and Amos*, 49; E. Bickerman, *Four Strange Books of the Bible*, 41.

[103]Schneider, "The Book of the Twelve," 104–5.

recently, some scholars have argued that Joel is dependent upon Jonah. Bergler has argued, for example, based upon tendencies elsewhere in Joel, that the author of Joel has directly appropriated the language of Jonah for his own compositional purposes.[104] Due to the difficulty in determining the chronological relationship of Joel and Jonah, Dozeman eschewed questions of literary dependence and instead evaluated the mutual relationships between Joel 2:13–14 and Jonah 3:9, 4:2 for the light that both texts shed upon one another and upon the descriptions of Yahweh's character as recorded in Exodus chapters 32–34.[105] Although their research goals differ, the works of both Bergler and Dozeman highlight the high degree of similarity between Joel and Jonah.

For example, Joel 2:13 and Jonah 4:2 are the only texts that expand the divine attributes listed in Exod 34:6 to include Yahweh's disposition to "repent from evil" (*wĕniḥām ʿal hārāʿâ*). The source of this expansion is Exod 32:12, 14, where Moses emplored Yahweh to "turn from [his] fierce wrath and repent of [the] evil" that Yahweh intended as retribution for the incident of the golden calf. Exod 32:12 likewise supplies the two verbs (*yāšûb wĕniḥām*) employed by both Joel and Jonah in the phrase "who knows whether [God] will turn and repent?"[106]

Another linguistic tie between Joel and Jonah is the use of the verb *ḥws* in the context of a discussion of divine mercy (Joel 2:17; Jonah 4:9–11).[107] The two books share thematic connections as well. Both prophets receive and convey messages of imminent

---

[104]Bergler, *Joel als Schriftinterpret*, 214–24. See also J. Magonet, *Form and Meaning: Studies in Literary Techniques in the Book of Jonah* (Sheffield: Almond Press, 1983), 73–77.

[105]Dozeman, "Inner-Biblical Interpretation," 209. See the similar comments of Sasson, *Jonah*, 23–24.

[106]Dozeman, "Inner-Biblical Interpretation," 220; Bergler, *Joel als Schriftinterpret*, 227–28.

[107]Dozeman, 209; Bergler, 225.

disaster.[108] Both books also link together a call to repentance
with the rituals of fasting and mourning.[109]

The literary relationships between Joel and Jonah not only
highlight their similarity but also cast their differences in high
relief. Both books address, albeit in different ways, the
significance of Israel's election upon Israel's relationship to the
nations. Joel, particularly chapter four and by extension the
Book of Obadiah as well, stresses the judgment due upon the
nations as a result of their treatment of the elect. Jonah, on the
other hand, teaches that Israel's election does not restrain
Yahweh's sovereign mercy toward all of Yahweh's creatures,
including the nations. As such, the juxtaposition of the books of
Joel and Obadiah, on the one hand, and Jonah, on the other,
forms a kind of merism with respect to the question of Israel and
the nations. In Joel and Obadiah, the salvation of Israel is brought
about through the judgment of the nations. In Jonah, the
salvation of the heathen people of Nineveh restores hope for the
possibility of salvation for a similarly penitent Israel. The
combination of affinities and polarities within the unit Joel-
Obadiah-Jonah reveals the literary and theological intelligence
and creativity behind their juxtaposition.

Beyond the literary connections between Jonah and the
books of Joel and Nahum, the placement of Jonah at the end of
the Book of the Twelve in 4QXII[a] may also have influenced the
position of Jonah in the LXX manuscript tradition. In the LXX
arrangement, Jonah is the sixth book in the collection. Rudolph
has observed that the first five books in the LXX sequence are
arranged in descending order according to book length.[110] He
argued that the position of Jonah in the LXX departed from the
principle of arrangement by length because Jonah provided an
appropriate conclusion to the first half of the Book of the
Twelve. This concluding function is precisely the function that
Jonah serves for the entire collection of the Book of the Twelve

---

[108]Dozeman, 210.

[109]Bergler, 224.

[110]*Haggai-Zacharja 1–8–Zacharja 9–14–Maleachi*, 296.

in 4QXII^a. The placement of Jonah at the end of the first half of
the LXX Book of the Twelve would therefore suggest that the
LXX arrangement was influenced by the placement of Jonah at
the end of the collection as attested in 4QXII^a. This possibility
lends further support to the conclusion that the position of Jonah
in 4QXII^a was chronologically prior to its positions in both the
LXX and the MT manuscript traditions.

Conclusion

Attention to the text-critical reconstruction of the *Vorlage* of
the LXX Minor Prophets reveals evidence as to why that
manuscript tradition preserved an arrangement of the Twelve
Prophets distinct from that of the MT. One reason that the LXX
Vorlage was not arranged like the MT is a negative one. One of
the linguistic associations that produced the MT sequence, the
connections between Amos 9:12 and Obadiah, was simply not
present in the text of the LXX *Vorlage*.

Beyond this negative reason against the sequence of the MT,
several positive reasons for the sequence of the LXX were
present. First, the numerous relationships of chronology,
language, tradition, and ideology between the books of Hosea,
Amos, and Micah were preserved in the sequence of the LXX.
Second, the same connection that united the MT of Amos with
the Book of Obadiah, a reference to Edom, was also present in
the text of Joel 4:19. This verbal association between Joel and
Obadiah was only one of a number of literary, thematic, and
theological points of connection between these two books.
Third, Joel and Obadiah displayed connections with the books
of Hosea, Amos, and Micah, a phenomenon that is commensurate
with the theory that an earlier collection of these eighth century
prophecies enjoyed a degree of authority and influence over
succeeding generations. Fourth, the depiction in Joel and
Obadiah of judgment against the nations is appropriate to the
succeeding books of Nahum and Habakkuk in the LXX Book of
the Twelve. Joel and Obadiah also share significant literary ties
to the Book of Nahum as well. Finally, the text of Jonah shares

remarkable linguistic and thematic connections with the Book of Joel that precedes it and with the Book of Nahum that follows it in the LXX textual tradition. The traditions of divine justice and judgment against the nations that bind together Joel, Obadiah, and Nahum are juxtaposed with the radical message of the Book of Jonah in a way that creates literary tension and initiates a dynamic play of perspectives that intensifies the respective messages of each book.

The limited freedom and creativity exercised by the ancient scribes and copyists of biblical literature was revealed in the textual alterations that were argued in Chapter Three to be present in the Hebrew *Vorlage* of the LXX Book of the Twelve. Beyond making minor changes within the text, a collection such as the Book of the Twelve presented an opportunity to exercise creativity in the manner in which the text was arranged. A general sense of chronology sometimes informed the arrangement, as illustrated in the grouping together of eighth century prophets (Hosea-Amos-Micah), seventh century prophets (Nahum-Habakkuk-Zephaniah), and post-exilic prophets (Haggai-Zechariah-Malachi). More important than chronology, however, was a method of associating the language and themes of various books in a way that created both a sense of unity and at times an unresolved tension. Some texts complemented one another, as in the way that the accomplishment of the fall of Samaria that was threatened by Hosea and Amos was applied to Jerusalem and Judah in the Book of Micah. Other texts were not so much joined together as juxtaposed, as in the case of Jonah and Nahum, or of Joel and Micah's contrasting picture of the gathering of the nations to Jerusalem.

The sense of integrity and creative arrangement in the LXX Book of the Twelve, however, does not diminish the similar unity and intelligibility of the MT Book of the Twelve. Rather, the presence of the techniques of association and juxtaposition in both the LXX and the MT confirms the conclusion that intentionality rather than randomness accounts for the formation and arrangement of the MT Book of the Twelve. The possibilities for the creative and coherent arrangement of the Minor

Prophets, however, were not exhausted by the MT sequence alone, as previous scholars seem to have assumed. The witness of the LXX to the existence of an edition of the Book of the Twelve comparable to that preserved in the MT is consistent with the conclusion, based on other manuscript evidence, that the production of sacred literature in ancient Israel was diverse and multiform.

CHAPTER 6

CONCLUSION: STAGES IN THE LITERARY AND CANONICAL DEVELOPMENT OF THE BOOK OF THE TWELVE

The thesis of the present study is that text-critical evidence may provide information about two issues that have appeared repeatedly in the history of scholarship on the Book of the Twelve, namely, the formation of the book and its relationship to the development of the Hebrew canon. The preceding chapters have examined the textual evidence of the LXX and 4QXII[a] and have evaluated it in relation to the received text of the MT manuscript tradition. The present chapter will summarize the results of this investigation and assess their importance as they relate to the issues of the formation and canonization of the Book of the Twelve. I will also attempt to weigh the implications of these results as they pertain to future research in the literary and canonical history of the Minor Prophets.

The Formation of the Book of the Twelve: Summary of Findings

The primary task of literary-critical analysis as it is currently practiced in biblical studies is to isolate, where possible, older materials within the received biblical text and to reconstruct the development of the text from its earliest identifiable stages of composition to its final textual form. Although the methodologies for such an enterprise have become highly refined over the course of the history of the discipline, literary analyses and their accompanying redactional reconstructions remain at best hypothetical, and such approaches have often produced diverse and often contradictory results.

The remarkable manuscript discoveries from the Judean Desert, however, have contributed both a new body of evidence and a new methodological perspective to the task of reconstructing the literary history of biblical texts. Because of the antiquity of some of the Qumran manuscript remains, it has become possible to trace the transmission history of some biblical books back to a time when the compositional development of those books was yet in progress. Due to the possible overlap between the literary history of biblical books and their textual history, it has been argued that certain textual remains may preserve concrete evidence of stages in the literary growth of biblical books prior to the final stage of composition and redaction that is preserved in the received text of the Masoretic tradition. The present study has sought to apply the methodological insights that have emerged from recent textual discoveries to the literary history of the Book of the Twelve. The results of such an examination may be summarized as follows.

The Evidence of 4QXII^a

Based upon both text-critical and literary-critical evidence, the last individual book to enter the Minor Prophets collection was most likely the Book of Jonah. Beyond the literary-critical observations concerning the possible date of the book, its primary themes, and its tenuous literary relationship to the remainder of the Minor Prophets corpus, the Book of Jonah has the least stable position within the arrangements of the Twelve in ancient manuscript witnesses. It occurs in three distinct positions, as illustrated by the following table.

Table 6.1. The Arrangement of the Twelve in Ancient Manuscripts.

	MT Sequence	LXX Sequence	4QXII[a] Sequence
1.	Hosea	Hosea	—
2.	*Joel*	Amos	—
3.	Amos	Micah	—
4.	*Obadiah*	*Joel*	—
5.	*Jonah*	*Obadiah*	—
6.	Micah	*Jonah*	—
7.	Nahum	Nahum	—
8.	Habakkuk	Habakkuk	—
9.	Zephaniah	Zephaniah	—
10.	Haggai	Haggai	Zechariah
11.	Zechariah	Zechariah	Malachi
12.	Malachi	Malachi	*Jonah*

Of the three positions of the Book of Jonah in ancient manuscripts of the Book of the Twelve, the position that it occupies in 4QXII[a] is the one that is most compatible with the conclusions of previous literary assessments of Jonah. I have therefore proposed that the placement of Jonah in 4QXII[a] represents the earliest position of the book within the Minor Prophets collection. The fact that Jonah ends with the artificial and arbitrary occurrence of the number twelve[1] suggests that the author or redactor of the book was aware of its position in the original collection of the Book of the Twelve.

If the conclusion is accepted that 4QXII[a] preserves the original placement of the Book of Jonah when it entered the Minor Prophets collection, then the question is raised concerning the sequence of the previous collection to which Jonah was appended. The question is a difficult one due to the fact that no book prior to the Book of Zechariah has survived in the text of 4QXII[a]. The arrangement of the eleven books other than Jonah,

---

[1]The number of inhabitants of Nineveh is given in Jon 4:11 as "more than twelve myriads," a number that reflects neither the approximate population of the city nor the most common means of expressing the number 120,000 in the Hebrew Bible. See above, Chapter Four.

however, is quite stable in both the MT and the LXX manuscript traditions. These two arrangements may therefore offer reliable options for reconstructing the order of books in 4QXII[a].

The primary difference between the two arrangements of the Minor Prophets preserved in the MT and the LXX is the placement of the books of Joel and Obadiah (see Table 6.1, above). As in the case of the Book of Jonah, I have concluded that the variant placements of the books of Joel and Obadiah in the manuscript witnesses support other literary evidence that these two books were inserted into a pre-existing collection of prophetical writings. Of the two placements of Joel and Obadiah in the MT and the LXX manuscripts, I have argued that the arrangement of the LXX preserves the earlier arrangement of the two books within the Minor Prophets collection.

The following data support the conclusion that the arrangement of Joel and Obadiah in the LXX is chronologically prior to the arrangement of these books in the MT. First, I argued in Chapter Five that the catchword connection between Amos 9:12 and Obadiah in the MT sequence of the Twelve was absent in the Hebrew textual tradition preserved in the LXX translation. The identical catchword, the proper name Edom, is present, however, in Joel 4:19, which is contiguous to the Book of Obadiah in the LXX. Second, of the two different catchwords that link the Book of Obadiah to its different positions in the MT and the LXX arrangements of the Twelve, I argued that the use of the word Edom as a catchword in the MT of Amos 9:12 is a secondary textual alteration of an earlier reading. The text of Joel 4:19, however, has been shown to be integral to its literary context. I have concluded therefore that the text of Amos 9:12 has been altered under the influence of Joel 4:19. Third, the books of Joel and Obadiah contain numerous literary and thematic ties to one another, and to both the broad context of the corpus of Hosea, Amos, and Micah that precedes them, and to the Book of Nahum that follows them in the LXX sequence (absent the Book of Jonah). The connection between the books of Joel and Obadiah and their context within the LXX arrangement is illustrated by, although certainly not limited to, the brief superscriptions of the two books. The language of Joel 1:1 is patterned after the introductory formulas in the preceding books of Hosea, Amos, and Micah, while Obad 1 "the vision of Obadiah," is similar to the superscription "the vision of Nahum the Elkoshite" in Nah 1:1.

Based upon a comparison of the arrangements of the eleven books of the Minor Prophets excluding the Book of Jonah in the MT and the LXX manuscripts, the LXX arrangement is most likely to have been the sequence of the first eleven books in 4QXII^a (see Table 6.2, below). Since I have argued above that the Book of Jonah was the last book to be added to the Minor Prophets collection and that its position in 4QXII^a is mostly likely to be the position in which it was placed when it entered the collection, then the reconstructed sequence of 4QXII^a is also proposed to be the sequence of the original compilation of the Book of the Twelve Prophets. Such a reconstruction of a partially attested scroll of the Minor Prophets may appear to be too hypothetical to merit acceptance, especially in the light of the criticisms that I myself have made of the speculative nature of literary-critical approaches to the Hebrew Bible. The difference between the present reconstruction of the sequence of books in 4QXII^a and other reconstructions of stages in the development of the Book of the Twelve, however, is that the present reconstruction has the additional merit of supporting textual evidence. The reconstruction of 4QXII^a, for example, although still hypothetical in nature, is based upon the following evidence: (1) the textual and literary evidence for the placement of the Book of Jonah as attested in 4QXII^a; (2) the textual and literary evidence for the coherence of the sequence of the books of Joel and Obadiah in the LXX Book of the Twelve; (3) the literary unity and the stable arrangement of the other nine books of the Minor Prophets as attested in both the LXX and the MT manuscript traditions (see Table 6.2, below); and (4) analogous examples of changes in the sequence of materials within manuscript traditions of the Hebrew Bible.[2]

Stages of Collection Prior to the MT

From the reconstructed arrangement of 4QXII[a], it is now possible to work backward chronologically to reconstruct stages in the collection of the Minor Prophets prior to the additions of the Book of Jonah and the books of Joel and Obadiah. The proposed development of the Book of the Twelve from the earliest stages that may be reconstructed from manuscript evidence with some degree of probability to the form of the book preserved in the MT may be described in the following table.

Table 6.2.—The Development of the Book of the Twelve according to Manuscript Evidence[3]

Book of IX	*Book of XI*	*4QXII[a]*	*LXX XII*	*MT XII*
1. *Hosea*	*Hosea*	*Hosea*	Hosea	Hosea
2. *Amos*	*Amos*	*Amos*	Amos	**JOEL**
3. *Micah*	*Micah*	*Micah*	Micah	Amos
4. *Nahum*	**Joel**	**Joel**	Joel	**OBADIAH**
5. *Habakkuk*	**Obadiah**	**Obadiah**	Obadiah	**JONAH**
6. *Zeph*	*Nahum*	*Nahum*	**JONAH**	Micah
7. *Haggai*	*Habakkuk*	*Habakkuk*	Nahum	Nahum
8. *Zech*	*Zeph*	*Zeph*	Habakkuk	Habakkuk
9. *Malachi*	*Haggai*	*Haggai*	Zeph	Zeph

---

[2]E. Tov, "Some Sequence Differences between the MT and the LXX and Their Ramifications for the Literary Criticism of the Bible," *JNSL* 13 (1987): 151–60.

[3]Names of books that occur in *italics* represent reconstructions that are not preserved in extant manuscripts; books that are underlined are argued to have been inserted into the collection listed in the preceding column; books that are in UPPER CASE LETTERS are argued to have been transposed from their position in the collection listed in the preceding column.

10.	—	*Zech*	Zech	Haggai	Haggai
11.	—	*Malachi*	Malachi	Zech	Zech
12.	—	—	**Jonah**	Malachi	Malachi

At least two prior stages of compilation may be reconstructed with a fairly high degree of probability. First, the eleven books other than Jonah in the LXX and the reconstructed 4QXII[a] arrangements of the Minor Prophets would comprise a stage of the collection prior to the Book of the Twelve. Second, I have argued that the literary and textual evidence suggests that the books of Joel and Obadiah were added to a pre-existing collection of nine books that was comprised of the books of Hosea, Amos, Micah, Nahum, Habakkuk, Zephaniah, Haggai, Zechariah, and Malachi. Although theoretically it is possible to argue for the existence of other stages of collection prior to these nine books, the extant manuscript witnesses offer no further corroborating evidence for such an enterprise.

Supporting evidence exists for the possibility of a "Book of the Nine" beyond the fact that the sequence of these books does not change in the manuscripts of the LXX and the MT textual traditions. First, there is a high degree of literary unity attested within the three chronologically-arranged subgroupings of Hosea-Amos-Micah, Nahum-Habakkuk-Zephaniah, and Haggai-Zechariah-Malachi.[4] Second, Nogalski has argued convincingly that the seams of the three sub-groupings that occur between the texts of Micah 7 and Nahum 1 and between Zephaniah 3 and Haggai 1 have been redactionally shaped in order to give unity to the collection.[5] Third, the chronological information within the

---

[4]An extensive treatment of the unifying features of these three subgroups of books may be found in the work of Schneider ("The Unity of the Book of the Twelve" [Ph.D. dissertation, Yale University, 1979]), whose observations still include many cogent and plausible explanations of the collection and unity of these nine books.

[5]*Redactional Processes in the Book of the Twelve*, BZAW 218 (Berlin: Walter de Gruyter, 1993), 103–109; idem, *Literary Precursors to the Book of the Twelve*, BZAW 217 (Berlin: Walter de Gruyter, 1993), 212–15, 220–21. Despite these

three subgroupings of prophets in the Book of the Nine fits into an overarching framework that is similar to the chronological framework that unites the three major prophetic books of Isaiah, Jeremiah, and Ezekiel.[6]

The Arrangement of the LXX Book of the Twelve

From the reconstruction of the arrangement of the Book of the Twelve preserved in 4QXII[a], it is possible not only to work backward to previous collections of the Minor Prophets, but also forward in time to the arrangements of the Twelve that are preserved in the LXX and the MT (see Table 6.2). From the reconstructed sequence of 4QXII[a], it is relatively simple to trace the transposition of the Book of Jonah, the latest book to be added to the Minor Prophets scroll, from the end of the scroll to its position prior to the Book of Nahum in the Hebrew *Vorlage* of the LXX. Three features relating to the placement of the Book of Jonah in the LXX serve to explain its origin. First, the central theme of Nineveh shared by Jonah and Nahum may have attracted these two books to one another in the transmission history of the Minor Prophets. The motivation for placing the two books adjacent to one another, however, is more difficult to determine. The juxtaposition of Jonah and Nahum may have been motivated by an attempt to balance the portrait of divine justice toward the nations that is contained in the books of Joel, Obadiah, and Nahum with the message of Yahweh's sovereign mercy in the Book of Jonah. Alternatively, the sequence of Jonah

---

observations, Nogalski does not argue for the existence of a Book of the Nine. His observations on the seams of the books of Micah, Nahum, Zephaniah, and Haggai are aimed at explaining the MT arrangement of the Twelve. The catchwords and other unifying features that he identifies, however, still apply to the nine book collection proposed here.

[6]D. N. Freedman, *The Unity of the Hebrew Bible* (Ann Arbor, MI: University of Michigan Press, 1991), 50–55. Although the affinities that Freedman observes are based upon the final form of the Book of the Twelve, his arguments are more convincing for a Book of the Nine, excluding the less chronologically-specific books of Joel, Obadiah, and Jonah.

and Nahum may have been an attempt to harmonize the reprieve extended to Nineveh described in the Book of Jonah with the acknowledged destruction of the city that is so graphically depicted in Nahum. This interpretation of Jonah is already present in the Targum of Jonah 4:5 and in one Greek textual tradition of the Book of Tobit.

A second feature that helps to explain the placement of Jonah in the Hebrew source text of the LXX is the degree of literary affinity shared by the books of Jonah and Joel. The literary and thematic parallels between these two books may have unified these writings across the boundaries of the intervening Book of Obadiah, which is itself also well integrated literarily with the Book of Joel. A third feature that helps to explain the placement of Jonah in the LXX is its position there at the conclusion of the first half of the Book of the Twelve. The Book of Jonah concludes the first six books of the Twelve, which otherwise are arranged in order of size from longest to shortest.[7] Since Jonah concluded the entire corpus of the Twelve in the arrangement of 4QXII[a], its placement at the end of the first half of the Twelve in the Hebrew *Vorlage* of the LXX may be dependent upon the position of Jonah in the earlier arrangement.

The Arrangement of the Twelve in the MT

According to the reconstruction of the formation of the Book of the Twelve proposed above, the arrangement of the Twelve in the MT textual tradition represents the final stage in the development of the Hebrew text of the collection. Since the MT arrangement of the Twelve has been the focal point of previous studies of the Book of the Twelve, the literary unity of that sequence has been well established. The contribution of the present study, therefore, is limited to a description of the manner in which the MT arrangement took shape.

---

[7]This observation about the role of Jonah within the first half of the LXX Book of the Twelve arrangement was made by W. Rudolph, *Haggai-Sacharja 1–8–Sacharja 9–14–Maleachi*, KAT 13/4 (Gütersloh: Gerd Mohn, 1976), 292.

The arrangement of the MT Book of the Twelve was accomplished primarily by incorporating the books of Joel, Obadiah, and Jonah into the sequence of the eighth century prophetic books of Hosea, Amos, and Micah. At least three factors seem to have made the transposition of these books possible. First, the books of Joel, Obadiah, and Jonah have no direct chronological markers. This fact made it necessary for the tradents of the Minor Prophets to rely on the literary features of these three books in order to relate the books to the remainder of the collection. The lack of chronological indicators may have presented both a problem and an opportunity for the tradents of the Minor Prophets, since the lack of specific information may have allowed them more freedom to incorporate these books within the subgrouping of the older prophetical writings. Second, the possibility that the books of Joel, Obadiah, and Jonah were late additions to an established collection of prophetic books would have also allowed the tradents of the Book of the Twelve more freedom in arranging these books within the collection. Since Joel, Obadiah, and Jonah would not have possessed as strong of a scribal tradition as the other books in regard to their position in the collection, these three books offered the tradents of the Book of the Twelve more flexibility in positioning them among the Twelve.

A third factor that may have influenced the incorporation of the books of Joel, Obadiah, and Jonah into the corpus of eighth century prophetic books was the continuing process of interpretation that facilitated the appropriation of the prophetic writings by successive generations of tradents and readers. By the time of the creation of the Book of the Twelve with the inclusion of the books of Joel, Obadiah, and Jonah, which according to the present reconstruction would not have taken place before the middle of the fifth century BCE, the collection of books comprised of Hosea, Amos, and Micah would already have possessed a lengthy history of transmission. The possibility of making editorial changes to the text of the eighth century corpus had probably decreased dramatically due to the growth of a somewhat stable textual tradition. The transposition of the books of Joel, Obadiah, and Jonah into the seams of the Hosea-Amos-Micah collection therefore may be seen to have had an interpretative effect by recontextualizing the message of an established corpus whose contents could perhaps no longer be altered by other means.

The recontextualization of the eighth century corpus with the incorporation of the books of Joel, Obadiah, and Jonah created a broader intertextual context for the reading of the older literary traditions. For example, the juxtaposition of the imagery of fertility in Hosea 14 with the description of agricultural blight in Joel 1 raises the question of the meaning of the promise of prosperity within the earlier tradition for the economically depressed post-exilic community that is reflected in the Book of Joel. Joel 1–2 resolves the tension between the unfulfilled promise of future weal and the present distress by projecting the promise into a new eschatological schema and by making the promise contingent upon a renewed commitment to religious and cultic institutions.

A similar contextual transformation may be seen in the relationship between Joel 4 and Amos 1–2. The description in Joel 4 of the future judgment of all nations, and specifically the regions of Phoenicia, Philistia, and Edom, combined with the echo of Amos 1:2 in Joel 4:16, recontextualizes the oracles against the nations in Amos 1–2 and gives them a possible future orientation.[8] Whereas the placement of the Book of Joel calls attention to the oracles against the nations in Amos 1–2, the Book of Obadiah in the MT plays upon the vision material in Amos 7–9, and particularly Amos 9. Nogalski has argued that the title "the vision of Obadiah," the similar language of Amos 9:2 and Obadiah 4, and the reference to the dispossession of Edom in Amos 9:12 and Obad 17–21 all serve to recast the vision of judgment upon Israel in Amos 9 into a prediction of future

---

[8]H. W. Wolff, *Joel and Amos*, Hermeneia Commentary, tr. W. Janzen, S. D. McBride, Jr., and C. Muenchow (Philadelphia: Fortress Press, 1977), 3.

judgment upon Edom in the Book of Obadiah.[9] These literary connections therefore bring the chronologically-specific material of Amos 9 forward into the generalized temporal context of the Book of Obadiah.

The relationship between Jonah and its context in the MT Book of the Twelve is less easily explained than the contexts of the books of Joel and Obadiah. Jonah has no direct or clearly identifiable linguistic ties with either Obadiah or Micah. A number of explanations have been offered for this sequence; each seems equally plausible and yet unsatisfactory. Wolff suggested that Obadiah was identified with the individual of that name who was mentioned in 1 Kings 18.[10] Thus the Book of Jonah followed the Book of Obadiah because the figure of Obadiah was chronologically prior to the figure of Jonah according to the Deuteronomistic History.[11] Schneider argues that Jonah precedes Micah in order to begin a section of books including Micah, Nahum, and Habakkuk that address the topic of Assyria.[12] Jonah precedes Micah because the prophet Jonah of 2 Kgs 14:25 was chronologically prior to the prophet Micah. A. Cooper has recently argued that Jonah's placement in the MT Book of the Twelve is based upon an association of the various appearances

---

[9] *Redactional Processes*, 61–69. I differ with Nogalski, however, on the manner in which the connections between Obadiah and Amos 9 came about. I argue that the MT text of Amos 9:12 is the result of the alteration of the Hebrew text preserved in LXX 9:12. I also argue that the superscription "vision of Obadiah" was originally composed to relate the book to the similarly entitled "vision of Nahum." As for the similarity between Obad 4 and Amos 9:2, the existence of such literary parallels between an essentially eighth century book and an exilic or post-exilic text should not be surprising. Compare, for example, Hag 2:17 and Amos 4:9, and Zech 13:5 and Amos 7:14.

[10] *Obadiah and Jonah*, 75. Nogalski (*Redactional Processes*, 270) follows Wolff's suggestion.

[11] Wolff's argument applies equally well to the arrangement of Jonah and Obadiah in the LXX.

[12] "The Unity of the Twelve," 113.

of the divine attributes in Joel 2:13–14, Jonah 4:2, Micah 7:18–20, and Nahum 1:3.[13] Nogalski argues that the placement of Jonah prior to Micah was accomplished by the additions of catchwords between Jonah 2:3–10 and Micah 7:19–20.[14] These catchwords link the salvation described in Micah 7:19–20 with the salvation experienced in Jonah. As I have argued in Chapter Five, the placement of Jonah after Obadiah in the MT Book of the Twelve appears to be dependent upon the sequence of the Hebrew *Vorlage* of the LXX Book of the Twelve. There, Jonah follows Obadiah almost accidentally due to Obadiah's position between the two books of Joel and Nahum with which Jonah shares significant literary affinities.

The only other possible tie between Jonah and its context in the MT Book of the Twelve occurs between Jonah and the Book of Micah. Rather than any linguistic or thematic connection existing within the texts of these two books, however, the possible relationship of Jonah and Micah occurs in the oral tradition about the historical career of the prophet Micah that has been preserved only in Jeremiah 26. A comparison of the Book of Jonah and the tradition about Micah in Jer 26:18–19 shows that both Micah and Jonah confronted a nation (Judah/Nineveh) with words of doom (Mic 3:12/Jon 3:4) that provoked the response of the king (Hezekiah/king of Nineveh) and led to a change of heart on the part of both the nation and the deity (Jer 26:19/Jon 3:10). A midrashic tradition of undetermined date even claims that Jonah's career included the proclamation of a message of judgment to Jerusalem that produced the same results as his mission to Nineveh and as

---

[13]"In Praise of Divine Caprice: The Significance of the Book of Jonah," in *Among the Prophets*, ed. P. R. Davies, JSOTSup 141 (Sheffield: JSOT Press, 1993), 159–63. See similar arguments by Schneider, "The Unity of the Book of the Twelve," 99.

[14]*Redactional Processes*, 266–69. See also Nogalski's arguments for a redactional linkage between Micah and Nahum which would have precluded placing Jonah prior to Nahum. "The Redactional Shaping of Nahum 1 for the Book of the Twelve," in *Among the Prophets*, 193–202.

Micah's preaching in Jerusalem.[15] This tradition seems to reflect the similarity between the careers of these two prophets, a similarity that is perhaps also reflected in the MT arrangement of the Book of the Twelve. When read in light of the tradition about the prophet Micah, therefore, the Book of Jonah in the MT Book of the Twelve provides a "historical" precedent for the interpretative oral tradition that lies behind the oracular material in the Book of Micah.

The Book of the Twelve and the Canonical Process

The great advantage of studying the Book of the Twelve from the vantage point of text-critical evidence is that such evidence provides insight not only into the issue of the formation of the book but also into its relationship to the history of the biblical canon as well. The manuscript evidence for the Book of the Twelve reveals a great deal about how these texts developed into a part of the exclusive collection of ancient Israel's literary and religious heritage. The conclusions of the present study regarding the Book of the Twelve and the growth of the biblical canon may be summarized as follows.

The Canonical Process

In Chapter Two I discussed the historical arguments for defining the term "canon" narrowly as a consciously-closed list of books. No reference to a fixed set of books of exclusively sacred status is directly attested prior to the end of the first century CE. This being said, however, there is also much evidence to indicate that many of the texts of the Hebrew Bible possessed both an exalted status and an authoritative function long before the relatively late date of conscious canonical closure. The present study employs the term "canonical process" to describe the interim period between the initial transmission and use of biblical books as valued and valuable texts, and their ultimate recognition as the exclusive corpus of the sacred

---

[15]*Pirqe R. El.* 10.

literature of ancient Israel.[16] Although theoretically the canonical process is a broad category that includes every aspect of the composition and transmission history of the biblical text, practically speaking, the dynamics of the canonical process are primarily exhibited, as argued repeatedly by J. Sanders, in the evidence for the textual transmission and (re)interpretation of the biblical text.[17]

Textual Alterations of an Interpretative Nature

The comparison in Chapter Three between the texts of the MT Book of the Twelve and the Hebrew *Vorlage* of the LXX demonstrated the contemporaneous relationship between the two processes of textual transmission and interpretation. Paradoxically, many of the interpretative changes that were attested within these two textual traditions demonstrate a degree of reverence for the text of the Minor Prophets even in the process of altering the reading of the text. For example, most of the textual alterations discussed in Chapter Three were in the form of harmonizations with language that was found in the surrounding literary context. In a sense, such harmonizations were an attempt to make the language of the text closer to other "biblical" language. Other examples of harmonizations attempted to answer specific exegetical questions raised by the reading of the source text. The method employed was often that of clarifying obscure language with additional language taken from the surrounding context, thereby explaining "Scripture" by "Scripture." Even the more lengthy textual additions such as the doxology in Hos 13:4 and the additions to Hag 2:5, 9, 14 were

---

[16]This description of the canonical process is most indebted to the discussion of E. Ulrich, "The Canonical Process, Textual Criticism, and Latter Stages in the Composition of the Bible," in *"Sha'arei Talmon." Studies in the Bible, Qumran, and the Ancient Near East Presented to Shemaryahu Talmon,* ed. M. Fishbane and E. Tov (Winona Lake, IN: Eisenbrauns, 1992), 267–91.

[17]See for example, Sanders's comments in *Canon and Community: A Guide to Canonical Criticism* (Philadelphia: Fortress Press, 1984), 32–33.

expressed in language that was either taken from or was similar to other biblical texts. It would appear that at the stage of the textual transmission of the Hebrew *Vorlage* of the LXX and the proto-MT texts, it was acceptable to introduce textual changes only under very limited conditions and only by means of language that conformed to a scriptural model.

Malachi 3:22–24

A specific text that is often cited as having canonical significance is Mal 3:22–24, which concludes the Book of the Twelve in the LXX and MT arrangements. The textual evidence is particularly helpful in examining the role of this passage in the canonical development of the Book of the Twelve. Although Mal 3:22 and 3:23–24 are generally thought to be two separate appendices to both the Book of Malachi and to the prophetic corpus as a whole, comparison of the LXX and MT texts presented a slightly different picture. First, the textual evidence is inconclusive regarding the question of the secondary nature of Mal 3:22, although a recent study has presented cogent arguments for its authenticity as a fitting summation of the message of the Book of Malachi.[18] The different text and placement of Mal 3:23–24 in the LXX, however, are argued to provide textual evidence in support of literary-critical arguments for the secondary nature of 3:23–24 within their present context. I have concluded, however, that Mal 3:23–24 was added to the Book of Malachi in the position and the textual form preserved in the LXX. The purpose of this addition appears to have been, as is often suggested, to explain the reference to the "messenger of the covenant" of Mal 3:1.

Although it appears that the original literary horizon of Mal 3:22–24 was limited to the Book of Malachi, the implications of these verses for the larger literary context of a collection of scriptural texts may be seen in the textual alterations attested by

---

[18]B. Glazier-MacDonald, *Malachi: The Divine Messenger*, SBLDS 98 (Atlanta: Scholars Press, 1987), 244–51.

the MT. There, the reference to Elijah is transposed to the end of the book following the reference to the Torah of Moses. The reading of the LXX, "Elijah the Tishbite," is also changed to reflect the title "Elijah the prophet," thereby explicitly establishing the figure of Elijah as a representative of prophecy after the time of Moses. Finally, the LXX reading "he will restore the heart of the parents to the children and the hearts of neighbors toward one another" is changed in the MT to "he will turn the heart of the parents toward the children and the heart of the children toward the parents." The suggestion that the prediction of generational reconciliation in Mal 3:23–24 is a reference to the generational strife of the Hellenistic crisis of the second century BCE might therefore apply not to the original text of Mal 3:23–24 but to the textual alteration that I have proposed to be reflected in the MT reading. In the context of its MT reading and placement, the reference in 3:22–24 to the Torah of Moses and to the return of Elijah the prophet may indeed encompass a literary horizon that includes a corpus of Scriptures containing the Torah and a collection of prophetic writings.

Jonah and the Canonical Process

Further illustration of the textual and intepretative dynamics of the canonical process may be seen in the different interpretations of the Book of Jonah in the manuscript traditions of the Book of the Twelve. A. Band, for example, has suggested that the inclusion of Jonah among the Twelve is illustrative of the canonical process.[19] Band interpreted Jonah as a parody of Israelite prophetic literature.[20] He concludes, however, that the book's parodic effect was eventually lost in the canonical context of the Book of the Twelve, where it was interpreted as an example of the literature that it originally sought to parody. Although I reject Band and Miles's characterization of Jonah as

---

[19]"Swallowing Jonah: The Eclipse of Parody," *Prooftexts* 10 (1990): 191–94.

[20]Band expands upon the work of J. A. Miles, Jr. "Laughing at the Bible: Jonah as Parody," *JQR* 65 (1974–75): 168–81.

parody, I agree with Band's conclusion that the placement of Jonah within the Book of the Twelve had definite interpretative effects, which may be summarized below.

In its placement in 4QXII[a], Jonah functions as a retrospective commentary on certain theological issues related to Israelite prophecy. The Book of Jonah addresses primarily the implications of the delay of divine justice against the nations as anticipated in certain prophetic writings. This delay had a negative impact upon both the post-exilic community that had expected an eschatological event of judgment against the nations, and upon the popular perception of Israel's prophets, who seemed responsible for encouraging false hope. The message of the Book of Jonah, communicated by means of an ironic, didactic narrative, is that the disappointment, disenchantment, and sense of injustice suffered by the survivors of the twelve tribes of Israel and by the twelve prophets who are representative of Israel's prophetic heritage are outweighed in the divine economy by the care that Yahweh the Creator has for the more than twelve myriads (Jon 4:11) of Yahweh's creatures. As such, Jonah provides a sophisticated defense of both the justice of Yahweh and the integrity of Yahweh's prophets.

Apparently, the creative talent of the author of the Book of Jonah allowed the book to be incorporated into the collection of Minor Prophets at a time of popular resistance to direct prophetic speech. The transposition of the Book of Jonah to its position in the Hebrew textual tradition preserved in the LXX is indicative of the acceptance of the book as prophetic literature. In the LXX arrangement of the Twelve, Jonah is interpreted not as a narrative reflection upon Israelite prophecy, but rather as an example of prophetic literature itself that is comparable with such prophetic texts as Joel and Nahum with which Jonah shares parallels in language and theme.

The placement of the Book of Jonah in the MT Book of the Twelve appears to be a further development in the intepretative history of Jonah. In the MT arrangement of the Twelve, Jonah is interpreted not in light of its primary message, but rather in light of the information that it contains about the eighth century prophet who is its central character. A similar emphasis upon the Book of Jonah as "history" has been observed in the literary character of the LXX *translation* of Jonah.[21] The placement of Jonah in the Hebrew source text of the LXX and the historical interests of the MT arrangement and the LXX translation demonstrate how the interpretation of the book developed first from a narrative postscript on Israelite prophecy to an example of Israelite prophetic literature and finally to an historical account of an eighth century prophetic figure.

Joel and Obadiah and the Canonical Process

The incorporation of the books of Joel and Obadiah into the Minor Prophets collection is in some respects similar to the trajectory followed by the Book of Jonah. In the LXX arrangement of the Twelve, which is proposed as the original placement of Joel and Obadiah within the collection, these two books occupy a position between the eighth century corpus of Hosea-Amos-Micah and the oracles against foreign nations contained in Nahum and Habakkuk. The structure of the two books of Joel and Obadiah when considered together fits well into this intermediate position. The central theme of judgment upon Israel that is described in Joel 1–2 in terms of natural disaster, military conquest, and the imminent judgment of the Day of Yahweh, hearkens back to the judgment upon Israel and Judah pronounced in the corpus of the eighth century prophets. Joel 3–4, however, and also Obadiah, take up the theme of a future judgment against all nations in the context of the Day of Yahweh tradition. These chapters thereby serve as an introduction to the oracles against the nations in Nahum and Habakkuk.

---

[21]L. Perkins, "The Septuagint of Jonah: Aspects of Literary Analysis Applied to Biblical Translation," *BIOSCS* 20 (1987): 43–53. Perkins argues that the tendency of the translator was to highlight features of the narrative that portrayed Jonah as an historical figure.

Unlike the Book of Jonah, however, Joel and Obadiah are composed in the form of prophetic books rather than as a prophetic narrative. The authors/editors of Joel and Obadiah apparently were able to secure their position within the Minor Prophets collection by imitating both the form and the language of earlier prophetic writings. Such a literary strategy would explain the density of intertextual echoes and allusions within these two books.[22] The strategy of gaining a place within the established literary tradition through conscious imitation of the tradition is similar to T. S. Eliot's description of the development of the literary canon.[23] Eliot suggested that the only way that an author could contribute to the established literary tradition, which Eliot described as preceding the author as an organic and perfect whole, was to absorb and embody the tradition so thoroughly that the author's own work could be imagined to have been pre-existent within the literary tradition itself. A process similar to the one described by Eliot might explain the incorporation of Joel and Obadiah into the Minor Prophets collection.

As the manuscript tradition of the MT illustrates, however, the books of Joel and Obadiah were not only accepted into the corpus of Minor Prophets, but also came to shape that corpus as well by means of their transposition within the collection of eighth century prophets. The influence of the books of Joel and Obadiah upon the reading of the entire corpus may be seen in the fact that traditional interpretations of the Minor Prophets dated the Book of Joel earlier than the books of Amos and Micah and the Book of Obadiah as the earliest of all the Twelve

---

[22]The intertextual nature of Joel and Obadiah is treated at length in S. Bergler, *Joel als Schriftinterpret* (Frankfurt am Main/Bern/New York: Peter Lang, 1988) and in Nogalski, *Redactional Processes*, 42–47, 61–77.

[23]Eliot, "Tradition and the Individual Talent," in *Selected Essays 1917–1932* (New York: Harcourt Brace & Co., 1963), 1–10.

Prophets.[24] The effect of the transposition of the books of Joel and Obadiah to their placement in the MT Book of the Twelve was to make these belated books appear to be not only the equal of the eighth century prophetic books, but the predecessors of the eighth century prophets as well.[25]

The mention of the traditional interpretations of the books of Joel and Obadiah calls attention to the fact that the interpretative dynamics of the canonical process continued in a wide variety of forms after the consonantal text of the Book of the Twelve achieved a point of fixity and standardization. It has in fact been suggested that, as a result of the stabilization of the consonantal Hebrew text, exegetical activity not only continued but actually increased due to the demands of continually appropriating a received tradition whose text had become sacrosanct.[26] The evidence of interpretative alterations that are attested in the textual transmission of the Book of the Twelve provides a vantage point from which one may look both back in time to the literary techniques employed in the composition and

[24]See the evidence of Jerome, the Talmud, and particularly the comments of the medieval commentator Abravanel that are summarized in Schneider, "The Unity of the Book of the Twelve," 2–4.

[25]The traditional interpretations of Joel and Obadiah as the predecessors to the prophetic books that they in fact imitate is akin to the psychoanalytic reading of T. S. Eliot's description of "tradition and the individual talent" found in H. Bloom, *The Anxiety of Influence* (New York: Oxford University Press, 1975). Bloom describes the poet's relationship to his/her predecessors not as a benign relationship with the "tradition," but rather, in terms of the Oedipal myth, as a struggle of a child against the threat of a father figure. The poet thus overcomes the "anxiety of influence" by struggling to rewrite the poetry of the predecessor in such a way as to make one's own work the "original" and the predecessor's work the imitation. A similar mode of allusion to a prior text is also described by the term "echo metalepsis" in J. Hollander, *The Figure of an Echo: A Mode of Allusion in Milton and After* (Berkeley: University of California Press, 1981).

[26]S. Cohen, *From the Maccabees to the Mishnah* (Philadelphia: Westminster Press, 1987), 193.

redaction of biblical texts, and also forward in time to the multifaceted interpretations and adaptations of the biblical canon that have emerged from late antiquity until the present. This twofold direction of inquiry, however, leads beyond the limits of the present study and points toward fertile ground for future research.

BIBLIOGRAPHY OF WORKS CITED

Ackerman, James S. "Satire and Symbolism in the Song of Jonah." In *Tradition and Transformation*, ed. B. Halpern and J. D. Levenson, 213–46. Winona Lake, IN: Eisenbrauns, 1981.

———. "Jonah." In *The Literary Guide to the Bible*, ed. R. Alter and F. Kermode, 328–41. Cambridge: Belknap Press, 1987.

Ackroyd, Peter R. "Some Interpretative Glosses in the Book of Haggai." *Journal of Jewish Studies* 7 (1956): 163–67.

Aejmelaeus, Anneli. "What Can We Know about the Hebrew *Vorlage* of the Septuagint?" *Zeitschrift für die Alttestamentliche Wissenschaft* 99 (1987): 58–89.

———. "Translation Technique and the Intention of the Translator." In *Proceedings of the VIIth Congress of the International Organization of Septuagint and Cognate Studies*, ed. C. Cox, 23–36. Atlanta: Scholars Press, 1989.

Albrechtson, Bertil. "Reflections on the Emergence of a Standard Text of the Hebrew Bible." *Vetus Testamentum, Supplements* 29 (1978): 49–65.

Alexander, T. Desmond. "Jonah and Genre." *Tyndale Bulletin* (1985): 35–59.

Allen, Leslie C. *The Books of Joel, Obadiah, Jonah and Micah.* New International Commentary on the Old Testament. Grand Rapids, MI: Eerdmans, 1976.

243

Amsler, Samuel. "Aggée, Zacharie 1–8." in *Aggée, Zacharie, Malachie.* Vol. XIc, Commentaire de l'Ancien Testament. Paris and Neuchatel: Delachaux and Niestle, 1981.

Andersen, Francis I., and David N. Freedman, *Hosea.* Vol. 24, The Anchor Bible. New York: Doubleday, 1980.

———. *Amos.* Vol. 24A, The Anchor Bible. New York: Doubleday, 1989.

Arieti, J. A. "The Vocabulary of Septuagint Amos." *Journal of Biblical Literature* 93 (1974): 338–47.

Auld, A. Graeme. "Prophets and Prophecy in Jeremiah and Kings." *Zeitschrift für die Alttestamentliche Wissenschaft* 98 (1989): 66–82.

Band, A. J. "Swallowing Jonah: The Eclipse of Parody." *Prooftexts* 10 (1990): 177–95.

Barr, James. *Holy Scripture: Canon, Authority, Criticism.* Philadelphia: Westminster, 1983.

———. *Comparative Philology and the Text of the Old Testament.* Oxford: Clarendon, 1968.

———. *The Typology of Literalism in Ancient Biblical Translations,* 279–325 in Mitteilungen des Septuaginta-Unternehmens, no. 15. Göttingen: Vandenhoeck and Ruprecht, 1979.

Barth, H. and Odil H. Steck. *Exegese des Alten Testaments.* 4th ed. Neukirchen-Vluyn: Neukirchener Verlag, 1973.

Barthélemy, Dominique. *Les Devanciers d'Aquila: Premiere Publication Integrale du Texte des Fragments du Dodecapropheton. Vetus Testamentum, Supplements* 10. Leiden: E. J. Brill, 1963.

———. "Redécouverte d'un chaînon manquant de l'histoire de la Septante." *Revue Biblique* 60 (1953): 18–29.

———. "L'Etat de la Bible juive depuis le début de notre ère jusqu'à la deuxième révolte contre Rome (131–135)." In *Le Canon de l'Ancien Testament: Sa formation et son histoire,* eds. J.-D. Kaestli and O. Wermelinger, 9–45. Genève: Labor et Fides, 1984.

————, D. W. Gooding, Johannes Lust and Emanuel Tov, *The Story of David and Goliath: Textual and Literary Criticism. Papers of a Joint Research Venture*. Orbis Biblicus et Orientalis, no. 73. Freiburg and Göttingen: University of Freiburg and Vandenhoeck and Ruprecht, 1986.

————. *Ezéchiel, Daniel et les 12 Prophètes*. Vol. 3, *Critique Textuelle de L'Ancien Testament*. Orbis Biblicus et Orientalis, no. 50/3. Freiburg and Göttingen: University of Freiburg and Vandenhoeck and Ruprecht, 1992.

Bartdke, Hans. "Prophetische Züge im Buche Hiob." In *Das Ferne und Nahe Wort: Festschrift Leonhard Rost*, ed. F. Masse, 1–10. Beihefte zur Zeitschrift für die Alttestamentliche Wissenschaft, no. 105. Berlin: Walter de Gruyter, 1967.

Barton, John. *Oracles of God: Perceptions of Ancient Prophecy in Israel after the Exile*. London: Basil Blackwell, 1986.

————. "'The Law and the Prophets': Who Are the Prophets?" *Oudtestamentische Studiën* 23 (1984): 1–18.

Beckwith, R. T. *The Old Testament Canon of the New Testament Church*. Grand Rapids, MI: Eerdmans, 1985.

Benoit, P., J. T. Milik, and R. de Vaux, *Les Grottes de Murabba'at*. Vol. II, Discoveries in the Judean Desert. Oxford: Clarendon, 1961.

Bergler, Siegfried. *Joel als Schriftinterpret*. Beiträge zur Erforschung des Alten Testaments und des antiken Judentums. Frankfurt an Main, New York, Paris: Peter Lang, 1990.

Berlin, Adele. "A Rejoinder to John A. Miles, Jr., With Some Observations on the Nature of Prophecy." *Jewish Quarterly Review* 66 (1976): 227–35.

Bewer, Julius. "Jonah." In *A Critical and Exegetical Commentary on Haggai, Zechariah, Malachi, and Jonah*. International Critical Commentary. Edinburgh: T & T Clark, 1912.

Beyer, H. W. "*kanon*." Vol. 3, *Theological Dictionary of the New Testament*, ed. G. Kittel and G. Friedrich, 596–602. Grand Rapids, MI: Eerdmans, 1968.

Bickerman, Elias. *Four Strange Books of the Bible: Jonah, Esther, Daniel, and Qohelet.* New York: Schocken, 1967.

———. *From Ezra to the Last of the Maccabees.* New York: Schocken, 1962.

Bleek, Johannes and Adolph Kampenhausen, eds. *Einleitung in das Alte Testament von Friedrich Bleek.* 3rd ed. Berlin: Georg Reiner, 1870.

Blenkinsopp, Joseph. *Prophecy and Canon: A Contribution to the Study of Jewish Origins.* Notre Dame and London: University of Notre Dame Press, 1977.

———. *A History of Prophecy in Ancient Israel: From the Settlement in the Land to the Hellenistic Period.* Philadelphia: Westminster, 1983.

Bloom, Harold. *The Anxiety of Influence.* New York: Oxford University Press, 1975.

Bogaert, P.-M. "De Baruch à Jérémie : Les deux rédactions conservées du livre de Jérémie." In *Le Livre de Jérémie: Le prophète et son milieu, les oracles et leur transmission,* ed. P.-M. Bogaert, 168–73. Bibliotheca ephemeridum theologicarum lovaniensium, no. 54. Leuven: Leuven University Press, 1981.

Bosshard, Erich. "Beobachtungen zum Zwölfprophetenbuch." *Biblische Notizen* 40 (1987): 30–62.

———, and Reinhard G. Kratz. "Maleachi im Zwölfprophetenbuch." *Biblische Notizen* 52 (1990): 27–46.

Brett, Mark. *Biblical Criticism in Crisis?: The Impact of the Canonical Approach on Old Testament Studies.* Cambridge: Cambridge University Press, 1991.

Brock, Sebastian P. "Translating the Old Testament." In *It Is Written: Essays in Honour of Barnabas Lindars, SSF,* ed. D. A. Carson and H. G. M. Williamson, 87–98. Cambridge: Cambridge University Press, 1988.

Brooke, George J. *Exegesis at Qumran: 4QFlorilegium in Its Jewish Context.* Journal for the Study of the Old Testament Supplement Series, no. 29. Sheffield: JSOT Press, 1985.

Bruce, F. F. "Prophetic Interpretation in the Septuagint." *Bulletin of the International Organization of Septuagint and Cognate Studies* 12 (1979): 15–26.

Budde, Karl. "Eine folgenschwere Redaction des Zwölfprophetenbuchs." *Zeitschrift für die Alttestamentliche Wissenschaft* 39 (1922): 218–29.

————. "Vermutungen zum 'Midrasch des Büches der Könige.'" *Zeitschrift für die Alttestamentliche Wissenschaft* 11 (1892): 37–51.

————. "Zu Text und Auslegung des Buches Amos." *Journal of Biblical Literature* 44 (1925): 63–122.

Burrows, Millard. "The Literary Category of the Book of Jonah." in *Translating and Understanding the Old Testament: Essays in Honor of Herbert Gordon May*, ed. T. H. Frank and W. L. Reed, 80–107. Nashville: Abingdon, 1970.

Carroll, Robert P. "Eschatological Delay in the Prophetic Tradition." *Zeitschrift für die Alttestamentliche Wissenschaft* 94 (1982): 47–58.

Cassuto, Umberto. "The Sequence and Arrangement of the Biblical Sections." In *Biblical and Oriental Studies*, Vol. I, tr. Israel Abrahams. Jerusalem: Magnes, 1973.

Cathcart, Kevin. "The Divine Warrior and the War of Yahweh in Nahum." In *Biblical Studies in Contemporary Thought*, ed. M. Ward, 72–76. Somerville, MA: Trinity College Biblical Institute, 1975.

Childs, Brevard. "The Canonical Shape of the Prophetic Literature." *Interpretation* 32 (1978): 46–55.

————. *Introduction to the Old Testament as Scripture*. Philadelphia: Fortress, 1979.

Clements, Ronald E. "Patterns in the Prophetic Canon." In *Canon and Authority*, ed. George W. Coats and Burke O. Long, 43–56. Philadelphia: Fortress, 1977.

————. "The Purpose of the Book of Jonah." *Vetus Testamentum, Supplements* 28 (1975): 16–28.

Cohen, Naomi. "From *Nabi* to *Mal'ak* to Ancient Figure." *Journal of Jewish Studies* 37 (1987): 12–24.

Cohen, Shaye. *From the Maccabees to the Mishnah*. The Library of Early Christianity, no. 7. Philadelphia: Westminster, 1987.

Cohn, G. H. *Das Buch Jona im Lichte der biblischen Erzählkunst*. Studia Semitica Neerlandica, no. 12. Assen: Van Gorcum, 1969.

Cooper, Alan. "In Praise of Divine Caprice: The Significance of the Book of Jonah." In *Among the Prophets: Language, Image and Structure in the Prophetic Writings*, ed. P. R. Davies, , 159–63. Journal for the Study of the Old Testament Supplement Series, no. 144. Sheffield: JSOT Press, 1993.

Coote, Robert. *Amos Among the Prophets: Composition and Theology*. Philadelphia: Fortress, 1981.

Craig, Kenneth. *A Poetics of Jonah*. Columbia, SC: University of South Carolina Press, 1993.

Crenshaw, James L. *Hymnic Affirmations of Divine Justice: The Doxologies of Amos and Related Texts in the Old Testament*. SBL Dissertation Series, no. 24. Missoula, MT: Scholars Press, 1975.

———. *Prophetic Conflict: Its Effect upon Israelite Religion*. Beihefte zur Zeitschrift für die Alttestamentliche Wissenschaft, no. 124. Berlin: Walter de Gruyter, 1971.

———. "Popular Questioning of the Justice of God in Ancient Israel." *Zeitschrift für die Alttestamentliche Wissenschaft* 82 (1970): 380–395.

———. "The Expression *mî yôdēaʿ* in the Hebrew Bible." *Vetus Testamentum* 36 (1986): 274–88.

Cresson, Bruce. "The Condemnation of Edom in Post-Exilic Judaism." In *The Use of the Old Testament in the New and Other Essays: Studies in Honor of William Franklin Stinespring*, ed. J. M. Efird, 125–48. Durham, NC: Duke University Press, 1972.

Cross, Frank M. *The Ancient Library of Qumran and Modern Biblical Studies*. Westport, CT: Greenwood Press, 1976.

————. "The Oldest Manuscripts from Qumran." *Journal of Biblical Literature* 74 (1955): 147–72.

————. "The Development of the Jewish Scripts." In *The Bible and the Ancient Near East: Essays in Honor of William Foxwell Albright*, ed. G. E. Wright, 170–254. Garden City, NY: Doubleday, 1965.

————. "The Evolution of a Theory of Local Texts." in *Qumran and the History of the Biblical Text*, ed. F. M. Cross and S. Talmon, 306–20. Cambridge: Harvard University Press, 1975.

Davis, Ellen. *Swallowing the Scroll: Textuality and the Dynamics of Discourse in Ezekiel's Prophecy*. Journal for the Study of the Old Testament Supplement Series, no. 78. Sheffield: Almond Press, 1990.

Delitzsch, "Wenn weisagte Obadja?" *Zeitschrift fur die gesamte Lutherische Theologie und Kirche* 12 (1851): 91–102.

Dozeman, Thomas. "Inner-Biblical Interpretation of Yahweh's Gracious and Compassionate Character." *Journal of Biblical Literature* 108 (1989): 207–23.

Dyck, Elmer. "Jonah Among the Prophets: A Study in Canonical Context." *Journal of the Evangelical Theological Society* 33 (1990): 63–73.

Eichhorn, J. G. *Einleitung in das Alte Testament*. Göttingen: C. E. Rofenbusch, 1824.

Eliot, T. S. "Tradition and the Individual Talent." In *Selected Essays 1917–1932*, 1–10. New York: Harcourt Brace & Co., 1963.

Facsimile of the Washington Manuscript of the Minor Prophets in the Freer Collection and Berlin Fragment of Genesis. Ann Arbor, MI: University of Michigan Press, 1927.

Fáj, A. "The Stoic Features of the Book of Jonah." *Instituto Orientale di Napoli, Annali* 34 (1974): 309–345.

Feuillet, A. "Les Sources du Livre de Jonas." *Revue Biblique* 54 (1947): 161–86.

————. "Les sens du livre de Jonas" *Revue Biblique* 54 (1947): 340–61.

Fishbane, Michael A. *Biblical Interpretation in Ancient Israel.* Oxford and New York: Clarendon and Oxford University Press, 1985.

———. "The Use, Authority, and Interpretation of Mikra at Qumran." In *Mikra: Text, Translation, Reading and Interpretation of the Hebrew Bible in Ancient Judaism and Early Christianity,* ed. M. J. Mulder, 347–55. (Philadelphia: Van Gorcum/Fortress, 1990.

———. "From Scribalism to Rabbinicism." In *The Garments of Torah: Essays in Biblical Hermeneutics,* 64–78. Bloomington, IN: University of Indiana Press, 1989.

Freedman, David N. "Headings in the Books of the Eighth Century Prophets." *Andrews University Seminary Studies* 25 (1987): 9–26.

———. "The Law and the Prophets." *Vetus Testamentum, Supplements* 9 (1962): 250–65.

———. "Canon of the OT." In *Interpreter's Dictionary of the Bible, Supplementary Volume,* 130–36. Nashville, Abingdon, 1976.

———. "The Earliest Bible." *Michigan Quarterly Review* 22 (1983): 167–75.

———. "Formation of the Canon of the Old Testament." In *Religion and Law: Biblical-Judaic and Islamic Perspectives,* ed. E. B. Firmage and B. G. Weiss, 315–31. Winona Lake, IN: Eisenbrauns, 1990.

———. *The Unity of the Hebrew Bible.* Ann Arbor, MI: University of Michigan Press, 1991.

Fretheim, Terence E. *The Message of Jonah: A Theological Commentary.* Minneapolis: Augsburg, 1977.

———. "Jonah and Theodicy." *Zeitschrift für die Alttestamentliche Wissenschaft* 90 (1978): 227–37.

Froula, Christine. "When Eve Reads Milton: Undoing the Canonical Economy." In *Canons,* ed. R. von Hallberg, 149–54. Chicago and London: University of Chicago Press, 1983.

Fuller, Russell E. *The Minor Prophets Manuscripts from Qumran, Cave IV.* Ph.D. dissertation, Harvard University, 1988.

Gelston, A. *The Peshitta of the Twelve Prophets.* Oxford: Clarendon, 1987.

Ginsburg, C. D. *Introduction to the Massoretic-Critical Edition of the Hebrew Bible.* First ed., 1897. Reprinted, New York: KTAV, 1966.

Glasson, T. F. "Nahum and Jonah." *Expository Times* 81 (1969/70): 54–55.

Glazier-MacDonald, Beth. *Malachi: The Divine Messenger.* SBL Dissertation Series, no. 98. Atlanta: Scholars Press, 1987.

Good, E. M. *Irony in the Old Testament.* London: SPCK, 1965.

Goshen-Gottstein, Moses H. "The Textual Criticism of the Old Testament: Rise, Decline, Rebirth" *Journal of Biblical Literature* 102 (1983): 365–99.

———. "Theory and Practice of Textual Criticism—The Text-critical Use of the Septuagint." *Textus* 3 (1963): 131–32.

Gosse, Bernhard. "La malédiction contre Babylone de Jérémie 51, 59–64 et les rédactions du livre de Jérémie" *Zeitschrift für die Alttestamentliche Wissenschaft* 98 (1986): 383–99.

Gottwald, Norman K. "Tragedy and Comedy in the Latter Prophets." *Semeia* 32 (1984): 83–96.

———. "Social Matrix and Canonical Shape." *Theology Today* 42 (1985): 307–21.

Greenspahn, Frederick E. "Why Prophecy Ceased." *Journal of Biblical Literature* 108 (1989): 37–49.

Guillory, "Canonical vs. Non-Canonical: A Critique of the Current Debate." *English Literary History* 54 (1987): 483–528.

———. "Canon." In *Critical Terms for Literary Study,* ed. F. Lentricchia and T. McLaughlin, 233–49. Chicago and London: University of Chicago Press, 1990.

Haller, Eduard. *Die Erzählung von dem Propheten Jona.* Theologische Existenz heute, no. 65. Munich: Chr. Kaiser, 1958.

Hammerschaimb, Erling. *The Book of Amos: A Commentary.* Tr. J. Sturdy. New York: Schocken, 1970.

Harrison, C. Robert, Jr. "The Unity of the Minor Prophets in the Septuagint." *Bulletin of the International Organization for Septuagint and Cognate Studies* 21 (1988): 55–72.

Haupt, P. "The Septuagint Addition to Haggai 2.14." *Journal of Biblical Literature* 36 (1917): 148–50.

Hermann, J. and F. Baumgärtel, *Beiträge zur Entstehungsgeschichte der Septuaginta.* Berlin/Stuttgart/Leipzig: Kohlhammer, 1923.

Hill, Andrew E. "Dating Second Zechariah: A Linguistic Reexamination." *Hebrew Annual Review* 6 (1982): 105–34.

Holbert, John C. "'Deliverance Belongs to Yahweh!': Satire in the Book of Jonah." *Journal for the Study of the Old Testament* 21 (1981): 59–81.

Hollander, John. *The Figure of an Echo: A Mode of Allusion in Milton and After.* Berkeley: University of California Press, 1981.

Hölscher, G. *Kanonisch und Apokryph: Ein Kapital zu der Geschichte des alttestamentlichen Kanons.* Leipzig: A. Deichert, 1905.

House, Paul. *The Unity of the Twelve.* Journal for the Study of the Old Testament Supplement Series, no. 77. Sheffield: JSOT Press, 1990.

Howard, G. "Some Notes on the Septuagint of Amos." *Vetus Testamentum* 20 (1970): 108–12.

Janzen, J. Gerald. *Studies in the Text of Jeremiah.* Harvard Semitic Mongraphs, no. 6. Cambridge: Harvard University Press, 1973.

————. "A Critique of Sven Soderlund's *The Greek Text of Jeremiah.*" *Bulletin of the International Organization of Septuagint and Cognate Studies* 22 (1989): 16–47.

Jepsen, Alfred. "Kleine Beitrage zum Zwölfprophetenbuch." *Zeitschrift für die Alttestamentliche Wissenschaft* 56 (1938): 85–200.

————. "Kleine Beitrage zum Zwölfprophetenbuch, II." *Zeitschrift für die Alttestamentliche Wissenschaft* 57 (1939): 242–53.

————. "Kleine Beitrage zum Zwölfprophetenbuch, III." *Zeitschrift für die Alttestamentliche Wissenschaft* 61 (1945–48): 95–114.

————. "Anmerkungen zum Buche Jona." In *Wort-Gebot-Glaube. Festschrift für Walter Eichrodt*, ed. J. J. Stam and E. Jenni, 297–305. Zürich: Zwingli Verlag, 1970.

Kaestli, J.-D. "Le récit de IV Esdras 14 et sa valeur pour l'histoire du canon de l'Ancien Testament." In *Le Canon de l'Ancien Testament: Sa formation et son histoire*, eds. J.-D. Kaestli and O. Wermelinger, 71–97. Genève: Labor et Fides, 1984.

Kaiser, "Wirklichkeit, Möglichkeit und Vorurteil. Ein Beitrag zum Verständnis des Buches Jona." *Evangelische Theologie* 33 (1973): 91–103.

Kapelrud, Arvid. *Joel Studies.* Uppsala: A.B. Lundequist, 1948.

Keil, Karl Friedrich. *Manual of Historico-Critical Introduction to the Canonical Scriptures of the Old Testament.* Tr. G. Douglas. 1st ed. 1892, reprinted Grand Rapids, Michigan: Eerdmans, 1952.

Keller, Carl A. "Jonas." In *Osée, Joël, Abdias, Jonas, Amos.* Vol. XIa, Commentaire de L'Ancient Testament. Paris, Neuchatel: Delachaux and Niestle, 1965.

————. "Jonas. Le Portrait d'un prophète." *Theologische Zeitschrift* 21 (1965): 329–40.

Kermode, Frank. "The Argument about Canons." In *An Appetite for Poetry*, 189–207. Cambridge: Harvard University Press, 1989.

Koch, Klaus. "Is Daniel also Among the Prophets?" *Interpretation* 39 (1985): 117–30.

————. "Haggai's unreines Volk." *Zeitschrift für die Alttestamentliche Wissenschaft* 79 (1967): 52–66.

Koole, J. L. "Die Bibel des Ben Sira." *Oudtestamentische Studiën* 14 (1965): 374–96.

Lacocque, André, and P.-E. Lacocque, *Jonah: A Psycho-religious Approach to the Prophet.* Columbia, SC: University of South Carolina Press, 1990.

Lambert, W. G. "Ancestors, Authors, and Canonicity." *Journal of Cuneiform Studies* 2 (1957): 9.

Landes, George. "Jonah, Book of." *The Interpreter's Dictionary of the Bible, Supplementary Volume*, 488–91. Nashville: Abingdon, 1976.

———. "Linguistic Criteria and Date of the Book of Jonah." *Eretz Israel* 16 (1982): *147–70.

———. "The Kerygma of the Book of Jonah." *Interpretation* 21 (1967): 3–31.

Lebram, J. C. H. "Aspekte der alttestamentlichen Kanonbildung." *Vetus Testamentum* 18 (1968): 173–89.

Lee, Andrew Y. "The Canonical Unity of the Scroll of the Minor Prophets." Ph.D. diss., Baylor University, 1985.

Leiman, Sid. *The Canonization of Hebrew Scripture*. Camden, CT: Arcon Press, 1976.

Lescow, Theodor. "Redaktionsgeschichtliche Analyse von Micha 1–5." *Zeitschrift für die Alttestamentliche Wissenschaft* 84 (1972): 46–85.

———. "Redaktionsgeschichtliche Analyse von Micha 6–7." *Zeitschrift für die Alttestamentliche Wissenschaft* 84 (1972): 182–212.

Levine, Etan. "Jonah as a Philosophical Book." *Zeitschrift für die Alttestamentliche Wissenschaft* 96 (1984): 235–45.

Liebermann, Saul. *Hellenism in Jewish Palestine*. NY: Jewish Theological Seminary, 1962.

Lifshitz, B. "The Greek Documents from the Cave of Horror." *Israel Exploration Journal* 12 (1962): 201–7.

Lightstone, Jack N. *Society, the Sacred, and Scripture in Ancient Judaism: A Sociology of Knowledge*. Waterloo, ON: Wilfrid Laurier University Press, 1988.

———. "The formation of the biblical canon in Judaism of late antiquity: Prolegomenon to a general reassessment." *Studies in Religion/Sciences religieuses* 8 (1979): 135–42.

Lohfink, Norbert. "Jona ging zur Stadt hinaus (Jona 4,5)." *Biblische Zeitschrift* NF (1961): 185–203.

Loretz, Oswald. "Herkunft und Sinn der Jona–Erzählung." *Biblische Zeitschrift* 5 (1961): 18–29.

Magonet, Jonathan. *Form and Meaning: Studies in Literary Techniques in the Book of Jonah.* 2nd ed. Bible and Literature Series, no. 8. Sheffield: Almond Press, 1983.

———. "Jonah, Book of." In Vol. III, *The Anchor Bible Dictionary,* ed. D. N. Freedman, 936–42. New York: Doubleday, 1992.

Mantel, Hugo. "The Nature of the Great Synagogue." *Harvard Theological Review* 60 (1967): 69–91.

Marböck, J. "Henoch-Adam-Der Thronwagen. 'Zu frühjüdischen pseudepigraphischen Traditionen bei Ben Sira.'" *Biblische Zeitschrift* 25 (1981): 103–11.

Marks, Herbert. "The Twelve Prophets." In *The Literary Guide to the Bible,* ed. R. Alter and F. Kermode, 207–32. Cambridge: Belknap, 1987.

Mason, Rex A. "The Relation of Zechariah IX–XIV to Proto-Zechariah." *Zeitschrift für die Alttestamentliche Wissenschaft* 88 (1976): 227–39.

———. "Some Examples of Inner-Biblical Exegesis in Zechariah 9–14." *Studia Evangelica* 7 (1982) 343–54.

———. *The Books of Haggai, Zechariah, and Malachi.* Cambridge Bible Commentary. Cambridge: Cambridge University Press, 1976.

———. *Preaching the Tradition: Homily and Hermeneutics after the Exile.* Cambridge: Cambridge University Press, 1990.

May, Herbert G. "'This People' and 'This Nation' in Haggai." *Vetus Testamentum* 18 (1938): 190–97.

Mays, James L. *Micah: A Commentary.* The Old Testament Library. Philadelphia: Westminster, 1976.

Metzger, Bruce. *The Canon of the New Testament: Its Contents, History, and Growth.* Oxford: Clarendon, 1987.

Meyer, Rudolph. "The Canon and the Apocrypha in Judaism." In Vol. 3, *Theological Dictionary of the New Testament*, ed. G. Kittel and G. Friedrich, 376–80. Grand Rapids, MI: Eerdmans, 1968.

————. "Bermerkungen zum literargeschichtlichen Hintergrund der Kanontheorie des Josephus." In *Josephus-Studien. Untersuchungen zu Josephus, dem antiken Judentum und dem Neuen Testament*, ed. O. Betz, K. Haacker, and M. Hengel, 285–99. Göttingen: Vandenhoeck and Ruprecht, 1974.

Meyers, Carol L., and Eric M. Meyers. *Haggai, Zechariah 1–8*. Vol. 25B, *The Anchor Bible*. Garden City, NY: Doubleday, 1987.

————. *Zechariah 9–14*. Vol. 25C, *The Anchor Bible*. New York: Doubleday, 1993.

Meyers, Eric M. "The Use of *torah* in Haggai 2:11 and the Role of the Prophet in the Restoration Community." In *The Word of the Lord Shall Go Forth: Essays in Honor of David Noel Freedman in Celebration of His Sixtieth Birthday*, ed. Carol L. Meyers and M. O'Connor, 69–76. Winona Lake, IN: Eisenbrauns, American Society for Oriental Research, 1983.

————. "Priestly Language in the Book of Malachi" *Hebrew Annual Review* 10 (1986): 225–37.

Miles, John A., Jr. "Laughing at the Bible: Jonah as Parody." *Jewish Quarterly Review* 65 (1974–75): 168–81.

Mitchell, H. G. "Haggai and Zechariah." In *A Critical and Exegetical Commentary on Haggai, Zechariah, Malachi, and Jonah*. International Critical Commentary. Edinburgh: T & T Clark, 1912.

Muraoka, Takamitsu. "Is the Septuagint of Amos viii 12–ix 10 a Separate Unit?" *Vetus Testamentum* 20 (1970): 496–500.

————. "In Defense of the Unity of the LXX Minor Prophets." *Annual of the Japanese Biblical Institute* 15 (1989): 25–36.

Nogalski, James D. "Redactional Layers and Intentions: Uniting the Writings of the Book of the Twelve." Ph.D. diss., University of Zürich, 1991.

———. *Literary Precursors to the Book of the Twelve.* Beihefte zur Zeitschrift für die Alttestamentliche Wissenschaft, no. 217. Berlin: Walter de Gruyter, 1993.

———. *Redactional Processes in the Book of the Twelve*, Beihefte zur Zeitschrift für die Alttestamentliche Wissenschaft, no. 218. Berlin: Walter de Gruyter, 1993.

———. "The Redactional Shaping of Nahum 1 for the Book of the Twelve." In *Among the Prophets: Language, Image and Structure in the Prophetic Writings*, ed. P. R. Davies and D. J. A. Clines, 193–202. Journal for the Study of the Old Testament Supplement Series, no. 144. Sheffield: JSOT Press, 1993.

O'Brien, Julia. *Priest and Levite in Malachi.* SBL Dissertation Series, no. 121. Atlanta: Scholars Press, 1990.

Olofsson, Stephan. *The LXX Version: A Guide to the Translation Technique of the Septuagint.* Coniectania biblica, Old Testament, no. 30. Stockholm: Almqvist & Wiksell, 1990.

Overholt, Thomas W. "The End of Prophecy: No Players without a Program." *Journal for the Study of the Old Testament* 42 (1988): 103–115.

Paul, Shalom. *Amos, A Commentary.* Hermeneia Commentary Series. Minneapolis: Fortress Press, 1992.

Perkins, Larry. "The Septuagint of Jonah: Aspects of Literary Analysis Applied to Biblical Translation." *Bulletin of the International Organization of Septuagint and Cognate Studies* 20 (1987): 43–53.

Pesch, R. "Zur konzentrischen Struktur von Jona 1." *Biblica* 47 (1966): 577–81.

Peters, Melvin K. H. "Why Study the Septuagint?" *Biblical Archaeologist* 49 (1986): 174–81.

Petersen, David L. *Late Israelite Prophecy: Studies in Deutero-Prophetic Literature and in Chronicles.* SBL Dissertation Series, no. 23. Missoula, MT: Scholars Press, 1977.

———. *Haggai and Zechariah 1–8.* The Old Testament Library. Philadelphia: Westminster, 1984.

Pfeiffer, E. "Die Disputationsworte im Buche Maleachi." *Evangelische Theologie* 19 (1959): 546–68.

Pierce, Ronald. "A Thematic Development of the Haggai-Zechariah-Malachi Corpus." *Journal of the Evangelical Theological Society* 27 (1984): 401–11.

————. "Literary Connectors and a Haggai-Zechariah-Malachi Corpus." *Journal of the Evangelical Theological Society* 27 (1984): 277–89.

Pisano, Stephen. "'Egypt' in the Septuagint Text of Hosea." In *Tradition of the Text: Studies offered to Dominique Barthélemy in Celebration of His Seventieth Birthday*, ed. G. J. Norton and S. Pisano, 301–308. Orbis Biblicus et Orientalis, no. 109. Freiburg and Göttingen: University of Freiburg and Vandenhoeck and Ruprecht, 1991.

Polley, Max. *Amos and the Davidic Empire: A Socio-historical Approach.* New York: Oxford University Press, 1989.

Prinsloo, Willem. *The Theology of the Book of Joel.* Beihefte zur Zeitschrift für die Alttestamentliche Wissenschaft, no. 163. Berlin: Walter de Gruyter, 1985.

Rabin, Chaim. "The Translation Process and the Character of the Septuagint." *Textus* 6 (1968): 1–26.

Reid, S. B. "The End of Prophecy in the Light of Contemporary Social Theory: A Draft." *Society of Biblical Literature Seminar Papers.* ed. K. H. Richards, 515–23. Atlanta: Scholars Press. 1985.

Rofé, A. *The Prophetical Stories.* 1st English ed. Jerusalem: Magnes, 1988.

Rogerson, J. W. "Dodekapropheton." Band IX, *Theologische Realenzyklopädie*, 18–20. Berlin, New York: Walter de Gruyter, 1982.

Rudolph, Wilhelm. *Joel, Amos, Obadja, Jona*, Vol. 13/2, Kommentar zum Alten Testament. Gütersloh: Gerd Mohn, 1971.

————. *Haggai-Sacharja 1–8–Sacharja 9–14–Maleachi.* Vol. 13/4, *Kommentar zum Alten Testament*. Gütersloh: Gerd Mohn, 1976.

Rüger, H. P. "Le Siracide: un livre à la frontière du canon." In *Le Canon de l'Ancien Testament: Sa formation et son histoire*, eds. J.-D. Kaestli and O. Wermelinger, 47–69. Genève: Labor et Fides, 1984.

Sanders, Henry A. *The Minor Prophets in the Freer Collection*. Ann Arbor, MI: University of Michigan Press, 1927.

Sanders, James A. "Text and Canon: Concepts and Method." *Journal of Biblical Literature* 98 (1979): 5–29.

———. *Canon and Community: A Guide to Canonical Criticism*. Philadelphia: Fortress, 1984.

———. *From Sacred Story to Sacred Text*. Philadelphia: Fortress, 1987.

———. "Cave 11 Surprises and the Question of Canon." *McCormick Quarterly* 21 (1968): 284–98.

———. "Hebrew Bible *and* Old Testament: Textual Criticism in Service of Biblical Studies." In *Hebrew Bible or Old Testament: Studying the Bible in Judaism and Christianity*, ed. R. Brooks and J. J. Collins, 41–68. Notre Dame: University of Notre Dame Press, 1990.

———. "Stability and Fluidity in Text and Canon." In *Tradition of the Text: Studies offered to Dominique Barthélemy in Celebration of his Seventieth Birthday*, ed. G. Norton and S. Pisano, 203–17. Orbis Biblicus et Orientalis, no. 109. Freiburg/Göttingen: Freiburg University Press/Vandenhoeck and Ruprecht, 1991.

———. "Canon. Hebrew Bible." In Vol. 1, *The Anchor Bible Dictionary*, ed. D. N. Freedman, 837–52. New York: Doubleday, 1992.

Sanderson, Judith. *An Exodus Scroll from Qumran: 4QpaleoExod^m and the Samaritan Tradition*. Harvard Semitic Monographs, no. 30. Atlanta: Scholars Press, 1986.

Sarna, Nahum M. "The Order of the Books." In *Studies in Jewish Bibliography, History, and Literature in Honor of I. Edward Kiev*. ed. Charles Berlin, 407–413. New York: KTAV, 1971.

Sasson, Jack. *Jonah*. Vol. 24B, The Anchor Bible. New York: Doubleday, 1990.

Schmidt, Ludwig. *"De Deo."* *Studien zur literarkritik und Theologie des Buches Jona, des Gesprächs zwischen Abraham und Jahwe in Gen 18:22ff. und von Hi. 1.* Beihefte zur Zeitschrift für die Alttestamentliche Wissenschaft, no. 143. Berlin: Walter de Gruyter, 1976.

Schmidt, W. "Die deuteronomistische Redaktion des Amosbuches." *Zeitschrift für die Alttestamentliche Wissenschaft* 77 (1965): 168–93.

Scholem, Gershom. "Revelation and Tradition as Religious Categories in Judaism." In *The Messianic Idea in Judaism and Other Essays on Jewish Spirituality*, 282–305. New York: Schocken, 1971.

Schneider, Dale A. "The Unity of the Book of the Twelve." Ph.D. diss., Yale University, 1979.

Sellin, Ernst. *Das Zwölfprophetenbuch.* 2nd ed., Vol. 12, Kommentar zum Alten Testament. Leipzig: Deichert, 1929.

Septuaginta, Vetus Testamentum Graecum. Vol. XIII *Duodecim Prophetae*, ed. Joseph Ziegler, 3rd ed. Göttingen: Vandenhoeck and Ruprecht, 1984.

———. Vol. VIII/5, *Tobit*, ed. R. Hanhart. Göttingen: Vandenhoeck and Ruprecht, 1983.

Sheppard, Gerald. "Canonization: Hearing the Voice of the Same God through Historically Dissimilar Traditions." *Interpretation* 34 (1982): 21–33.

Silberman, Louis. "Unriddling the Riddle: A Study in the Structure and Language of the Habakkuk Pesher (1QpHab)." *Revue Qumran* 3 (1961–62): 323–64.

Skeham, Patrick W. "Qumran and the Present State of Old Testament Text Studies: The Masoretic Text." *Journal of Biblical Literature* 78 (1959): 21–25.

———, and Alexander A. DiLella. *The Wisdom of Ben Sira.* Vol. 39, The Anchor Bible. Garden City, NY: Doubleday, 1987.

Smart, James D. "Introduction and Exegesis of the Book of Jonah." In Vol. VI, *The Interpreter's Bible*, 869–94. New York: Abingdon, 1956.

Smith, Barbara Herrnstein. "Contingencies of Value." In *Canons*, ed. R. von Hallberg, 5–39. Chicago and London: University of Chicago Press, 1983.

————. *Contingencies of Value: Alternative Perspectives for Critical Theory*. Cambridge: Harvard University Press, 1988.

Smith, David L. *Religion of the Landless: The Social Context of the Babylonian Exile*. Bloomington, IN: Meyer–Stone Books, 1989.

Smith, J. M. P. "Malachi." In *A Critical and Exegetical Commentary on Haggai, Zechariah, Malachi, and Jonah*. International Critical Commentary. Edinburgh: T & T Clark, 1912.

Smith, Jonathan Z. "Sacred Persistence: Towards a Redescription of Canon." In *Approaches to Ancient Judaism, Vol. 1: Theory and Practice*, ed. W. S. Green, 11–28. Missoula, MT: Scholars Press, 1978.

Smith, Morton. *Palestinian Parties and Politics That Shaped the Old Testament*. London: SCM, 1971.

Soderlund, Sven. *The Greek Text of Jeremiah: A Revised Hypothesis*. Journal for the Study of the Old Testament Supplement Series, no. 47. Sheffield: JSOT Press, 1985.

Soisalon-Soininen, I. "Beobachtungen zur Arbeitsweise der Septuaginta-Ubersetzer." In *Isac Leo Seeligman Volume: Essays on the Bible and the Ancient World III*, ed. A. Rofe and Y. Zakovitch, 319–29. Jerusalem: E. Rubenstein, 1983.

Steck, Odil H. *Der Abschluss der Prophetie im Alten Testament: Ein Versuch zur Frage der Vorgeschichte des Kanons*. Biblisch-Theologische Studien, no. 17. Neukirchen: Neukirchener Verlag, 1991.

————. "Der Kanon des hebräischen Alten Testaments." In *Vernunft des Glaubens: Festschrift zum 60 Geburstag von Wolfhart Pannenberg*, ed. J. Rohls and G. Wenz, 231–52. Göttingen: Vandenhoeck and Ruprecht, 1988.

Steuernagel, Carl. *Lehrbuch der Einleitung das Alte Testament*. Tübingen: J. C. B. Mohr, 1912.

Sundberg, A. C., Jr. *The Old Testament of the Early Church.* Harvard Theological Studies, no. 20. Cambridge: Harvard University Press, 1964.

———. "Reexamining the Formation of the Old Testament Canon." *Interpretation* 42 (1988): 78–82.

Swete, Henry B. *Introduction to the Old Testament in Greek.* Cambridge: Cambridge University Press. 1914.

Swanson, T. N. "The Closing of the Collection of the Holy Scriptures: A Study in the History of the Canonization of the Old Testament." Ph.D. diss., Vanderbilt University, 1970.

Talmon, Shemaryahu. "The Textual Study of the Bible—A New Outlook." In *Qumran and the History of the Biblical Text,* ed. F. M. Cross and S. Talmon, 321–400. Cambridge, MA: Harvard University Press, 1975.

———. "The OT Text." In *The Cambridge History of the Bible,* Vol. I, From the Beginnings to Jerome, ed. P.R. Ackroyd and C. F. Evans, 159–99. Cambridge: Cambridge University Press, 1970.

———. "DSIa as a Witness to Ancient Exegesis of the Book of Isaiah." *Annual of the Swedish Theological Institute* 1 (1962): 62–72.

Textuz, M. "Deux fragments inedits der manuscripts de la Mer Morte." *Semitica* 5 (1955): 38–39.

Thackeray, Henry St. J. *A Grammar of the Old Testament in Greek according to the Septuagint.* Cambridge: Cambridge University Press, 1909.

———. "The Greek Translators of the Prophetical Books." *Journal of Theological Studies* 4 (1902–3): 78–85.

———. *The Septuagint and Jewish Worship: A Study in Origins.* London: Oxford University Press, 1920.

Tov, Emanuel. *The Greek Minor Prophets Scroll from Nahal Hever (8HevXIIgr).* Vol. VIII, Discoveries in the Judean Desert. Oxford: Clarendon Press, 1990.

———. *The Use of the Septuagint in Text-Critical Research.* Jerusalem: Simor, 1981.

————. *The Septuagint Translation of Jeremiah and Baruch—A Discussion of an Early Revision of Jeremiah 29–52 and Baruch 1:1–3:8.* Harvard Semitic Mongraphs, no. 8. Missoula, MT: Scholars Press, 1976.

————. "L'incidence de la critique textuelle sur la critique littéraire dans le livre de Jérémie." *Revue Biblique* 79 (1972): 189–99.

————. "Exegetical Notes on the Hebrew *Vorlage* of the LXX of Jeremiah 27 (34)." *Zeitschrift für die Alttestamentliche Wissenschaft* 91 (1979): 73–93.

————. "Some Aspects of the Textual and Literary History of the Book of Jeremiah." In *Le livre de Jérémie: Le prophète et son milieu, les oracles et leur transmission,* ed. P.-M.Bogaert, 145–67. Bibliotheca ephemeridum theologicarum lovaniensium, no. 54. Leuven: Leuven University Press, 1981.

————. "The Literary History of the Book of Jeremiah in the Light of Its Textual History." In *Empirical Models for Biblical Criticism,* ed. Jeffrey Tigay, 213–37. Philadelphia: University of Pennsylvania Press, 1985.

————. "Recensional Differences Between the MT and LXX of Ezekiel." *Ephemeridum theologicarum lovaniensium* 62 (1986): 89–101.

————. "Some Sequence Differences Between the MT and the LXX and their Ramifications for the Literary Criticism of the Bible." *Journal of Northwest Semitic Languages* 13 (1987): 151–60.

————. "The Nature and Background of Harmonizations in Biblical Manuscripts." *Journal for the Study of the Old Testament* 31 (1985): 3–29.

————. *Textual Criticism of the Hebrew Bible.* Minneapolis/ Assen/Maastricht: Fortress Press/Van Gorcum, 1992.

Trible, Phylis. "Studies in the Book of 'Jonah.'" Ph.D. diss., Columbia University, 1963.

Tucker, Gene M. "Prophetic Superscriptions and the Growth of a Canon." In *Canon and Authority,* ed. George W. Coats and Burke O. Long, 57–70. Philadelphia: Fortress, 1977.

Ulrich, Eugene. "The Canonical Process, Textual Criticism, and Latter Stages in the Composition of the Bible." In *'Sha'arei Talmon': Studies in*

the Bible, Qumran, and the Ancient Near East Presented to Shemaryahu
Talmon, ed. M. Fishbane and E. Tov, 267–91. Winona Lake, IN:
Eisenbrauns, 1992.

——. "Horizons of OT Textual Research at the Thirtieth Anniversary of
Qumran Cave 4." *Catholic Biblical Quarterly* 46 (1984): 612–36.

——. "Double Literary Editions of Biblical Narratives and Reflections on
Determining the Form to Translate." In *Perspectives on the Hebrew
Bible: Essays in Honor of Walter J. Harrelson*, ed. J. L. Crenshaw, 101–16.
Macon, GA: Mercer University Press, 1988.

Utzschneider, Helmut. *Künder oder Schreiber? Eine These zum Problem der
"Schriftprophetie" auf Grund von Maleachi 1,6–2,9.* Beiträge zur
Erforschung des Alten Testaments und des antiken Judentums, no.
19. Frankfurt an Main: Peter Lang, 1989.

Vawter, Bruce. *Job and Jonah: Questioning the Hidden God.* Ramsey, NJ: Paulist
Press, 1983.

Walters, Stanley. "Hannah and Anna: The Greek and Hebrew Texts of 1
Samuel 1" *Journal of Biblical Literature* 107 (1988): 385–412.

Wanke, Gunther. "Die Entstehung des Alten Testaments als Kanon." Band
VI, *Theologische Realenzyklopadie*, 1–7. Berlin and NY: Walter de
Gruyter, 1980.

Waard, Jan de. "Translation Techniques Used by the Greek Translators of
Amos." *Biblica* 59 (1978): 339–50.

Watts, John W. "Text and Redaction in Jeremiah's Oracles against the
Nations" *Catholic Biblical Quarterly* 54 (1992): 432–47.

Weimar, Peter. "Obadja: Eine redaktionskritische Analyse." *Biblische Notizen*
27 (1985): 94–99.

——. "Jon 4,5. Beobachtungen zur Entstehung der Jonaerzählung"
Biblische Notizen 18 (1982): 86–109.

Weiser, Artur *Das Buch des XII Kleinen Propheten*, Vol. 24, Das Alte Testament
Deutsch. Göttingen: Vandenhoeck and Ruprecht, 1967.

Wildeboer, G. *Die Entstehung des Alttestamentlichen Kanons*. Gotha: Friedrich Andreas Perthes, 1891.

Willi-Plein, Inna. *Vorformen der Schriftexegese innerhalb des Alten Testaments. Untersuchungen zum literarischen Werden der auf Amos, Hosea und Micha zurückgehenden Bücher im hebräischen Zwölfprophetenbuch*. Beihefte zur Zeitschrift für die Alttestamentliche Wissenschaft, no. 123. Berlin: Walter de Gruyter, 1971.

Wilson, Robert R. *Prophecy and Society in Ancient Israel*. Philadelphia: Fortress, 1980.

Wolfe, Rolland E. "The Editing of the Book of the Twelve." *Zeitschrift für die Alttestamentliche Wissenschaft* 53 (1935): 90–129.

Wolfenson, L. B. "Implications of the Place of the Book of Ruth in Editions, Manuscripts, and Canon of the OT." *Hebrew Union College Annual* 1 (1924): 151–78.

Wolff, Hans Walter. *Joel and Amos, A Commentary*. tr. W. Janzen, S. D. McBride, and C. Muenchow, Hermeneia Commentary Series. Philadelphia: Fortress, 1979.

————. *Obadiah and Jonah: A Commentary*. Tr. M. Kohl. Minneapolis: Augsburg, 1986.

————. *Dodekapropheton 1. Hosea*. Vol. 14/1, Biblische Kommentar: Altes Testament. Neukirchen-Vluyn: Neukirchener Verlag, 1965.

————. *Dodekapropheton 2, Joel und Amos*. Vol. 14/2 in Biblische Kommentar: Altes Testament. Neukirchen-Vluyn: Neukirchener Verlag, 1969.

————. "Schwerter zu Pflugscharen—Missbrauch eines Prophetenwortes?" Praktische Fragen und exegetische Klärungen zu Joël 4,9–12, Jes 2,2–5 und Mi 4,1–5." *Evangelische Theologie* 44 (1984): 280–92.

Würthwein, Ernst. *The Text of the Old Testament: An Introduction to Biblica Hebraica*. tr. Erroll F. Rhodes. Grands Rapids, MI: Eerdmans, 1979.

Yee, Gale. *Composition and Tradition in the Book of Hosea*. SBL Dissertation Series, no. 102. Atlanta: Scholars Press, 1987.

Younger, K. L. Jr., W. W. Hallo, and B. F. Batto, eds. *The Biblical Canon in Comparative Perspective*. Vol. 4, *Scripture in Context*. Lewiston/ Queenston/Lampeter, NJ: Mellen, 1991.

Ziegler, Joseph. "Die Einheit der Septuaginta zum Zwölfprophetenbuch." *Beelage zum Vorlesungsverzeichnis der Staatl. Akademie zu Braunsberg*, 1–16. Göttingen: Vandenhoeck and Ruprecht, 1934–35.